SCREENWRITING DOWN TO THE ATOMS

DIGGING DEEPER INTO THE CRAFT OF CINEMATIC STORYTELLING

MICHAEL WELLES SCHOCK

SCRIPTMONK INDUSTRIES

ISBN 978-0-9888487-0-2

First Edition
Originally published Jan 18, 2013. Last update August 31, 2015.

SCREENWRITING DOWN TO THE ATOMS

ACKNOWLEDGEMENTS

The author would like to thank Merav Ronen, Krystal Quinones, and David Urbina for their notes and suggestions; Michael Dwyer for his cover photography; and Nir Studnitski, for had it not been for his stubborn arguments, many parts of this book may have never been born.

CONTENTS

RECOMMENDED VIEWING

The following twelve films are used frequently throughout this book for demonstrative purposes. The author strongly suggests readers become familiar with these films before proceeding.

Alien
(1979)
screenplay by Dan O'Bannon
story by Dan O'Bannon and
Ronald Shusett

American Beauty
(1999)
written by Alan Ball

Back to the Future
(1985)
written by Robert Zemeckis &
Bob Gale

The Bourne Identity
(2002)
written by Tony Gilroy and
William Blake Herron
adapted from a novel by Robert
Ludlum

Chinatown
(1974)
written by Robert Towne

Die Hard
(1988)
written by Jeb Stuart and Steven
E. de Souza
adapted from a novel by
Roderick Thorp

The Godfather
(1972)
screenplay by Mario Puzo and
Francis Ford Coppola
based on the novel by Mario Puzo

*The Lord of the Rings: The
Fellowship of the Ring*
(2001)
screenplay by Fran Walsh,
Philippa Boyens & Peter Jackson
based on the novel by J.R.R.
Tolkien

The Matrix
(1999)
written by Andy & Lana
Wachowski

Raiders of the Lost Ark
(1981)
screenplay by Lawrence Kasdan
story by George Lucas and Philip
Kaufman

Rocky
(1976)
written by Sylvester Stallone

Star Wars (aka *Episode IV: A New
Hope*)
(1977)
written by George Lucas

SUGGESTED ADDITIONAL VIEWING

These films are also mentioned within the text. Though not required, it will be helpful to be knowledgeable of them as well.

Casablanca
(1942)
screenplay by Julius Epstein,
Philip Epstein, and Howard Koch
adapted from a stageplay by
Murray Burnett and Joan Alison

Citizen Kane
(1942)
written by Herman J.
Mankiewicz & Orson Welles

Fargo
(1996)
written by Joel & Ethan Coen

Finding Nemo
(2003)
screenplay by Andrew Stanton,
Bob Peterson, & David Reynolds
story by Andrew Stanton

Raging Bull
(1980)
screenplay by Paul Schrader and
Peter Savage
based on a book by Jake LaMotta
with Joseph Carter and Peter
Savage

Saving Private Ryan
(1998)
written by Robert Rodat

Schindler's List
(1993)
screenplay by Steven Zaillian
adapted from a book by Thomas
Keneally

The Shawshank Redemption
(1994)
screenplay by Frank Darabont
adapted from a short story by
Stephen King

Shrek
(2001)
screenplay by Ted Elliot & Terry
Rossio, Joe Stillman, and Roger
SH Schulman
adapted from a book by William
Steig

The Sixth Sense
(1999)
written by M. Night Shyamalan

INTRODUCTION
WHY "DOWN TO THE ATOMS"?

What does "screenwriting down to the atoms" mean? What does this book aim to do that others on the subject do not?

This author is familiar with most screenwriting guides available to developing writers. In my earlier years, I was much like yourself, devouring every book on the subject I could find. Unfortunately, no matter how much I read, I was still left with questions. Big questions. Questions these books would not or could not answer. I soon realized that the vast majority of guides suffer from the same flaw: superficial approaches based on speculation or imitation that fail to do more than scratch the subject's surface. They may give the rudimentary mechanics of the craft, but the reader's grasp of the subject remains hollow underneath.

The biggest problem with how screencraft is taught to young and aspiring writers is not one of technical instruction, but one of philosophy. Many teach the subject as if they were telling readers to build a house. Only they build these houses without first laying the foundation. Without a firm understanding of the principles beneath the principles, any attempt at screenwriting will remain rickety, rootless, and ready for collapse. Screencraft is like an iceberg. Most of its substance lies under the surface. If writers wish to find success, they must be allowed to dig deeper.

Dramatists usually approach screencraft from the outside-looking-in. They take a collection of films considered successful, find similarities, and then command writers to copy the formula. Unfortunately, this approach only suggests what seems to work for the particular films under analysis. Every cinematic story is unique, with its own particular problems and needs. Quite often, the dramatists' commandments are only applicable to a select number of films. This ends up locking readers into a rigid mindset where they can only imitate and not innovate, rendering them incapable of adjusting their knowledge to the special requirements of their individual stories. The rules of screencraft must be flexible enough to adapt to the needs of the story, not the other way around.

In contrast, this book approaches its subject from the inside-looking-out. It seeks to explain not only how screencraft works, but more importantly WHY it works. To do so, it puts the entire field under the microscope to seek out the most basic of the most basic of the most basic. When scrutinized, much of what we assume to be true proves untrue. What we believe to be simple turns out complex. Meanwhile, many areas which at first seem quite complicated reveal themselves to be elegantly simple at heart. From these basic fundamentals emerge an intricate web of universal guidelines every cinematic story must obey in order to connect with an audience on an intimate, emotionally-satisfying level, regardless of the story's particular content or form. This is what "screenwriting down to the atoms" means. This is what this book intends to do.

This guide is not meant as the be-all, end-all of screenwriting knowledge. It only provides a suitable starting point from which to move forward. Much of narrative study remains uncharted territory. This book picks up where its predecessors have left off, and makes up where others have fallen short, by not only expanding upon proven concepts, but by pushing forward with new discoveries that illuminate the mysteries of the craft in clearer detail than ever before. With this knowledge, developing screenwriters take a giant leap forward in their ability to comprehend and execute their craft, paving the way for the next generation of cinematic storytellers. Whether this be your first introduction to screenwriting or the continuation of years of study, this author hopes to give all the knowledge and inspiration you need to create powerful, effective stories audiences cannot help but love and enjoy.

CHAPTER 1
CLEANING THE SLATE

Where to begin? The path from unseasoned amateur to skilled professional is a long journey, and as with any journey, those most likely to succeed are those who are the best prepared from the start. In my experience, the greatest stumbling block in the way of developing screenwriters is not what they have learned or have yet to learn, but the harmful misconceptions they bring with them before they even begin. The longer these notions go unchallenged, the more harm they will do the writer, so it is best to expose and eliminate them from the start. The purpose of this opening chapter is to clear the reader's mind of the most common of these misconceptions. You may find some of what follows encouraging. Other material you may find difficult to accept. Regardless, a writer free of illusions is the most ready to learn, and most likely to reach healthy, productive results.

As anyone who has ever made a serious go of screenwriting will attest, writing movies is the only skilled profession in the world which seemingly everyone believes they are already an expert. A casual mention of his or her work at a cocktail party will have a screenwriter cornered by everyone from grocery clerks to dental hygienists trying to impart some sort of million-dollar advice. Most people assume that just because they have seen a lot of movies, they know how to write one themselves. However, this is the same as believing one can be a gourmet chef simply because he or she has eaten a lot of good meals. Moviegoers see only the finished product. Most viewers know nothing about the complex processes that went into making that film such an entertaining experience. Behind every good screenplay lies a complex collection of rules, logic, and structure that took the writer years to master. Anyone who wishes to write movies must accept that, like any other field of study, screenwriting takes time and effort to learn.

You will not learn how to write a great screenplay overnight. Hollywood itself took decades to figure this out. For every *Casablanca* or *Gone With the Wind* produced during Hollywood's Golden Age, there were a hundred more films that wound up on the scrap heap of history as artists strove to find the most effective approach to the cinematic form. The cinematic stories of today are the result of a gradual refinement of ideas that took over a century to develop. The good news is most of this knowledge is now available for you to learn. The bad news is the bar has been raised much higher for those seeking entry into the profession. If one wishes to compete, one must first know the rules of the craft and become their master.

To start things simply, movies are a form of storytelling. So are novels, plays, children's books, and the tales told around the campfire. All forms of storytelling share the same basic rules. In addition, each form also follows unique rules specialized to its mode of telling. The storytelling found in cinema is not the same as that found in a book. Nor is it the same as a play. A screenplay's story is written to be dramatized by actors, photographed with cameras, pieced together through editing, and then presented to an audience as a finished whole. This mode of execution forces cinema to tell its stories with strict rules different than any other storytelling form. This gives cinema's storytelling certain strengths and weaknesses; its own set of needs, as well as a wide array of limitations.

These needs and limitations are further compounded by a film's required length. Feature-length films (the films you see in the local theater and the subject of this book) have an established running time of 80-140 minutes, (although the expected norm is 90-120). This required length forces a feature-length film to follow different rules than a 22-minute television episode, or a 9-minute short film, or a 30-second commercial.

Because of such physical requirements, screenwriting becomes just as much of an intellectual and analytical pursuit as it is a creative one. I will not be so bold as to claim screenwriting as the most difficult form of writing, but I will say it is the most complex. Screenwriters must not only follow more rules and limitations than any other type of storyteller, but are also expected to fill those boundaries with fresh and original content audiences will find entertaining. The demand for originality met with the necessity for order, forces a balancing act that takes a screenwriter years to master.

Do not be discouraged, however. Although screenwriting is far from easy, *anyone* can learn it with proper patience. Screenwriting is not a talent. A talent is something with which one must be born. Screenwriting is a SKILL. And skills can be learned. All one needs to write a great movie is, 1. A good deal of creativity (which can be nurtured), 2. A bit of smarts (you're on your own there), and most importantly, 3. A desire to learn the craft, combined with the dedication to become its master. This book can give you the knowledge, but it is up to you to supply the dedication. Those who find success are those who want it the most and are willing to take the time and effort to get it. Which reminds me of a story...

TORTOISES AND HARES

Here is a tale many of you know well. A Tortoise and a Hare decide to have a race. The speedy Hare thinks the race will be easy, so it quickly becomes lazy and distracted. The Tortoise, on the other hand, keeps its head down and plods forward, one step at a time. Because the Tortoise handles the long haul with focus and dedication, it reaches the finish line while the Hare does not.

How does this relate to screenwriting? Well, it seems every newcomer starts out thinking he or she is going to be a Hare. They believe all they have to do is finish one script and they will be on their way to fame and fortune. Unfortunately, this expectation never pans out. In fact, it falls short by a thousand miles. If there is one hard and fast rule about screenwriting, it is that the first script you write will not be very good. In fact, the odds are it will be absolutely *awful.*

There is virtually no escaping this. No matter how much raw talent one starts with, it is inconceivable for anyone to get something as subtle and complex as screenwriting perfect on their first try. Like any other worthwhile endeavor, it takes time and practice. Developing writers must write. A lot. In screenwriting, victory comes to the Tortoise and never the Hare. On average, a beginner must complete five to ten screenplays before his or her ability reaches a professional level. That is five to ten FULL screenplays, 90-120 pages apiece, with multiple revisions. This may sound like a lot of work, but with a little experience, you will quickly understand the necessity. Every writer must work through a series of growing pains. Skill tends to develop along a predictable pattern, a pattern so clear that an experienced studio reader can pick up a script and tell right away if it is the writer's first, second, or third attempt. Book learning can help pick up the pace of this development, but every writer must still grind through script after script, rewrite after rewrite, before he or she has sharpened his or her skills to a competent level.

Some may point out exceptions to this rule. Yes, there have been a lucky handful who found phenomenal success with their first efforts. Callie Khouri's first script was *Thelma & Louise,* which was not only produced, but won the 1991 Academy Award for Best Original Screenplay. Diablo Cody had identical success with her script *Juno* in 2007. However, sixteen years passed between these amazing freshman efforts. During the interim, tens of thousands of first screenplays were written, not to mention just as many second, third, and fourth attempts that never saw the light of day. Often these first-time success stories turn out to be more legend than fact.

Many believe Sylvester Stallone had never attempted to write anything prior to *Rocky,* but this is not true. Stallone not only wrote several previous script, but even had one optioned that was never produced. Stallone found success by putting in time and hard work, just like everyone else.

You may feel discouraged by this. You do not want to think of your first scripts as nothing but practice. You may even get sick at the thought of the story you love never amounting to anything substantial. Do not feel this way. Write your first scripts with every intention of success. Just don't be Hare-brained about it. Stay honest with yourself and keep expectations reasonable. Do not think of your first scripts as throwaways, but stepping stones. Your ability will increase exponentially with each script you finish. After five or more, you will be amazed at how far you have come. Then if you wish, you can return to your early scripts and really take them to the next level. Plus, who knows? The passion you put into your early work may push it beyond expectations. It has happened before, and can happen again.

First-time writers are not the only ones who fall prey to the Hare mentality. It can inflict itself upon even experienced writers. Most of us would like to believe all we have to do is finish one or two drafts and the script will be perfect and ready to sell. But this is never true. Anyone who believes a script is finished after one draft needs to hear a little wisdom from Ernest Hemingway:

"The first draft of anything is shit."

My apologies for Papa's salty language, but he has a point. First drafts stink. It does not matter how experienced you are, or how many scripts you have written. Your first draft will stink. This is what first drafts do. If even Hemingway admits his first drafts are no good, what chance do the rest of us have?

No screenwriter can hit a story out of the park with a single swing. There is no decent film in theaters today that did not need ten, twelve, or even twenty revisions to get things right. Rocky took forty drafts before it was perfect. Forty! Anyone who thinks he or she can achieve equal success with one measly draft is either self-deluded or a fool.

The truth is, a first draft is not *supposed* to be perfect. This is not what it is for. The first draft is known as the "puke draft," meaning the goal is to simply vomit all the ideas out of your head and on to the page so they can exist in manageable form. Once you can see your ideas in black-and-white, the real work can begin. Successive drafts are where the story really begins to take shape. What is rough becomes refined. What is confused becomes clear. Each new draft becomes twice as good as the previous.

The old phrase "writing is rewriting" is absolutely true. *Citizen Kane* (1941) is considered by many to be the finest film ever made. However, I have an early draft of *Kane,* and guess what? It is not very good. The finest film ever made started out as a lousy first draft. So do all films. Perfection takes time. Quit too early and your polished gem of a screenplay will remain just another cruddy old rock.

CALLING OUT THE CRITICS

This book, like others on the topic, approaches the cinematic story from an academic point of view. It analyzes the craft to reveal rules and concepts under its surface. Yet, despite the widespread popularity of this approach, there are those who still remain skeptical. They declare it unnecessary to learn the rules of screencraft. Some even call it a waste of time. I admit there are a lucky few who do not need instruction. These are the "natural storytellers," people seemingly born with an intuition on how stories should be put together. But, for the remaining 99.5% of us, we need a little help. This is what screencraft is for. It illuminates the darkness by turning on a light.

Some of you may still have doubts. The critics make a lot of noise, and on the surface, their arguments seem valid. However, a closer look dispels their logic in a puff of smoke. This section presents the three most popular arguments against the study of the craft, followed by simple logic to render them false.

THE REBEL FALLACY

"I'm a rebel! I don't need to learn anything! I make my own rules!" When industry professionals hear this, it usually translates as, "I'm too lazy to learn how to do things the right way." While this may be true for some, the rebel attitude usually arises out of a fear that formal guidelines will stifle creativity. However, this fear holds about as much water as believing the rules of English grammar limit our ability to speak. The rules of speech do not limit communication. They merely organize it so it may be understood. Without rules, speech becomes the ramblings of a madman.

The same concept applies to screencraft. Rules, structures, and guidelines do not stifle creativity. They merely organize it into a form the audience can understand and appreciate. Without form and order, a story becomes confused and chaotic. Like pillars supporting a building, rules and structure merely give creativity room to operate while keeping the roof from caving in.

Yet perhaps you really are a rebel. You see yourself as a nonconformist, eager to find new paths and challenge old ideas. This is fine. Modern cinema needs more innovators. But a rebel needs a plan. He or she cannot go about breaking rules randomly. That only results in chaos. History provides many examples of individuals who challenged the establishment and won. Why not look at them and discover how they found success?

Everyone knows Mohandas Gandhi led India to independence against the British Empire. However few know that before this Gandhi earned a law degree at the University of London. Gandhi was able to wage a political battle against the British Empire because he had an intimate knowledge of the British and their system of law. The same goes for Nelson Mandela or Vladimir Lenin. Martin Luther changed the Western world with his 16th century revolt against the Catholic Church. However, Luther began as a Catholic priest and friar who knew church theology frontwards and back. Pablo Picasso turned the 20th century art world on its ear with styles that defied all categorization. But, before he managed to warp reality, Picasso was a master of the traditional styles of his day.

The parallels are clear. These were all highly educated persons who were able to rebel against the system only because they first knew that system through and through. They did not make trouble randomly. That would have accomplished nothing. If one wishes to revolt, it must be done properly. You have to know the rules before you can break them.

Without understanding what you want to do differently and why, you will not know what must be done to pull it off. Arbitrary rule-breaking will turn a story into a mess. Traditional story structure gives a narrative a sense of balance the audience finds enjoyable. If a piece of the structure is randomly altered or removed, the balance must be compensated elsewhere. Fail at that, and the movie will no longer be a pleasant experience. Without knowing what you reject and why, any cinematic rebellion will end up as nothing more than an arbitrary experiment, with success coming purely by luck.

THE OLD TIMER FALLACY

Some critics love to point out that the scribes of Hollywood's Golden Age were able to pen masterpieces like *Casablanca* or *Citizen Kane* without the aid of any academic training. If writers did not need it then, why do we need it now? It is true that the old-time writers did not need formal book-learning. However, this was only because they had something no screenwriter has today – on the job training.

Old Hollywood was nothing like Hollywood today. Screenwriters were contracted employees, working for a studio on a permanent basis. Writing movies was like any other 9-to-5 job. The writers would show up at the studio each morning, go to their offices, and work on whatever the bigwigs told them to write. This allowed a number of breaks for young writers. First, it allowed them to rub elbows with the veterans of the industry and gain the benefit of their experience. Second, beginning writers were given the opportunity to start at the bottom and work their way up. First assignments were usually cheap B-movies where quality was not of high concern. If a writer showed promise, he or she was elevated to more important projects.

By that time, the writer had already finished a half-dozen B-scripts, enough experience to make the next assignment a breeze.

Such advantages do not exist in Hollywood today. Screenwriters are expected to break in at the top. If a script is not already as good or better than what is already in theaters, it will never gain recognition. Without on the job experience, modern writers are left with only one substitute: self-education.

THE MYSTIC FALLACY

These critics are the most troublesome. They are also the most prone to shooting themselves in the foot. Mystics tend to view any creative endeavor as a magical, even religious process. To them, "Art" is a holy thing, making any attempt to dissect it blasphemy. Therefore, mystics shun the study of craft and put all their faith in natural talent or inspiration. Unfortunately, talent and inspiration alone are not enough to find success in the highly-structured field of feature filmmaking. Without a foundation of formal knowledge to back up creativity, screenwriting becomes a completely hit-or-miss pursuit. While right-brain creativity is indispensable, a story will fail without proper form and structure.

Despite their passion, mystics seem to miss the higher purpose of screencraft's rules and structures. The storyteller's ultimate goal is to give an audience a pleasing mental and emotional experience. The storyteller can best accomplish this by first understanding how the audience's minds will react to whatever occurs on the screen. Audiences depend on the storyteller to have some skill at guiding their interest and emotions. Books such as this are at heart nothing more than an organized collection of patterns found to be successful at doing this. Through generations of study and observation, writers and scholars alike have found effective and efficient ways to elicit interest, excitement, and emotion from a viewing audience. Screencraft unites the creative with the formal to bring about the best possible story experience.

Though a newcomer may begin with little formal knowledge, there is one quality he or she must possess from the start. Screenwriters must love to write, and must feel certain that this is a path they want to stick with to the end. Screenwriting is not a profession for dabblers. Nor for hobbyists. Only those with true commitment will find success. Despite the glitz and glamor of Hollywood, the profession of screenwriting is about as glamorous as that of a monk. And, if success is to come, a writer must be as dedicated as one. You must be willing to spend hours each day in solitude, scribbling one scene after another. You must be a ravenous scholar of all things cinematic. You must put up with years of skepticism, apathy, and even rejection as you slowly sharpen your skills. But in the end, the rewards greatly outweigh the sacrifices. There is no more satisfying thrill than to see one of your own creations brought to life on the silver screen. If this appeals to you, then welcome aboard. It is always good to have another monk in the monastery.

CHAPTER 2
IT'S ALL ABOUT THE AUDIENCE

Imagine you are the head of a corporation, one that produces some sort of product. The product could be anything: refrigerators, fabric softener, dog food, whatever. Your product goes through a lot of hands before it reaches the consumer. There is the executive who initiates the product, the designer who develops it, and the manufacturer who produces it. It then travels to the wholesaler who distributes it, followed by the retailer who sells it. Along the way come dozens of others, also necessary for your product's success, with responsibilities ranging from advertising to transportation. Now ask yourself, out of all the people connected to your product, who is the most important? Who do you depend upon most for success?

The answer? None of the above. A savvy businessperson knows the most important person is always the *consumer,* the person who will actually use the product. The product is made for the consumer. Should the consumer dislike the product, none will be purchased, and the corporation will go out of business. Everyone else on the corporate chain exists for the sole purpose of making the end user happy.

In this regard, screenwriting has everything in common with business. Once a script is finished, hundreds, even thousands of talented, high-paid individuals will come together to bring that movie to the eyes and ears of the audience. But without the approval of that audience, all the work will amount to nothing. Audiences are the end users of the Hollywood product. The movie was created for them and no one else. Therefore, it is the audience whom everyone must aim to please. The reasons go far beyond the economic necessity of the box office. The industry may need ticket sales to make money, but let us put the commercial aspect aside and focus upon what it means to find success as a storyteller.

I use the word storyteller, and not screenwriter, because "screenwriter" is simply the name of an occupation. Storytelling, on the other hand, is a cultural tradition that has existed since the beginnings of human history. And since those beginnings, a storyteller's success or failure has been built upon his or her ability to understand and connect with an audience. Between the storyteller and the audience there exists an intimate bond. The two are connected, as if by an invisible cord through which the story travels. It is a *relationship*. One of responsibility on the side of the storyteller, and of trust on the side of the audience. Professional screenwriters interact with many different people in the course of their careers; producers, executives, actors, directors; but no relationship is more important than the one they have with their audience. It is the most important business partnership a cinematic storyteller will ever have.

STORYTELLERS AND AUDIENCES: A BRIEF HISTORY

Unfortunately, the practical realities of modern cinema often make it difficult for newcomers to understand the storyteller-audience relationship, or even recognize that it exists. As storytelling has evolved through the ages, each innovation has had the unfortunate side effect of distancing the storyteller from its audience, making this all-important connection more and more difficult to achieve.

Storytelling originated as a very simple affair. Before the invention of written language, all storytelling was done face-to-face. This created an intimate, one-on-one relationship between storyteller and audience. Storytellers could tell whether their story had its desired effect by simply looking into their listeners' eyes. They could then adapt their methods in the moment, reacting to the audience as the audience reacted to them.

With the invention of the written word, storytellers became one step removed from their audiences. Though the storyteller was still allowed to tell his or her story directly to the audience, the face-to-face intimacy was gone. Although the written word allowed the storyteller to reach many more audiences for many years, the separation in time forced storytellers to rely on experience or insight to predict how their audience might react.

Storytelling's next innovation was staged drama. This step also distanced storyteller from audience, but rather than separating the two sides by time, the stage separated them by space. The storyteller was no longer allowed to speak directly to his or her audience. Instead, he or she had to transmit the story through the filter of actors. Because of this, the storyteller became invisible to the audience. He or she was left as a force who could only control the story from behind the scenes.

The invention of cinema strained the once intimate storyteller-audience relationship even further. The cinematic storyteller gets the worst of both worlds, removed from his or her audience by both space *and* time. Cinematic storytellers face the same difficulties as their theatrical counterparts, but unlike theater, a cinematic story may take years, even decades, to reach its audience. Meanwhile, that story goes through the hands of many other artists, shaping and altering it along the way. The practical realities of the medium have created a gulf between storyteller and audience so wide that the two sides risk losing sight of each other.

However, despite this separation, the bond between storyteller and audience still exists in the cinema and remains as important as ever. Unfortunately, many would-be screenwriters do not realize this. They see the gap, but do not recognize the audience on the other side. This results in stories that ignore the audience's needs. These stories are then met with boredom, apathy, or even disgust, all because storytellers did not live up to their responsibilities. The story is meant to please the audience. Fail at that, and the story will fail altogether.

A great screenwriter must always have the audience in mind, even though that audience is far, far away. He or she must know at any given moment what the audience will think, what they will feel, what they know, and what they will WANT to know. Our ancestral storytellers could figure this out by simply looking into their audiences' eyes. Cinematic storytellers must be far more perceptive. We must learn to look forward into our future audience's minds. Despite the distance, the campfire of the ancient story-teller still exists – even though it resides on the other side of the screen.

A storyteller's responsibility to an audience goes far beyond giving enter-tainment. Storytellers fulfill an even more important role in society. To understand why, we must first realize:

WHY STORIES EXIST

Everybody loves stories. Stories make us feel good. When we were child-ren crawling into bed, we all wanted some wise, guiding figure to take us on an adventure. We still want this as adults. This is what movies are for. Movie stars may be called "box office draws," but people do not go to movies to see acting. Neither do they go for special effects. Nor do they come for brilliant photography or dazzling camerawork. People the world over love movies, need movies, cannot get enough of movies simply be-cause they want to be *told a story.*

But why is this? Why do we crave stories? Why is it that every society since the beginning of time has developed storytelling as part of its culture? What is the root of this universal affection?

> *"This world in itself is not reasonable, that is all that can be said. But what is absurd is the confrontation of this irrational and the wild longing for clarity whose call*

*echoes in the human heart... it binds them one to the
other as only hatred can weld two creatures together."
- Albert Camus, author/philosopher*

Stories exist because all people on earth, regardless of race, culture, or creed, share a deep-seeded psychological NEED for the order and meaning contained in a story's events. Stories do more than provide entertainment or emotional satisfaction. They act as a tool to help make sense of the world and cope with the problems and issues around us.

Whether one admits it or not, the world is a chaotic place. Life is unpredictable. Disasters strike without warning. People grow sick and die. Injustices go unpunished, while tragedies are inflicted upon the innocent. Human existence can feel like a constant struggle against events well beyond our control.

Yet, despite the chaos, deep inside every human heart exists a desperate need to believe that, yes, we do have control over our lives, that there is order in the universe, and that everything happens for a reason. To maintain sanity, human beings instinctively seek out methods to the madness. This is why religion is so comforting. This is why scientists explore the world. And likewise, this is why people create stories.

This is story's great social function. Stories give the world a sense of order and meaning. In a story, everything happens for a reason. Events have order and structure. Actions have purpose and consequence. Stories reassure us that problems can be overcome, that what is wrong can be put right, and that everyone can find happiness if they are just willing to try. In this way, stories calm our fears, give meaning to chaos, and explain the unexplainable.

People fear the unknown. So, since the beginning of time, we have used story to explain what available methods could not. When the early Greeks looked to the sky with wonder, they had no way to understand the nature of the sun. So, they explained it with stories of a god in a fiery chariot. The ancient Japanese were plagued by inexplicable earthquakes. Rather than fear the unknown, they calmed their anxiety with a tale of a giant unruly catfish. The Inuit of the Arctic North had no scientific means to explain their nightless summers and long dark winters. No matter. A story about a crow and a stolen ball of daylight was all they needed.

Modern society continues to use stories to release anxieties and calm its fears. *Star Wars* assuaged Cold War worries with a message that tyranny could not overcome hope. *The Matrix* comforted Computer Age nightmares that technology might one day overshadow the human spirit. *Raiders of the Lost Ark* gives a timeless reassurance that the ambitions of the cruel will always be held in check by the actions of the just. Look at any successful film, and you will find the hopes and fears of the time and place it was created, fashioned into a form to give order and meaning.

Cinematic storytellers must recognize their social responsibility. The storyteller is someone to whom the world flocks, for not only entertainment, but comfort and hope. However, the storyteller's success in this role depends largely upon the attitude with which he or she approaches it.

SERVANT AND SHEPHERD

Some working in the film industry operate under the misconception that since they are on the end with all the money, with all the control, and with the authority to choose which stories get made and how to make them, they are the masters in the storyteller-audience relationship. If this were true, why is every studio executive, every producer, every agent and manager locked in a constant struggle to foresee what the audience wants next? Why do they tear their hair out to come up with the next big idea? Whether those at the top wish to admit it or not, the power in the relationship does not lie with them, but with the audience. Like entertainers to the ancient kings, the audience is the master and the storyteller is the servant. Displease the master, and you will not last very long.

The point is, whether you are telling a story to an audience of millions or to your granddaughter Sally, *you* are doing it for *them*. True storytelling is a selfless task. A storyteller must surrender him or herself to the audience's needs. A real storyteller gives his or her all to the audience and expects nothing in return except appreciation.

However, there is a flip side to this. Once storytellers learn to surrender themselves to the audience's needs, they gain the ability to turn the tables and seize power in the relationship. The storyteller's willing servitude convinces the audience to grant him or her access to their minds. The storyteller can then crawl inside the audience's heads to push buttons and pull strings to summon thoughts and emotions at will. With the audience's permission, the storyteller gains the ability to control WHAT the audience thinks and WHEN they think it. The storyteller then transcends to a state where he or she is both servant and master at once.

A storyteller holds the audience's minds in his or her hands. However, with this power comes responsibility. A storyteller cannot be a trickster or an abuser. Any manipulation should be done only for the audience's ultimate benefit. The storyteller must act as the audience's shepherd, leading it through the story as one would guide a blind man by the arm. Even in this position of power, the storyteller must continue to respect the audience's needs. Fail to do so, and they will revoke access to their minds and reject the story as well.

To maintain this balance between the roles of servant and shepherd, the storyteller must strive to do two things. The first is respect the audience. The second is understand the audience. Understanding the audience will be easy once you realize that you are already an expert on cinematic audiences. After all, you have been a member of one thousands of times. You already know how it feels when a storyteller has you in good hands. You also know when a less competent storyteller is trying to cheat you, manipulate you, or force you to believe situations you find implausible or absurd. The audience is not some mysterious band of fickle and unpredictable others, but individuals exactly like yourself. They react the same way you react. The storyteller must put him or herself into the audience and experience the story from the same viewpoint as they would any other film. Respecting the audience becomes easy after this point. Because what fool would deny respect to themselves?

CHAPTER 3
THE BASIC OF THE MOST BASIC

Screencraft can start to feel very complicated, very quick. The cinematic storyteller must learn to keep hundreds of story elements in perfect balance, while at the same time give the audience an experience they find original and entertaining. This seems like a tall order. But, where to begin? At the beginning, of course. We learn to read by first learning the alphabet. We begin mathematics by first learning to count. So, we begin our exploration of the cinematic story by first asking:

WHAT IS A "STORY"?

The question is misleadingly simple. Everyone knows what a story is, but defining the term proves surprisingly difficult. What exactly makes a story a *story*? What specific traits does a story possess to separate it from things which are clearly not?

At first glance, one might define a story as a series of events involving one or more persons. However, a mere series of events does not constitute a story. This, for instance, is not a story:

> "I woke up this morning. I showered. I sat in traffic on the way to work. I talked to my boss during lunch. I drove home and made dinner."

Just because events occur in chronological order, it does not necessarily mean those events create a story. Such a narrative will fail to hold an audience's attention for more than the shortest period of time. So, what is the difference between a story and a mere series of events? It all comes down to four basic qualifications. First,

1. A story is about a PROBLEM and the resolution of that problem.

Take a look at the basic ideas behind four well-known stories:
- A jaded expatriate re-encounters the woman who broke his heart (*Casablanca*).
- A mafia family is threatened by its violent rivals (*The Godfather*).
- The children of two warring families fall in love ("Romeo & Juliet").
- Pigs in poorly-constructed homes are threatened by a Big Bad Wolf ("The Three Little Pigs").

What do these ideas have in common? They all involve characters dealing with a PROBLEM.

Stories are all about problems, whether that problem be physical or emotional, intimate or cosmic, concrete or abstract. The return of the old lover, the rivals' aggression, the forbidden romance, the Big Bad Wolf; the sudden arrival of these problems trigger characters to take action. Without a problem, a story would never begin. The remainder of the story unfolds as characters take action to deal with that problem. In *Casablanca*, Rick spends the story debating whether or not to help his ex-lover. In *The*

Godfather, Michael Corleone takes actions to protect his family. Romeo and Juliet go to great lengths to continue their romance. The Three Little Pigs run for better shelter.

Why are problems so central to storytelling? As learned in the previous chapter, stories exist as social therapy. They provide the appearance of order and meaning in a chaotic world. By presenting a problem and then the quest for its solution, a story becomes a transformation from *chaos to order* – from an unstable situation into one where everything has been resolved. This in turn gives the audience comfort and reassurance. When the audience sees characters face and defeat problems, they feel much more confidence in their ability to deal with problems in their own lives. Stories tell us that no matter how bad things may be, no problem is insurmountable. In this way, a problem and its solution give a story its meaning.

2. Stories are about HUMAN BEINGS.

A story cannot exist without *characters.* To put it a better way, stories are about people. People doing things; speaking, acting, loving, fighting, wanting, needing. A documentary on soil erosion may present a fascinating problem, but it does not contain a story unless it focuses upon a human being dealing with that problem. Stories are reflections on our humanity. They help us better understand ourselves and others by presenting us with people to whom we can follow and relate.

Though some stories contain characters who are not physically human, these characters are human nonetheless. Though the lead may be a bunny rabbit, a robot, or an animate teddy bear, the characters have been *anthropomorphized* – that is, given human traits and behavior. They are simply people in a different form, exhibiting the same emotions, urges, and anxieties as their fully human counterparts. Even live-action franchises starring real animals anthropomorphize their heroes by giving those animals an intelligence and range of emotion far beyond their natural capability. Because of this, audiences are able to connect with non-human characters as well as they could any human being.

3. A story is unified by a PREMISE.

No matter how thick the novel or epic the film, all good stories are simple at their heart. Events revolve around a small handful of characters. All actions occur in response to a single problem or related group of problems. All elements work together to express a single set of ideas. Good stories can be summed up in a few words. *The Bourne Identity* is the story of a man trying to regain his memory. *Finding Nemo* is about a father searching for his son. *The Sixth Sense* is about a man helping a troubled boy. This basic summary is called the STORY PREMISE.

In the simplest terms, the premise is what the story is "about." If you saw a movie, and a friend asked what it was about, you would proceed to relate the premise. If the movie had a strong premise, the task is easy; "It is about a woman who loses her job and has to find a new life," or "It was about a guy who had to take over for Santa Claus on Christmas Eve." If it lacked a strong premise, all you might be able to say is, "I don't know. A lot of things. It was confusing."

A story's premise must be established at its very beginning. As a story opens, the audience must quickly learn what characters occupy the story, the world those characters live in, and the problems those characters face. This is the who, what, where, and why of the story. These specific elements are what make each premise unique. There could be a thousand stories about a father searching for his son like *Finding Nemo,* or of a man helping a troubled boy like *The Sixth Sense,* but the specific who, what, where, and why of each premise is what makes these stories unique.

Around 355 BC, Aristotle wrote *Poetics,* the first known study of dramatic theory. According to Aristotle, the best dramas possessed a "unity of action," a "unity of place," and a "unity of time." Simply put, he meant a play should be unified around a single course of action, taking place in a single location, occurring within a single frame of time (ideally a single day). Though modern drama has proven Aristotle's limitations on time and space far too strict, he was absolutely right in one regard: a good story must be unified in its action.

A story achieves unity of action by establishing a premise at its beginning, and then sticking to that premise until the story's end. For example, the premise of *The Bourne Identity* is, "An amnesiac secret agent attempts to recover his memory while avoiding forces who wish to capture him." Every one of *Bourne's* events relate to this premise. Because of this, *Bourne* has unity of action. If on the other hand the story were to suddenly switch focus onto a new set of characters, or if Jason Bourne were to abruptly abandon his quest, or if aliens were to appear and change the story into science fiction, the story would lack unity. The addition of persons or events outside of the original premise will not improve a story. It will only make it muddy and confused. Fail to stick to a premise, and the story will revert back into a mere series of events.

Recall the rambling non-story I presented at the top of this chapter ("I woke up this morning. I showered. I sat in traffic...) Its events are not unified by a premise. Each statement is arbitrary and unrelated. However, this series of events can be turned into a story if one simply establishes a premise at its start:

> "I woke up late this morning and realized I had yet to book a flight to my sister's wedding. Since I only had time to shower, I hoped to take care of it from the office before I started my day's work. Unfortunately, traffic was heavy and I arrived late. I could not find the time to do it at lunch either because my boss corralled me into a twenty-minute conversation. After lunch, things got too hectic, so I decided to wait until I got home. By then the flight had sold out, and there was nothing left to do but make dinner."

Do you see the difference? This is no longer a list of random events. Everything is now unified around a single idea. The premise has given each instance meaning in relation to the whole.

Most movies are unified by action. They contain a single storyline relating to a single problem. However, it is possible for a film to contain multiple disconnected storylines as long as the premise continues to unify events through time, place, character, and/or theme. This approach is more difficult, but there have been notable successes. *Pulp Fiction* (1994) is made of a series of episodes told out of chronological order. Though these episodes are more or less unrelated in terms of action, they remain unified by character (the characters from one storyline also appear in others), time (all events occur within the same few days), and theme (each episode revolves around violent men facing ethical decisions). *City of God,* the 2002 film about life in a Rio de Janeiro slum, has an even more episodic storyline. Yet its various stories remain unified. All episodes work together to tell the history of a single location, seen through the eyes of a single character, with events that converge to express a single theme.

4. A story is told in a STRUCTURED ORDER.

A story's events must occur in logical order. THIS happens, which then causes THAT to happen. Little Red Riding Hood is sent on an errand to grandma's house. Because of this, she travels into the forest. Because of this, she meets the Big Bad Wolf. Because of this, Little Red tells the Wolf where she is going. Because he has learned this, the Wolf races to grandma's house, devours grandma, and disguises himself in her clothing. Because this has happened, the Wolf is able to fool Little Red when she arrives.

This cause and effect relationship is known as CAUSALITY. Every event occurs as a result of that which has occurred before it. If events are random or disconnected – if Little Red were on her way to grandma's house, but then climbed Jack's beanstalk, then took a nap, and then visited the Three Bears – this would be a series of events and not a story due to the lack of causality.

Causality demonstrates the biggest difference between story and real life. Real life lacks structure. Things happen out of the blue. Actions taken often fail to generate results. Meanwhile, distractions intrude and interfere. Stories, on the other hand, comfort audiences with a world where everything is organized and logical. In a story, everything makes sense. Every cause has an effect, and every effect a cause. Some beginners find difficulty because they believe a story is supposed to be just like real life. It is not. Stories are not a reflection of reality, but an *analogue* of reality. They present us the world *as we would like it to be.*

So in conclusion: What is a Story?

A STORY is a series of events, about HUMAN BEINGS, dealing with a PROBLEM, unified by a PREMISE, told in a STRUCTURED ORDER.

Anything that does not fit this definition is not a story and will not have what it takes to hold an audience's interest. This may seem elementary, but it is not uncommon to find amateur scripts that lack one or more of these basic qualifications. A script without a story cannot hope to do anything but fail. It creates a wandering, pointless experience that makes its audience restless and bored. Do not automatically assume your script tells a story. Look at it and confirm that it indeed meets these four qualifications. Without them, all your writing will amount to nothing.

We may now know what a story is, but this supplies only half the equation. "Storytelling" is a two-part term. First, there is the "story." Then, there is the "telling." It is not enough to simply have a good story. Equally important is how that story is told. Even the best of stories can be sunk by poor telling. So, with that said, we must ask–

HOW DOES ONE "TELL" A STORY?

To be more specific to our purposes, how does one tell a *cinematic* story? Storytelling has many forms: novels, stage plays, operas, anecdotes, comic strips, dirty jokes, even song lyrics. Each tell a story in a different way, each with its own inherent advantages and limitations. But how does cinema tell its story?

Cinema is possibly the most complex form of storytelling. It is definitely the most complex art form. Most methods of storytelling use only words to communicate. Some only images. Others only sound. Cinema, on the other hand, uses words, images, sounds, light, movement, color, time, space, editing, and camerawork. Where does one begin to break down something so densely layered?

To find out, we must put the entire field under the microscope. We start once again by seeking the most basic of the most basic of the most basic.

THE ATOMS OF CINEMA

Consider the word "atom." Though used most often in chemistry, the word itself refers to any element so basic that it cannot be broken down into smaller units. Its origin dates back to the fifth century BC, when the Greek philosopher Democritus proposed (quite rightly) that everything in the universe was made of tiny particles. He believed that if one had a knife sharp enough, an apple could be sliced thinner and thinner, until it came to a point where it could be sliced no further, down to the very particles that held it together. Democritus called these particles atoms – Greek for "uncuttable."

Not only was Democritus' idea revolutionary, but so was his approach. He knew the key to study was to first break the subject down to its MOST BASIC ELEMENT. The whole is best understood by first identifying the tiniest building blocks by which everything is constructed.

Nearly every legitimate field of science is built upon a most basic element. Chemistry procured the word atom for itself to label the swirling particles that make up matter. The chemistry atom is uncuttable. If an atom were split, the result would not be two half-atoms, but a useless scatter of subparticles. Biology is the study of life. Its most basic element is a single living cell. A single cell can carry out all requirements of life, but if cut into smaller parts, it ceases to function. Sociology studies behavior in human societies. Societies are made up of individuals, making a single person sociology's most basic element.

Any field of study will suffer until it discovers its most basic element. Chemistry was a rather hit or miss pursuit before the theory of atomic structure. Biology developed slowly until cells were discovered inside a piece of tree cork. Identifying the most basic element makes an entire field far easier to comprehend.

But can this method be applied to cinema? Does cinematic storytelling have a most basic element? Many would refuse to even consider the question, simply because chemistry and biology are sciences while cinema is an art. People tend to segregate art and science into isolated categories. Nevertheless, can an understanding of an art be found in the same manner as a science?

To answer the question, it is first necessary to figure out what it means to call cinema an art.

WHAT IS "ART"?

Art. It is a word of such high and mighty connotation that many dare not define it. In this case, let us first ask, why do people create art? Works of art have no practical purpose. Officially, art must be non-utilitarian in nature, meaning it has no use other than the aesthetic. A beautifully-crafted sculpture is art, but a beautifully-crafted lamp is not. A novel can be art, but the book you read now is not. If art has no practical use, then what is its purpose?

The answer is found in the artistic process itself. The artistic process is made of three parts: the artist who creates the work, the medium the artist works through (paint, dance, music, etc.), and finally the audience who ultimately receives the work. One must not overlook the importance of the audience. It is the audience who brings the process to its completion. Art without an audience is like the proverbial tree falling in the woods. What is the point of a novel that is never read? Music that is never played? A film that no one sees? "Artistic expression" implies a second party to whom the artist's efforts are addressed. Only the most vain of artists would create something to put in a closet. Real artists create because they have something to express to the world: an idea, an opinion, an emotion... Artists create in order to communicate. *Art* is about *communication*.

Art is the communication of meaning, from artist to audience, through a creative medium.

Since the purpose of art is to communicate meaning, how then is meaning communicated in something such as literature? Through words, of course. The most basic element of literature – its atom – is a single word. An author can communicate meaning with one word, but not with a single letter or detached syllable. It is by the accumulation of words into larger structures that the novelist makes his or her art. The art of dance communicates through movement. Its most basic element is a single movement of the body. Music is made of a collection of singular notes. Painting is an accumulation of individual brush strokes. Photography is the manipulation of individual photons of light. Thus, we see that like science the arts have their own atoms. Each has a basic building block with which the artist constructs a greater meaning.

However, things become far more complicated when it comes to cinema. Cinema combines elements from nearly every art form; from photography, to theatre, to music, to the graphic and plastic arts. In addition, cinema has its own unique attributes, such as the ability to elongate or compress time, or to change perspective through editing. If cinema contains the most basic elements of all other art forms plus elements of its own, what could possibly be the single, most basic building block of cinema itself? Can cinema be boiled down to a single element? Or is it just a hodgepodge?

The search proves difficult. Cinema's most basic element cannot be a single image, since that would ignore cinema's use of sound. It is not a spoken word, since dialogue makes up only a small part of any film. It also cannot be a single scene, or a shot within that scene, because both of these elements can be broken down further.

It turns out the answer is right under our nose. Cinema is an art. Art communicates. And what is transmitted by the act of communication?

Information.

The cinematic experience is created by a constant transmission of story information from storyteller to audience. Whether it be seen or heard, everything presented to the viewer is part of an intentional act of communication. Every detail; a line of dialogue, the look of a room, an expression on an actor's face, an off-screen sound effect, exists to advance the story with NEW INFORMATION. If a character is murdered, that is information. If someone reveals a secret, that is information. If a character walks across the room, that is information. It is through this steady flow of information, communicated one piece at a time, that the cinematic storyteller makes his or her art. Each piece builds upon that which preceded it, advancing the narrative and developing the audience's comprehension of the story as a whole.

This is cinema's atom: the communication of a single piece of information from storyteller to audience; whether it be communicated by audio, visual, or any other means. Cinematic storytellers make their art through the creative control of this information – knowing what information to give and when to give it. By gradually accumulating this information the audience is able to understand, and enjoy, the cinematic narrative.

So, to return to our original question: How is a cinematic story told?

A cinematic story is told through the creative communication of information, given one piece at a time, from Storyteller to Audience.

How the storyteller chooses to communicate makes all the difference. Have you ever heard two people tell the exact same joke and watch it generate a huge laugh for one, yet nothing but silence for the other? The difference was not the joke, but how that joke was told. This is what is meant by story-*telling*: the proper and effective execution of a story's information. Good storytellers know how to communicate information in a way audiences will best understand and appreciate. The true skill of storytelling comes not simply from the story, but from how that story is *told*.

A full explanation of story atoms and their proper execution is beyond the scope of this chapter. Both will be expanded upon later. For now, we are going to put away our microscopes and shift focus onto a more pressing question. We may know what makes a story a story, but now how does a cinematic storyteller construct that story?

CHAPTER 4
THE GOLDEN KEY

We have defined story. We have established the importance of the audience. Now we will marry these concepts to learn how one constructs a cinematic story capable of pleasing the audience. The next three chapters cover the ins and outs of PLOT.

Plot is the organized arrangement of everything that physically "happens" in a story. A car explodes. Lovers kiss. Someone learns a secret. If it moves the story forward through physical action (that is, action we can see or hear), it belongs to plot.

Recall from the previous chapter that a story must be told in a structured order. Plot and structure are almost synonymous. It is the organized arrangement of events that *gives* story its structure. The plot is like the skeleton of a story. It supports the entire body because every bone has been put in the right place. To achieve this perfect state, a plot must follow certain principles which govern what events must occur, when.

Though feature films appear complicated on the surface, the principles behind good plot structure are simple. Behind all the trappings of screencraft lies one fundamental, yet largely-ignored concept that has provided the foundation of every great story ever told. This is the golden key of storytelling, the seed from which all plot originates, the device that unites every element into a single whole. Prepare yourself, for you are about to unearth buried treasure.

It is called the STORY SPINE.

Now to be honest, some use of the word "spine" has been bandied about in the screenwriting community for decades. However, it has remained unclear just what the Story Spine is and how it should be used. This is unfortunate, since I can honestly say from personal experience that an incomprehension of the Story Spine has been the main cause for failure in over 90% of the screenplays I have ever read. To say that again:

Over 90% of screenplays fail because the writer does not understand the Story Spine!

The Story Spine is the key to successful storytelling. If a storyteller should learn only one thing about the craft, it must be this.

WHAT IS THE STORY SPINE?

If plot is the skeleton of a story, the Story Spine, as the name implies, is the backbone. Take a look at the skeleton of any animal and you will notice that the backbone forms the core of its structure. It runs the entire length of the animal, from head to tail. It connects every part of the body, uniting its anatomy into a functioning whole. It contains the spinal cord through which movement is controlled. Sever the spine and the animal is as good as dead.

In the same way, the Story Spine runs the entire length of a story, starting at its beginning and continuing unbroken to its end. It unites all characters, events, and ideas into a functioning whole. It contains the motivating force that propels a story forward. Without a Spine, a story is lifeless.

Last chapter, we established that a story must be about characters – dealing with a problem – unified by a premise – told in a structured order. The Story Spine accomplishes all of this and more. Its structure, a) contains the essential information of the story's premise, including the problem and characters, b) provides the motivating force that causes the premise to develop into a structured narrative, and most importantly, c) *orientates the audience* to understand what is going on, who is important, where the story is going, and why they should care. Simply put, the Story Spine turns a story into a *story*. Without a Spine, a story will not properly exist.

Let me repeat that:

Without a Story Spine, a story will not exist.

Let me repeat it again:

WITHOUT A STORY SPINE, A STORY WILL NOT EXIST!!!

Have I made it clear just how important the Story Spine is?

The Story Spine begins with a single character. Most stories revolve around the actions of one person. This is the story's hero, the central figure, the person the audience should care most about. In dramatic terms, this character is called the PROTAGONIST (meaning "the first actor"). A story is then constructed around the protagonist from five simple components:

A. The protagonist's main STORY PROBLEM,

B. The protagonist's main STORY GOAL that, once achieved, will overcome that problem,

C. The PATH OF ACTION the protagonist takes to reach that goal,

D. The MAIN CONFLICT – a force that opposes the protagonist's actions, and

E. The STAKES that push the protagonist onward in spite of the conflict's opposition.

Drawn as a diagram, the Story Spine looks like this:

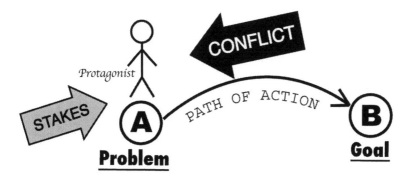

All five components must be present for the Story Spine to exist. Like the engine of a car, if only one part is removed, the entire machine ceases to function. It does not matter how well-constructed the other components are, they can never overcome the absence of the missing piece.

The Story Spine is a concept that predates the cinema. In fact, it is as old as storytelling itself. Whether it was by experience or instinct, the greatest storytellers have always understood that the most audience-pleasing stories were those that contained a Problem, Goal, Path of Action, Main Conflict, and Stakes. Let us imagine, fifty thousand years ago, there was a caveman storyteller named Og. Here is a story Og might have told his people:

Gorak the Mammoth Hunter

> "Many seasons ago, there was a terrible winter. No animals could be found for hunting, and it was feared the tribe would starve. So, Gorak, the bravest of all hunters, set out to find the food to save his people. Gorak searched for days, over hills and mountains, through snow and wind, but found nothing. Then, at the point of starvation, Gorak saw a single giant mammoth in the valley below. Gorak knew such a beast could kill him, yet he had no choice. He attacked the mammoth. There was a fierce

battle. Gorak killed the mammoth, and with the meat, the tribe survived the winter."

Though this is a simple story, it is a complete story, since it contains all five elements of the Story Spine. Its protagonist has a PROBLEM; Gorak's tribe has no food. A GOAL; to find food. A PATH OF ACTION; Gorak searches for, and eventually battles with the mammoth. CONFLICT; Gorak deals with bad terrain, harsh weather, and a mammoth who will not go down without a fight. And, STAKES; if Gorak succeeds, the tribe will survive. If he fails, everyone will die.

Since Og's story was a complete story, its audience found it memorable and entertaining. However, if it had lacked even one of its five components, the story would have failed. Let us take a closer look to find out why.

1. THE STORY PROBLEM

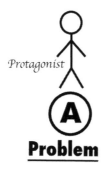

Once again, stories are all about problems. The arrival of a problem is what causes the story's action to begin.

Nearly every story begins with the protagonist carrying on with his or her normal, everyday life. They perform their normal, everyday actions, and interact with the people and things in their normal, everyday world. This life may be pleasant, or it may be horrid. It may be dull, or exciting. Whatever it is, it represents the protagonist's *status quo*. The daily life of *American Beauty*'s Lester Burnham is one of drudgery and humiliation, so this is what we see when his story begins. James Bond's daily routine involves chasing down international criminals in exotic locations, so this is what opens every Bond film.

Before long, a problem arises to disrupt this routine. The problem may be a threat. It may be a challenge. It may be both. No matter what it is, the problem must be something significant enough to uproot the status quo and throw the protagonist's life into disarray. Terrorists take over the building (*Die Hard*). Marty McFly finds himself stuck in the past (*Back to the Future*). Marlin's son is abducted (*Finding Nemo*).

The moment of the problem's arrival is called the INCITING INCIDENT. Sometimes, the problem is huge and life-threatening from the start. *Independence Day* (1996) begins with the appearance of alien spacecraft over every major world city. At other times, the problem starts small, but then grows in severity. The problem in *Alien* begins with a simple distress signal from the reaches of space. Regardless of whether the problem starts out large or small, the protagonist cannot ignore it. The Story Problem puts the protagonist into a situation where he or she absolutely cannot continue on with life until the problem is solved. John McClane *must* do something about the terrorists. Marty McFly *must* find a way home. Marlin *must* get his son back. This is the only way to return life to normal.

The inciting incident is thus the catalyst that sparks the adventure. It is dynamite that starts a landslide. Until it occurs, the characters have little or no reason to take action. Because of this, storytellers should not wait too long to introduce the Story Problem. The longer the delay, the longer the audience must wait for the story to get moving. A story cannot truly begin until the hero is confronted by something he or she feels MUST be acted upon, NOW.

In a handful of stories, rather than disrupt the status quo, the Story Problem *is* the status quo. In other words, the protagonist's problem does not arrive suddenly. It has instead been present for some time. However, the protagonist has either failed to recognize the problem, or has chosen to submissively put up with it. *American Beauty* is one of these stories. In this case, the inciting incident occurs when an event forces the protagonist to recognize he or she has a problem and then *choose to do something* about it. *American Beauty*'s Lester Burnham is willing to put up with the misery of his daily life until he experiences an "awakening" at the sight of his daughter's friend Angela. This event becomes the catalyst that motivates Lester to stand up for himself and fight back.

Once the inciting incident occurs, everything the protagonist does should be part of a clear and focused effort to overcome the Story Problem. Nothing should distract from the protagonist's quest. The Story Problem must create a situation where all other worries or concerns become insignificant in comparison. To illustrate, let's say you are at home, beginning a day in your life as normal as any other. With it will come the stresses and responsibilities you face every day. Only this morning, you step from your bedroom and find a man-eating tiger in your living room. Well, that's a pretty big problem that has been thrust into your life, isn't it? Suddenly, all other worries become insignificant. You are not willing, and certainly not able, to perform any other task until you get rid of that tiger.

I sometimes find scripts in which the writer does not bother to create a Story Problem. With no inciting incident, these scripts become nothing more than a series of pointless episodes where characters wander like zombies from one place to another without purpose or direction. The characters never accomplish anything of significance, simply because there is no urgent situation compelling them to do so. If the characters have no reason to do anything, why should the audience care to watch them do it? Other times, beginning writers throw their protagonists headlong into action and adventure, but never create a Story Problem to explain why. When this happens, all the hero's actions, no matter how impressive, seem pointless. Imagine "Gorak the Mammoth Hunter" without a Story Problem. Let us say the tribe is not starving to death. Gorak now has no reason to risk his life in search of food. Yet, he still travels many miles, faces the elements, and fights to the death with a dangerous beast. This tale would have confused Og's audience. They would no doubt ask, "Why Gorak go hunt? Why he risk life? Gorak not brave. Gorak stupid!" A story without a problem will lack any purpose.

2. THE STORY GOAL

Once the protagonist recognizes the Story Problem and feels compelled to take action, the next step is to establish a *goal.* The STORY GOAL is a certain accomplishment that the protagonist believes, once achieved, will overcome the Story Problem and return life to what he or she wishes it to be. The Story Goal is the problem's hoped-for solution. In *Die Hard,* terrorists have taken over Nakatomi Tower. John McClane hopes to defeat them. In *Back to the Future,* Marty is stuck in the year 1955. His goal is to return to his own time. In *Finding Nemo,* Marlin's son has been abducted. His goal is to get his son back again.

If we think of a story as a physical journey, the Story Problem is what first pushes the protagonist out the door. The Story Goal is his or her end destination. Without a Story Goal, the protagonist has no place to go. I sometimes find scripts that establish a Story Problem, but not a Story Goal. In these scripts, the protagonists recognize their problems but never DO anything about it. Imagine this story: "Gorak's tribe is starving. Gorak never does anything about it. Everyone dies." A story without a goal lacks direction and will ultimately lead nowhere.

Reaching the Story Goal will bring the stability back to the protagonist's world, either by restoring the status quo, or by improving life from what it was when the story began. Marty McFly's Story Goal is to restore the status quo. He wishes to return to 1985, exactly as he left it. The goal in *Alien* is also restorative. A monster is loose aboard the ship. The crew wishes to eliminate the monster so the ship can be safe once again. In contrast, the

Story Goal of *American Beauty* is progressive in nature. Lester Burnham hates his life, so he wishes to improve it. Likewise, *Star Wars* begins with the galaxy enslaved by an evil empire. The goal is to improve life by defeating that empire.

Once the protagonist chooses a goal, his or her path should not waver from it. No distractions. No side trips. A good story forces the protagonist to have a one-track mind. There is a tiger in your living room. It does not make any sense to do anything other than try to get that tiger out.

In the same way, a protagonist must be one hundred percent committed to reaching this goal. No backing down, no quitting. Hesitation and half-stepping make weak action. In cases where the hero starts out reluctant, the storyteller must quickly put the hero into a situation where he or she is *forced* to become dedicated, or else. No matter how many times the hero may fail, or how badly, he or she must be willing to keep going until either the goal is achieved, or the hero is met with a final, irreversible defeat.

Once a storyteller matches a Story Problem to a Story Goal, something very important happens. The audience asks a question. They wonder, "Will the hero achieve this goal?" This is called the MAJOR DRAMATIC QUESTION. Will Marty McFly get back to 1985? Will John McClane defeat the terrorists? Will Marlin find Nemo? This is the moment that hooks the audience into the story. They continue to watch because they wish to know the answer. Therefore, to keep the audience glued to their seats, this question must not be answered until the story's very end.

Reaching the Story Goal answers the Major Dramatic Question (MDQ). The Story Problem has been overcome, stability has been restored, and the story must come to an end. Should characters reach their goals too early, they will be left with nothing to do for the rest of the film. The audience then grows bored because there is nothing more to hold their interest. The James Bond film *Casino Royale* (2006) is one such story marred by a prematurely achieved Story Goal. *Casino Royale* asks, "Will Bond defeat the villain Le Chiffre?" Only Le Chiffre is killed with thirty minutes left in the film! What then follows is a long, dull sequence in which Bond does little more than lay about because his job is finished. The audience, on the other hand, is left checking their watches, wondering why the movie will not end.

Casino Royale then tries to overcome this mistake by giving Bond a new Story Problem and Goal with only minutes left in the film. However, this error is even more egregious than the first. *Royale* basically attempts to create a brand new story right at the point when everything should be wrapping up. A story can have only one Story Spine, and with it only one Story Problem and one Story Goal. Switching Story Goals is like trying to change horses in midstream. It will confuse the audience, lose the narrative's direction, and disallow the unity of action a good story needs.

3. THE PATH OF ACTION

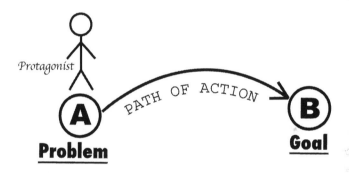

The Story Problem begins a story. Reaching the Story Goal ends it. The Path of Action is everything in between. It is the road the protagonist travels on his or her adventure. Though some stories involve a literal journey (*The Wizard of Oz, The Lord of the Rings: The Fellowship of the Ring, Finding Nemo*), the Path of Action is usually a metaphorical road, one made of all actions the protagonist must take to overcome the problem and bring the story to an end. After all, victory is not going to fall into the protagonist's lap. He or she must DO something to get it.

This path can never be easy. A goal easily achieved has little value. What if Gorak did not need to spend days on end searching for the mammoth? What if he simply found the mammoth standing outside his camp, patiently waiting for a spear through its heart? This story would not have impressed its audience. The goal was reached with far too much ease, making the hero's actions not very heroic at all.

The more characters must struggle for what they want, the bigger the victory will be when they finally get it. If the audience sees the hero go through enough trouble, make enough hard choices, put enough at risk, the story's outcome will be perceived as emotionally satisfying. The Path of Action must be a journey filled with tests and trials. This not only makes a story exciting and unpredictable, but meaningful at its end.

As with any journey, the Path of Action must always MOVE FORWARD. Characters must push towards their goal with each and every scene until they reach the journey's end. When people speak of "pace," or "momentum," they refer to the rate which the plot advances down its Path of Action. Constant forward progress is what separates a good Path of Action from a poor one. Every event should do something to advance the story. A story is like a shark. If it stops moving, it dies. The moment you pause your story, allow your protagonist to stop pursuing the goal, or send the narrative onto an unrelated tangent, tension will fade and the audience will lose interest.

The Path of Action is where most scripts falter. Typically, things go wrong in one of two ways.

The first occurs when writers create protagonists unwilling to take strong, willful action towards the Story Goal. Instead, these protagonists are content to sit and wait for the problem to resolve itself. These stories move at a snail's pace, if they move at all. It is up to the protagonist, and the protagonist alone, to be the active force that makes things happen. Success cannot simply fall into the hero's lap. He or she must earn it through hard work. Only then will the audience find the outcome satisfying.

An even worse mistake occurs when writers send the plot off its proper Path of Action into unrelated tangents. When people say a script has "gone off its spine," they mean characters have stopped pursuing the Story Goal and are now mucking about in areas with little to do with the story's original premise. Like a hiker who leaves the marked trail, the story has lost its way. The audience then grows frustrated as it watches events wander aimlessly in the woods.

Remember that the audience has been hooked into the story by the Major Dramatic Question. They continue to watch because they want to know, "Will the hero achieve X?" Therefore, in order to maintain the audience's interest, every event should somehow relate to this original question. Unrelated plot tangents damage a story by stalling forward progress and distracting from it's focus. Think of your story as a freight train. Connecting its point of departure and its final destination is a single length of track. The train must stay on its tracks. Jump the rails, and the result will be a disaster.

4. THE MAIN CONFLICT

Imagine I interrupted your busy day to tell you this story:

> "This morning, I couldn't find my dog Rex. I got really worried
> because Rex is very old, and if he got out, he would get lost. So,
> I threw on my coat, grabbed my keys, opened the front door –
> and there he was on the doorstep."

At this point, you would probably feel pretty annoyed at me. I just wasted your time with a completely uneventful story. How was that in any way interesting?

Nothing is less exciting than a story where everything goes as planned. People will not listen very long to a tale on how nice your day was, how well the children behaved last night, or how perfect you find the weather. These stories are not very interesting. They contain no drama. The stories people want to hear, the stories that never have a problem gathering an audience, are stories where *everything goes wrong*. Why? Because these stories contain CONFLICT. Conflict is what makes a story interesting. Conflict creates drama.

Conflict is something with which we are all familiar. We face it every day. Whenever something stands in the way of what we want, that is conflict. When any goal is made more difficult, that is conflict. If any person, thing, or event makes life harder than it already is, conflict is the result. Conflict is what makes life hell. It is also what makes it so very interesting.

Conflict excites and titillates the human mind. Though few like to experience conflict directly, we all enjoy observing conflict within safe, controlled boundaries. Conflict is the reason people love sports. It is the cause of our fascination with crime, politics, romantic quarrels, and celebrity gossip. It is also the source of the dramatic excitement we feel when watching a movie.

Conflict creates DRAMA. One cannot exist without the other. It is hard to define drama as opposed to conflict, since the terms are practically one and the same. When someone calls a situation "dramatic," they mean it is filled with conflict. Story drama, in a way, is nothing more than the structured presentation of a conflict through the actions of characters.

Though the exact psychological reasons for our love of conflict are unknown, the evidence seems to suggest something as simple as human curiosity. When two things come into conflict, whether it be an argument, a fistfight, or a suitcase that will not close, it creates a situation in which the outcome is unclear. This uncertainty raises questions. And when the human mind has questions, it experiences a natural urge to pay attention until an answer is found. The longer the situation remains in doubt, the longer we remain interested. Think of a sporting event. If one team jumps out to an insurmountable lead, the fans grow disinterested since they can already foresee the game's result. On the other hand, if the score goes back and forth, keeping the outcome in doubt, the fans remain on the edges of their seats. They are excited by the uncertainty.

I sometimes find scripts by writers who have yet to learn the importance of conflict. In these scripts, characters breeze through the narrative with no trouble at all. Nothing ever goes wrong. Everybody gets along swell. Sounds pleasant, doesn't it? It's not. It is as dull as eight hours of vacation slides. Without conflict, there is no drama. Without drama, there is nothing to hold the audience's interest.

However, the Story Spine cannot make do with just any random collection of conflicting events. A clear and focused plot requires a MAIN CONFLICT. Here is how it works: The protagonist has a goal. He or she takes action to reach that goal. Now, in order for these actions to be dramatic (that is, filled with conflict), *something must stand in the protagonist's way.* There must be a singular force that does not want the protagonist to succeed. This force then takes action to stop the protagonist. Whenever the protagonist pushes forward, this force pushes back. This creates the story's Main Conflict.

The source of this conflict is called the FORCE OF ANTAGONISM. In most cases, this force is another character, known as the ANTAGONIST. Antagonists are usually easy to spot: Hans Gruber in *Die Hard,* Darth Vader in *Star Wars,* Apollo Creed in *Rocky.* These characters block the hero's path to success. They do not want the hero to win and will do whatever it takes to stop it from happening. In other cases, the force of antagonism comes not from one character, but from the protagonist's general situation as a whole. Stories of wilderness survival find the hero threatened by a combination of weather, lack of food, and dangerous animals. Films that address social issues often involve a protagonist taking on society at large. Yet, even in these cases, it is best if the writer chooses one character or thing to act as a tangible representative for the conflict as a whole. For example, the conflict of *Schindler's List* does not come from a single person, but from the entire culture under the Nazi regime. However, the storytellers chose to channel most of this conflict through the actions of a single character, Amon Goeth (Ralph Fienes).

In certain stories, the protagonist can even be his or her own force of antagonism. These stories contain protagonists who are constantly defeated by their own deeply flawed behavior, rather than by the actions of others. This creates a Jekyll & Hyde-type situation where the protagonist is his or her own worst enemy. Jake LaMotta in *Raging Bull* (1980) is one such character. Jake wants happiness and success like anyone else, however it is his own jealous, self-destructive behavior that always brings him ruin. If these characters are to succeed, they must do so by overcoming themselves.

No matter where the force of antagonism originates, it is essential that this force *directly oppose* the protagonist's actions from the beginning of the story to its end. It must be the protagonist's shadow, dogging him or her every step of the way. The force of antagonism does not just block the protagonist's actions, but is DEAD SET against them and is willing to do everything possible to cause the protagonist to fail. This creates a scenario where only one side can win. This is called a *unity of opposites*. For example, the heroes of the *The Matrix* wish to free humanity by destroying the Matrix. This brings them into conflict with the Agents, artificial men designed to protect the Matrix. Since the destruction of the Matrix would mean the end of the Agents and all they know, the Agents are willing to do everything possible to stop the heroes. In *The Lord of the Rings,* the antagonist Sauron wants to find the One Ring so he may conquer Middle Earth. In opposition, Frodo and his allies wish to destroy the ring to stop this from happening. This creates a head-to-head struggle where both sides have no choice but to fight against each other until one is defeated.

Generally, a story with one strong source of conflict creates far better drama than one composed of multiple smaller conflicts. One might think more villains would equal more drama, but the opposite is true. Dividing screen time amongst multiple forces of antagonism splinters the Path of Action into several directions, creating confusion and disallowing unity of action. Each antagonist will then seem only half as powerful as each dilutes the importance of the others. If you have a hard time believing this, take a look at a movie such as *Spider-man 3* (2007) and try not to be convinced that the story would have been better served with one antagonist instead of three. The Story Spine gets its power from its simplicity. One protagonist. One Story Goal. For the most dramatic conflict, one mighty force should stand in the way.

5. THE STAKES

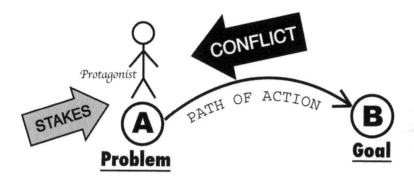

So now, the hero has a problem, he or she has chosen a goal, and takes action – only to encounter enormous resistance from the force of antagonism. Once this happens, what motivates the hero to keep going? If conflict makes the Path of Action so difficult, dangerous even, what stops the hero from deciding the goal is no longer worth the struggle? If the protagonist is to continue taking action in the face of overwhelming conflict, there must be a darn good reason. There must be a counter-force pushing the protagonist onward. This force is called the STAKES.

The stakes are "what's in it" for the protagonist. They are what the protagonist has to gain should he or she win (happiness, freedom, stability), versus the consequences that will occur should he or she lose (death, ruin, loss of loved ones). Stakes keep the protagonist personally invested in the situation. The protagonist is not in this for fun and games. He or she keeps fighting because there is something hanging in the balance. Something important. Something he or she desperately wishes to gain, or something he or she fears to lose.

If John McClane succeeds in *Die Hard,* he will be reunited with his family. If he fails, he and many others will die. If Jason Bourne succeeds in *The Bourne Identity,* he will not only regain his sense of self, but also his freedom. If he fails, he will permanently lose that freedom, and possibly his life as well. If Rocky wins his fight with Apollo Creed, he will receive the respect and recognition of the whole world. If he loses, all he will get is humiliation.

Like conflict, stakes are something we constantly deal with in daily life. With every important decision comes an internal weighing of what is to be gained or lost. For instance, many people dislike their jobs. Yet, they do not quit. They keep doing something they dislike because there is something at stake. If they continue to work, they will receive a steady paycheck. If they quit, they will lose the means to support themselves. As long as what is to be won or lost continues to outweigh the displeasure one must put up with, people will willingly suffer the daily grind.

Writers and actors alike speak of a character's *motivation.* Simply put, motivation is the impulse that causes people to act. It explains why characters do what they do. Motivation is a natural outcome of stakes. In any given situation, what is to be won or lost puts pressure on a character, which in turn motivates him or her to act in a certain way. If a story lacks stakes, characters will seem to behave without motivation. The characters do things, but the audience does not understand why. Consider another lost dog story. This time, the story contains conflict, but lacks stakes:

> "Last month, I went looking for this lost dog. I searched for days. In the morning. At night. In the sun. In the rain. I even took a sick day from work so I could keep at it. It took forever, but I finally found the dog."

Anyone listening would undoubtedly sense something was missing and ask :

"I don't understand. Was this your dog?"

"No."

"Did it belong to a friend?"

"No."

"Was there a reward?"

"No."

"...Are you insane?"

Life is hard enough. No one is willing to take on any more trouble than they must unless there is a darn good reason. Having a character run head-long into risky situations without good reason will not be considered heroic. It will be seen as pointless, foolish, even suicidal. These actions will not make sense unless there is something to be won, something to be lost, or even better, both.

Stakes explain why the hero cares about the situation. They also explain why the audience should care as well. Actions without consequences have little meaning to an audience. If nothing good comes from victory, or nothing bad from failure, why should the result matter at all? On the other hand, if the audience cares about a character and then understands something bad will happen should that character fail, the audience becomes emotionally invested in the outcome. The audience roots for the hero to succeed because they know and fear what will happen if the hero should not. Clear, identifiable stakes allow the audience to understand the deeper significance behind story events. They are not just watching a conflict, but a conflict with consequences. Consequences the audience cares about as much as the characters.

Take another look at the diagram of the Story Spine. The Main Conflict creates a massive force pushing against the protagonist. The Stakes provide a counter-force pushing back. If the protagonist is going to stay in the fight, the force pushing forward must be just as strong, or even stronger than the forces aligned against the hero. In great stories, heroes face incredible amounts of risk. To remain plausible, that which is to be won or lost must outweigh the risk. Why *must* Neo and his friends destroy the Matrix? They are putting their lives in danger when it is far safer to simply hide from the machines. Neo and his friends choose to take on the risk because they know the fate of humanity lies in their hands. The benefit to be won outweighs the risk necessary to get it. Why *must* Indiana Jones find the Ark of the Covenant before the Nazis? In this case, Indy does not have much to gain, but he does have everything to lose. If the Nazis find the Ark first, they will use it to conquer the world. The cost of failure greatly outweighs the risk. Gorak cannot give up when he realizes the mammoth may kill him. Gorak is fighting for the survival of his tribe, and that is far more important than his personal safety.

In great movies, the stakes are HUGE. In *The Godfather,* the fate of Michael Corleone's entire family is at stake. In *Die Hard,* the lives of dozens of people. In *Star Wars,* the freedom of the entire galaxy. However, stakes need not be on such a grand scale to be considered huge. In *Rocky,* the title character's sense of self-worth is at stake. That may not mean anything to the person sitting next to him on the bus, but it means the world to him. A stranger may see little at stake in Dr. Malcolm Crowe's attempts to help Cole in *The Sixth Sense.* However, Crowe is haunted by the memory of another boy he failed in the past. Crowe will not be able to live with himself if he fails with Cole as well. Though these stakes may not be on an earth-shattering scale, what is important is that they *seem* huge to the protagonist. These characters still fight like their lives depend on it, because what they have to gain or lose is incredibly important to them.

Problem. Goal. Path of Action. Conflict. Stakes. It is surprisingly simple. Yet these five components, when properly used, always have and always will hold the key to great storytelling. Everything else within storytelling is simply an embellishment upon this basic design. With that said, we move deeper into the structure of plot to reveal how the Story Spine expands to create an entire cinematic narrative.

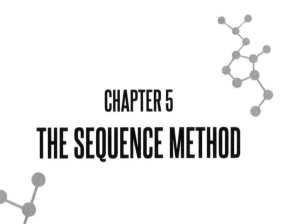

CHAPTER 5
THE SEQUENCE METHOD

Here again is the Story Spine:

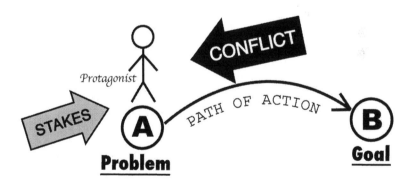

This diagram was designed to be simple and straightforward so it may ilus-trate the basics of any story, regardless of what form that story may take. However, as we move from examining all storytelling in general to the feature-length cinematic story in particular, we find that the Spine becomes a bit more complicated in a certain area. A more accurate representation would look something like this:

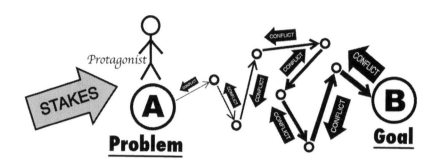

In the first diagram, the Path of Action is represented by a single line traveling straight from Problem to Goal. This might suggest that a protagonist need only take a single set of actions to reach his or her goal. While this may be sufficient for short forms of story, such as a folk tale or anecdote, a feature-length film must hold an audience's attention for ninety to over one hundred and fifty minutes. This creates a problem. If an audience must watch a protagonist pursue the same course of action scene after scene, with no change or variation, the story will quickly become repetitive and dull. The audience will lose interest because nothing is DEVELOPING. And development requires *change*.

A good plot depends largely upon the pace at which development occurs. Too little development, and the story will move like pond water. On the other hand, if development is too quick or chaotic, the plot becomes confusing and erratic. If a cinematic story is to move at a proper pace while maintaining focus and direction, the long, winding Path of Action must have a structure of its own.

Take a look at the updated diagram. Its Path of Action is not made of one straight line, but many small segments, all twisting and turning their way to the ultimate goal. These are called STORY SEQUENCES. Story sequences can be thought of as "legs" in the protagonist's journey. Like the chapters in a novel, story sequences break up the long cinematic narrative into a series of smaller, more discrete units of action. The Path of Action is not one long, plodding marathon after a far-off finish line, but rather a series of sprints.

In each sequence, the protagonist pursues a separate, more immediate SEQUENCE GOAL. Sequence goals exist as direct subsets of the main Story Goal. When a story begins, the ultimate Story Goal is very far away. To reach it, the protagonist must take things step by step. In each story sequence, the protagonist pursues a smaller, related goal. Each of these smaller goals have the cumulative effect of moving the protagonist closer and closer to the ultimate prize. To provide a simple illustration, let us say you are required every morning to get to your workplace by 8:00 AM. This is your ultimate goal. But to achieve this, you must first accomplish a series of smaller, more immediate goals. First, you must wake up, take a shower, and get dressed. Then you must catch the bus. Once on the bus, you must reach your destination. Finally, with whatever time remains, you must get to your work station and start your day. Each of these smaller, more immediate tasks require their own specific actions and come with their own difficulties. Yet if successful, every sub-goal works to get you closer and closer to your final destination.

Each story sequence is brought to an end by a TURNING POINT. These are represented by the small white circles on the diagram. Turning points are events that create a dramatic and permanent change in the story situation. As the name suggests, they literally turn the course of the story in a new direction by bringing the action of one sequence to an end and throwing the hero headlong into the next. This typically occurs either because the protagonist has reached the sequence sub-goal, or because something forces the protagonist to abandon the current course of action and shift attention to a new, more urgent task. After the turning point, a new story sequence begins in which the protagonist pursues a new sequence goal. The value of turning points cannot be underestimated. They provide the story's most important events. Like the evenly-spaced columns that support a building, turning points create the rhythmic structure that give a story its ultimate shape and form.

Here is how all of this works:

The inciting incident thrusts a Story Problem into the protagonist's life. In reaction, the protagonist establishes a Story Goal. However, reaching this goal will be no simple task. So, the protagonist begins by first taking action towards a closer, more immediate sub-goal. This is usually something small and practical, the simplest action the character thinks will get what he or she needs with the smallest amount of risk. So, if the character's problem is that she has been evicted from her apartment, her first action would be to talk to her landlord. If the hero's wife has been kidnapped, his first action would be to contact the police. The protagonist has every reason to believe that this simple, low-risk action will succeed. It will either solve the problem, or at least get the ball rolling towards its eventual resolution. Unfortunately, this is not the case. Something gets in the way.

The landlord slams the door in the woman's face. The police do not believe the man's story. The protagonist has encountered an OBSTACLE. Obstacles are roadblocks on the Path of Action. They are walls that spring up to prevent the protagonist from reaching his or her goal through the current line of action. The obstacle could come from any number of sources. It may be another character (the antagonist blocks the hero's actions), an event outside of the character's control (the man gets in a car wreck on the way to the police station), or perhaps new information (the man learns *he* is the prime suspect in his wife's disappearance). No matter what the source, the obstacle is more than just an annoyance. It stops the hero dead in his or her tracks. It must be an *insurmountable* obstruction that makes it impossible for the hero to make any more progress through his or her current efforts. To see the difference: Heavy traffic on the way to work is not an obstacle. It may make things difficult, but you will still reach your goal through the current line of action. Running out of gas is an obstacle. It stops you dead in your tracks and forces you to take new action if you wish to continue on towards your destination.

When confronted by an obstacle, the protagonist faces a choice. He or she can either give up, or decide to do what it takes to get around that obstacle. To do so, the protagonist must find a *new* course of action. This creates a turning point. It launches the story in a new direction after a new immediate goal.

So begins the second leg of the protagonist's journey. However, this time actions must be a little bigger. The small, low-risk actions taken previously did not work. The protagonist must one-up him or herself, put forth some more effort, and become willing to take on a little risk. So, failing with her landlord, our evicted heroine decides to contact her estranged sister in hope that she will take her in. Our hero with the kidnapped wife now seeks the help of a private investigator. The protagonist hopes these stronger actions will prove more successful than the last. But, something happens once again.

Another obstacle blocks the hero's way. The evicted woman's sister wants nothing to do with her. The only detective willing to take the man's case is an unreliable drunk. What to do now? We have reached another turning point. The protagonists cannot quit at this point. The stakes have grown too high. They have no choice but to begin yet another course of action towards another immediate sub-goal. The woman decides to learn why her sister hates her. The man decides to investigate the kidnapping himself. So begins the third leg of the Path of Action.

The journey on this leg becomes even tougher. It requires more effort and holds more risk. Yet, hope urges our heroes onward. The protagonists believe that some way, somehow, this new set of actions will pull them through. But then, something happens. Again. And again. The plot continues to develop in this manner, sequence after sequence, turning point after turning point, until the story's climactic end, where the hero, weak and exhausted from the long journey, finally reaches the Story Goal he or she set out to attain so long ago.

Let's look at how this works in one of our study films. *The Lord of the Rings: The Fellowship of the Ring* is the story of Frodo Baggins, an unlikely hero who must protect a magic ring from the forces of evil. At the start, Frodo's task is rather simple. He must take the ring to the city of Bree where he will meet Gandalf the Wizard at the Prancing Pony Inn. Frodo believes that once this is accomplished his work will be over.

Only this proves more difficult than Frodo originally believed. An unforeseen development creates an obstacle. He is discovered by a Ring Wraith, an undead creature sent to find the ring and kill its bearer. Frodo cannot continue his mission on his current path. If he does, the Wraith will kill him. Frodo must find a new course of action.

This creates a turning point. To continue, Frodo must pursue a new immediate goal: to escape the Wraith. So begins a new story sequence. Frodo's actions meet success this time. He escapes the Wraith and reaches Bree. However, Frodo's victory is short-lived. Another obstacle meets Frodo at the Inn. Gandalf is nowhere to be found.

What to do now? Bree is filled with danger, and the Wraiths are still after Frodo. Without Gandalf's protection, the ring will surely be found. This forces Frodo to make another story-changing decision. Backed into a corner, Frodo decides to accept the aid of a stranger and continue the ring's journey on his own.

This begins a third sequence. Here Frodo must put forth more effort and take on more risk. Frodo has a new immediate goal: to take the ring to Rivendale, where he will find protection. This course of action goes well at first, but an obstacle arises once more. The Wraiths find them, and Frodo is poisoned by one of their blades.

This obstacle creates another turning point. Frodo will die unless he receives first aid. If this happens, the entire mission will fail. So begins a new story sequence with a new immediate goal: to save Frodo's life. Frodo reaches this goal with the help of his allies and is healed. However, Frodo's troubles are not allayed for long.

The story turns once more as a band of heroes gather to decide what must be done with the ring. At this point, it seems Frodo has finished his task and can go home. However, another obstacle arises to prevent this. It becomes clear that Frodo is the only one amongst the heroes capable of resisting the ring's power. Frodo must once again choose to continue his adventure and begin the next story sequence.

Note that story sequences are never arbitrary. They do not go into tangents or pursue areas unrelated to the Story Spine. No matter how the obstacles may alter his path, Frodo continues to move in the same direction. Every action he takes either gets him one step closer to his ultimate goal, or works to ensure his survival so he may continue this quest. Though the story may twist and turn in new directions, the end destination always remains the same.

To illustrate further, let us say you are taking a cross-country trip from Dallas to Denver. Denver, of course, is your ultimate destination. So, you start with what seems like the easiest and safest route. But, a distance down the road you find there is a detour. You are forced to turn off onto another highway. This road is not as convenient, but it will still get you where you wish to go. Unfortunately, a hundred miles down this new road you find that the route has been closed due to flooding. Because of this, you must backtrack and find yet another road that will bypass the flooding. So, you turn off onto a small winding road that cuts through the mountains. This road is tougher, but according to the map, it will still get you to Denver. Only then, you find that this route has been blocked as well. With no remaining choice, you turn onto a dirt road that is not even on the map and hope, *hope* that this road will get you where you need to go. Though the route of your journey is constantly forced in new directions, the end goal remains the same. You are still trying to get to Denver.

STRUCTURE WITHIN THE SEQUENCE

Last chapter, we established that every good story is formed by a five-component structure called the Story Spine. Story sequences can be thought of as smaller, interrelated *sub-stories*. No story can exist without a spine, and these smaller sub-stories are no exception. Each story sequence then finds focus and direction by paralleling the structure of the main narrative through their own SEQUENCE SPINES.

A sequence spine operates exactly like the Story Spine, only on a smaller scale. It contains a sequence problem, a sequence goal, a sequence path of action, a main sequence conflict, and sequence stakes. To illustrate, let's use the sequence in *Fellowship* where Frodo flees the Wraith. Frodo's sequence problem: The Wraith has discovered him. Frodo's sequence goal: To escape the Wraith. Frodo's sequence path of action: He and his comrades flee. Frodo's sequence conflict: The Wraith will not let him get away. Frodo's sequence stakes: If he fails to escape, he will be killed and the Wraith will take the ring.

Sequence spines are not independent from the main Story Spine. Just as story sequences are not separate, independent narratives but rather interdependent sub-narratives that work together to create the story as a whole, each sequence spine is merely a subset of the main Story Spine. Sequence spines do not exist for their own purpose, but to develop the main Spine and serve its needs. Each component of the sequence spine is merely a smaller and more immediate expression of its larger counterpart. Each sequence problem is a direct result of the Story Problem. Each sequence goal is a more immediate step taken towards the main Story Goal. Each sequence conflict comes as a result of the main Story Conflict. The stakes of each sequence are directly connected to the main Stakes. And finally, the sequence's path of action is really nothing more than a small segment of the story's Path of Action as a whole.

We see these connections quite well as Frodo flees the Wraith. The Wraith has discovered Frodo (sequence problem) because the Wraith has been sent by the antagonist Sauron to find the ring. Therefore, the sequence problem is a direct result of the main Story Problem. Escaping the Wraith (sequence goal) will allow Frodo to continue his pursuit of his main Story Goal. So, success with this goal is necessary for Frodo to reach his ultimate goal. Since the Wraith (the source of the sequence conflict) is a minion of Sauron, it is as if Sauron himself pursues Frodo. So, the sequence conflict is directly related to the Main Conflict. If Frodo fails in this sequence (sequence stakes), the forces of evil will claim the ring. This will not only mean doom for this sequence, but for the story as a whole. Finally, every action Frodo takes in this sequence path of action becomes a small part of the overarching Path of Action Frodo must take to reach the story's end.

Thus, the action of any sequence is never random or isolated, but rather exists to continually develop and build upon the action of the main Story

Spine. Like how the branches of a tree grow outwards while remaining connected to their root, sequence spines allow story sequences to develop the plot's action down various paths while remaining connected to the story's original source. This separate-yet-unified structure keeps a two-hour movie from drifting or wandering off course, no matter how many twists and turns its plot may take. Everything remains connected. If a sequence contains a spine with components that do not support and relate to the main Story Spine, it becomes like a branch that has broken off the tree. It is not connected to anything, nor does it lead to anything else. It creates little more than a tangent of irrelevant actions that will distract from the story and skew it off course.

Even if the narrative, for one reason or another, must turn down a path where actions do not directly relate to the main Story Spine, the sequence spine must still connect to the overall structure in an indirect manner. Let us look at a hypothetical screenplay that must turn down such a road. It follows a knight who must save the life of a dying queen. At a certain turning point, the knight learns that the queen can be saved with the help of a particular wizard. Unfortunately, the wizard is locked in a castle guarded by a monster. This sets up a new story sequence: the rescue of the wizard. Even though the action in this sequence has nothing directly to do with saving the queen, each element of the sequence spine still relates to the main Spine indirectly. The sequence problem is that the wizard is held prisoner. Since the wizard is necessary to save the dying queen, this problem is connected to the main Story Problem. The sequence goal is to free the wizard. Doing so will move the hero one step closer to his main Story Goal. The sequence conflict comes from the monster. Even though the monster is unique to this sequence, it is still connected to the Main Conflict. By standing in the way of the immediate goal, it also indirectly blocks the knight's ultimate goal. The same goes for the sequence stakes. If the knight fails, he will not gain the help of the wizard. If this happens, the queen may die.

A sequence's action should be self-contained. This means that once a sequence begins, no unrelated material should interrupt the action until either the sequence goal is achieved, or an insurmountable obstacle arises to force the sequence to an end. Interrupting a sequence with material unrelated to its spine will cause the sequence to lose focus and momentum. Look at *The Bourne Identity. Bourne* requires its story to constantly switch back and forth between Jason Bourne and the antagonist Ted Conklin to keep the audience updated on both fronts. However, every time Jason Bourne begins the pursuit of a new sequence goal, the film sticks with that pursuit until Bourne reaches his next turning point. His actions are never interrupted by material from Conklin until those actions are finished. Thus, instead of interrupting the momentum of Bourne's sequences, the Conklin material acts almost like a commercial break that gives the audience a breather between each episode.

MORE ON TURNING POINTS

As previously suggested, a sequence can end with one of two results. The protagonist can reach the sequence goal, or an unexpected event may force the protagonist to abandon his or her goal in favor of a new course of action.

When a sequence results in success, it creates a *positive* turning point. Events end on an up-beat. The knight kills the monster and saves the wizard. The knight has claimed a small victory and can now take a moment to catch his breath before turning his attention to the next step of the plan.

However, more often than not, a sequence does not end in success. The hero is unexpectedly confronted by an insurmountable obstacle that either makes victory impossible or throws him or her in an even more threatening situation. Let us say the knight kills the monster, only to discover the wizard has been dead for years. This is an unexpected setback. A failure. This creates a *negative* turning point. The knight must now find a new course of action that will compensate for this defeat and allow him to continue on-ward. Or perhaps, while distracted by the monster, the knight is ambushed and captured by his enemy. This unexpected development has put the knight in an even more threatening situation. He can no longer think about the wizard. He must find a new goal and a new course of action to escape this new predicament.

If given the choice between a positive or negative turning point, it is more dramatic to go with the negative. Audiences expect the hero to succeed. Positive turning points reinforce these expectations. So, a story with nothing but positive turning points will lack the drama that comes from unpredictability. On the other hand, a swift change from bad to worse will surprise the audience. The Major Dramatic Question is then thrown into further doubt, and the audience has a new reason to fear for the hero's welfare. For best results, use a healthy mix of positive and negative. This keeps the action unpredictable, and thus more engaging for the audience.

DEVELOPMENT & ESCALATION

A great cinematic plot does more than twist and turn with every story sequence. Its events must also increase in intensity as the story progresses. People often compare an exciting movie to a roller-coaster. This thrilling experience is made possible by two things: DEVELOPMENT and ESCALATION.

We have already discussed development to some degree. Development occurs whenever any action or event, no matter how large or small, causes the story situation to undergo change. New characters appear, secrets are revealed, alliances are made, friends are betrayed, actions are taken by protagonist and antagonist that move both closer and closer to the story's climactic end. In a great story, the only constant is change. No scene should pass that does not in some way alter the dramatic landscape.

Story situations always seem rather simple at their beginnings. Goals are clear, problems seem straightforward, and the necessary actions appear cut-and-dry. But as the hero starts to meet obstacles and turning points, the situation becomes progressively more and more complex. Each turning point provides an event that complicates what has existed before, until the situation grows into an increasingly difficult state of affairs. If one would look back on a story after it has reached its end, it should be astounding that such extreme circumstances could have ever come from such a simple beginning.

To have any profound effect, this change must be *irrevocable* change. Each event must alter the dramatic landscape in an irreversible manner. Once a man sleeps with his best friend's wife, he cannot undo that action. Once a character is killed, that person cannot come back to life. If a secret is revealed, the cat cannot be put back in the bag. A change that can be easily reversed is no change at all. At best, it becomes a dramatic cul-de-sac that leads the story in a circle, only to return it to where it began. Irrevocable change, on the other hand, forces the situation to move forward, simply because there is no going back. Bridges have been burnt, and the hero must push onwards, no matter how ugly the situation has become.

Though essential for a well-told story, development alone will not be enough to create the most exciting movie experience. With development must come a second element. **Escalation.**

> *"You want to know how you get Capone? They pull a knife,*
> *you pull a gun. He sends one of yours to the hospital, you*
> *send one of his to the morgue."* - The Untouchables (1987)

Take another look at the updated Story Spine:

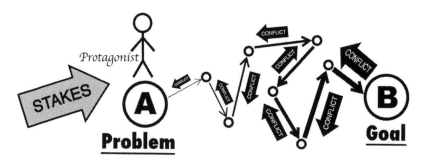

You will notice that after each turning point, the line segments grow thicker and thicker. Likewise, the arrows representing conflict grow larger and larger. This is because turning points do more than push the story in a new direction. They also escalate the level of conflict. Actions must increase in significance as the story advances. Things must grow more intense. More dangerous. More risky. Like a snowball rolling downhill, the plot gains both size and speed as it goes.

A protagonist begins the Path of Action with the smallest action he or she thinks will find success. However, an obstacle forces the protagonist to escalate. The smallest action is not enough. The hero must go bigger. So the hero takes a larger action, but the next obstacle proves this action to be insufficient as well. The hero must go even bigger, and then bigger, and then bigger. This continues until the story's climax, where the protagonist has no choice but to take the BIGGEST action possible. One huge effort. With everything on the line.

John McClane shows a steady escalation of action in *Die Hard*. When the terrorists invade, John's first reaction is to hide. This does little to help, so John then pulls the fire alarm. This also fails, so John tries to contact the police via radio. A policeman arrives, but the cop does not notice anything suspicious. John escalates further by smashing a window. The policeman still does not notice. Finally, John throws a dead body out the window to get the cop's attention. John did not go straight to such an extreme action. He was forced to gradually escalate his behavior thanks to a string of lesser actions that met nothing but failure.

However, conflict is a two-way street. The unity of opposites locks protagonist and antagonist into a conflict only one can win. So, whenever the protagonist escalates his or her actions, so must the antagonist. Every time John McClane takes greater effort to reach his goal, Hans Gruber responds with an even greater effort to stop him. When John first pulls the fire alarm, Hans sends only one man to find him. When John tries to contact the police, Hans send three more. Finally, when John steals a bag of detonators, Hans feels it is necessary to do everything he can to find John and kill him. This back and forth escalation of actions turns the plot into an increasingly intensifying contest of wills. Both sides push at each other harder and harder, until the conflict pushes the situation all the way to the edge. In the end, only one side will win, while the other will be pushed over the edge into oblivion.

As the protagonist's actions escalate, so must his or her level of *dedication*. Each obstacle draws a line in the sand. Once encountered, protagonists must ask themselves whether they are willing to do what it takes to cross that line. In doing so, the protagonist becomes more committed to his or her Story Goal, and as an added consequence, willing to take on more *risk*. When a story begins, the hero's dedication is usually quite weak. He or she takes small actions that require minimal risk. However, as the hero encounters obstacle after obstacle and repeatedly makes the decision to continue rather than quit, the hero's dedication builds to a point where he or she is willing to do anything to achieve success. By the time the story reaches its climax, the protagonist has become so committed that he or she will risk any danger to come out on top.

Let us use Jake Gittes of *Chinatown* as an example. Jake first shows very little personal dedication to his detective work. That is, until someone plays him for a sap. This offense motivates Jake to summon a little dedication and take on some risk to find the culprit. This ends with him getting roughed up by hired goons. While this would make some decide to quit, Jake only becomes more determined. He ups the ante and dives even deeper into the mystery. Likewise, when Luke Skywalker is first asked to leave home and join the Rebel Alliance, he is reluctant. His dedication is low. He fears the risk. Then, he finds his family murdered by Imperial Troopers. This turning point forces Luke to take on a little risk and dedicate himself to a new life. However, Luke does not suddenly turn gung-ho. His dedication remains middling and he continues to do all he can to avoid danger. It is not until Luke finds himself trapped aboard the Death Star that he decides to commit himself fully. Luke crosses the line in the sand and chooses to become a hero.

For both Jake and Luke, the snowball continues to roll. Sequence by sequence, turning point by turning point, their stories continue to escalate, turning a once simple setup into an increasingly intense and complicated situation. This continues until the story's climax, where the roller-coaster, at its highest point, hurtles downward to an exciting and satisfying resolution

Story sequences provide the basic method by which the cinematic narrative finds structure. However, over the past few decades, writers and dramatists alike have further organized this method into a more complicated, yet highly effective model known as *3-Act Structure*. This will be the topic of the next chapter.

CHAPTER 6
ON THREE-ACT STRUCTURE

For decades, instruction on the craft has revolved around a story model known as 3-Act Structure. For the uninitiated, 3-Act Structure is based upon the idea that stories best suited for the cinematic medium are those with plots that unfold in three clear sections. A beginning, a middle, and an end —or as some say, a unit of setup, a unit of development, and a unit of resolution. This three-part pattern has been found to be very successful at giving a feature film's events a dramatically satisfying rise and fall. This view has grown so popular that it has become the industry standard of Hollywood storytelling.

Yet despite its ubiquitous presence, 3-Act Structure's role in cinematic storytelling is largely misunderstood. Many treat 3-Act Structure as if it were a method of story creation. It is not. It is simply a standardized pattern used to organize story sequences into a form proven dramatically sound for the feature-length film. The 3-Act Structure provides no narrative action on its own. All story action originates from the Story Spine. The 3-Act model is merely an empty mold that exists to house the Story Spine and carry out its needs. A writer can follow the 3-Act model to a tee and still meet failure if he or she ignores the Story Spine.

So, what exactly is an ACT and how are they used? In cinematic terms, an act is really nothing more than a grouping of consecutive story sequences. In the traditional view, the first two to three sequences make up the FIRST ACT, the next five to seven sequences compose the SECOND ACT, and the final three to four sequences create the THIRD ACT. Story sequences are grouped in such a manner because their content works together to accomplish larger movements of plot. In the first act, the premise is established and the action of the Spine is brought into motion. The Second Act develops and escalates the story situation. The Third Act contains the build-up to the event that will resolve the Story Spine, that event itself (known as the MAIN STORY CLIMAX), and the final material that brings the story to a close. Some stories will contain more sequences within each act, some less. It all depends on how much development and escalation the particular story requires. Three-hour epics such as *Titanic* or *The Godfather* will have far more sequences in each act. However, it should be noted that no matter how long the film, every cinematic story is still told in three acts, and three acts only.

You may wonder, if acts are no more than groups of story sequences, what is the point of this model? Why not ignore all of this and carry out the Story Spine using the sequence method alone? In truth, one can create a perfectly acceptable narrative by sticking to the methods covered in Chapters 4 & 5. But doing so would ignore the enhanced dramatic potential the 3-Act model can bring. Movies are long, and audiences are easily distracted. The beauty of 3-Act Structure is that it has found over decades of study that audiences are kept best engaged when certain sequences and turning points perform certain duties, depending upon where they occur in the narrative. The 3-Act model provides a dramatic rise and fall to events that keeps the audience interested and involved. It takes the sequence method and enhances it one step beyond.

Here is a visual representation of traditional 3-Act Structure. Each column represents a story sequence. As you can see, dramatic conflict escalates with each sequence, moving the story on a constant upward trajectory until it reaches its climactic end.

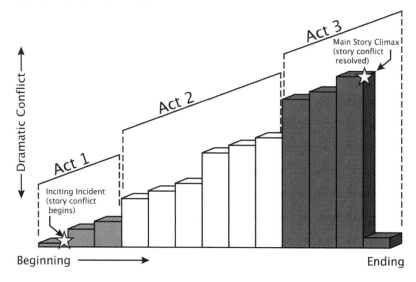

You should notice a significant jump in dramatic conflict at the end of each act (as well as halfway through the 2nd Act, which will be addressed shortly). While every turning point should provide some degree of development and escalation, the turning point that ends each act must provide a far greater boost than usual. Think of these as "super-turning points." They contain events of such significance that they not only turn the next sequence in a new direction, but lay a course for the next entire series of sequences to follow. These events, the END OF 1ST ACT TURNING POINT, the END OF 2ND ACT TURNING POINT, and the MAIN STORY CLIMAX (which is in fact the final turning point of the third act) are – along with the inciting incident – the most important moments of the entire story. Collectively known as the MAJOR DRAMATIC TURNING POINTS, these events are what give the cinematic narrative its three-part form. Each Major Dramatic Turning Point performs certain special duties in addition to those of a regular turning point. These additional duties will be covered in detail later this chapter.

But what of this sudden boost in dramatic conflict halfway through the second act? How does this fit into the pattern? It turns out that 3-Act Structure has a dirty little secret, one that newcomers are rarely told. Most dramatists insist that a cinematic story has only three acts and only three major dramatic turning points. They then offer a model whereby the first act covers the first quarter of a story, the second act the next two quarters, and the third act the final quarter. (See the diagram below.)

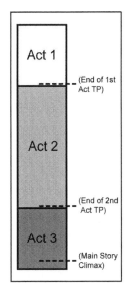

However, one look at this model should raise obvious questions. Why are the lengths of the acts so out of proportion? Why is the second act twice as long as the others? What is the logic behind this incongruity? The truth is, there is no logic behind it. The model is inaccurate. And this inaccuracy has been a cause for failure in countless attempts at screenwriting.

Many writers falter in the second act due to its supposed extreme length. The second act is expected to last from forty-five minutes to over an hour, but the End of 1st Act Turning Point gives only enough dramatic momentum to last halfway through. After this point, momentum slows, conflict sags, and the plot loses direction. Like a car driving through a desert on half a tank of gas, the story runs out of fuel before it reaches the next station.

However, great films do not have this problem. Their second acts do not only maintain momentum in their latter halves, but actually escalate in intensity. How do they do this? Simple. Their writers know something most amateurs are never told. Proper cinematic structure contains a *fourth* major dramatic turning point, situated smack-dab in the middle of the second act. This is called the MID-2ND ACT TURNING POINT. Now, many dramatists do recognize the existence of the Mid-2nd Act Turning Point (or Midpoint, as it is more commonly known). However, few are fully aware of its actual purpose. The Mid-2nd Act Turning Point is an event that behaves just like an end-of-act turning point. Why? Because it IS an end-of-act turning point. The truth is, the second act is not one long, drawn out act as so many writers are told, but rather *two separate acts* of equal length separated by a major dramatic event.

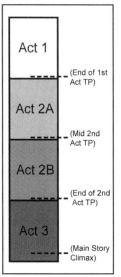

This division can be seen clearly in any of our study films. The course of action taken in Act 2A is very different from that taken in Act 2B.

Star Wars

Act 2A: The heroes find a way off Tatooine.

Mid-2nd Act Turning Point: The heroes are captured by the Death Star.

Act 2B: The escape from the Death Star.

Raiders of the Lost Ark

Act 2A: The search for the Ark.

Mid-2nd Act Turning Point: The Ark is found, but stolen by Nazis.

Act 2B: The fight to get the Ark back.

Rocky

Act 2A: Rocky Balboa flounders in his attempts to prepare to fight Creed.

Mid-2nd Act Turning Point: Mick offers to train Rocky.

Act 2B: Rocky grows strong under Mick's training.

Die Hard

Act 2A: John tries to contact the police.

Mid-2nd Act Turning Point: The police arrive, but make the situation worse.

Act 2B: John fights against both Hans and the police.

Here we see 3-Act Structure's dirty little secret. It is completely misnamed! The most effectively-structured cinematic story is not composed of one short act, one very long act, and then another short act, but *four* acts of equal length. This simple alteration gives balance and parity to the formerly lop-sided model. With four major dramatic turning points, spaced evenly throughout the narrative, the story no longer has a problem maintaining focus and momentum from its beginning to end. Every twenty to thirty minutes, the story encounters an explosion of development and escalation that drastically alters its course in a new direction.

(Note: Though there are in fact four acts in this structural model, I have not renumbered the acts 1, 2, 3, & 4. The terminology of the craft, inaccurate as it may be, has already been firmly established in this area. Therefore to avoid confusion, this model will still be referred to as 3-Act Structure. The "third act" will continue to indicate the story's final act, and any mention of the "second act" implies Acts 2A & 2B in combination.)

THREE-ACT STRUCTURE: A GUIDED TOUR

That was the general. Now come the specifics. The rest of this chapter maps out 3-Act Structure piece-by-piece to illustrate how each sequence and turning point works to create, develop, and resolve the Story Spine in the most dramatically effective manner. As you will see, each sequence and turning point has certain specific duties it must perform in addition to those already covered in Chapter 5, depending on where it occurs in the narrative.

THE FIRST ACT

Some dramatists refer to the first act as the "Setup Act." However, the first act does more than this name suggests. The purpose of the first act is to: a. establish the story's characters and premise, b. initiate the action of the Story Spine, and then c. lead the protagonist past a *point of no return.*

ACT 1, SEQUENCE 1 – THE SETUP SEQUENCE

The opening sequence of any film has a clear and simple duty. It establishes all information the audience must know before the story action begins so the audience may understand who people are, what is going on, and what type of story to expect. Though the setup sequence typically lasts ten to fifteen minutes, the "story" proper has not yet begun. The inciting incident has not yet invaded the protagonist's life and the Main Conflict has yet to engage. Though the Story Problem may already be lurking in the background, it has not yet forced the protagonist to take action. The setup instead provides the *status quo,* as mentioned in Chapter 4. Think of the opening sequence as the setting up of pieces on a chess board. Each piece must be in the right place before the game can begin.

The first thing a setup must do is communicate the rules by which the story will operate. Usually, this means establishing the genre, style, and tone. Audiences have different expectations for different genres. Communicating this information upfront tells the audience how they should react to events. So, if the story is a comedy, a light, humorous tone should be clear from its opening moments so the audience knows they should not take future events too seriously. If it is an action film, it should open with material that conveys the intensity inherent to the genre so the audience may brace themselves for the thrill-ride to follow. If a story communicates the wrong tone at its start, it may result in GENRE CONFUSION. The audience is orientated to expect one type of story when it is in fact another. This mismatch of expectations puts the audience out of step, leaving them unable to properly appreciate later events because they have been led to view them from the wrong angle.

In some genres, a story's rules go beyond style and tone. Genres such as fantasy or sci-fi take place in worlds that function differently than the one with which we are familiar. To follow the story, the audience must know the special rules by which this world operates. If a story exists in a world where vampires and black magic are possible, the storyteller must establish these facts early. Otherwise, the audience will become confused when a seemingly realistic story suddenly takes a supernatural turn. It is like the legal concept of full disclosure. The audience will accept any bending of reality as long as all deviations are admitted up front. This does not always require a long explanatory voiceover like the one which opens *The Lord of the Rings: The Fellowship of the Ring. Star Wars* quickly establishes its universe through simple action in its opening scenes. Right from the start, the audience is given spacecraft, combat, robots, a princess, an evil warlord, and a mysterious power later known as the Force. This allows the audience to quickly understand the type of universe it will deal with, turning wild fantasy into something concrete and easy to believe.

The setup's next duty is to establish the protagonist. Ideally, the protagonist should be introduced as soon as possible. The protagonist does not have to be the first person on screen, but at some point in the opening minutes the protagonist must be presented in such a way that clearly states *this* is the hero, this is the person we should fix our attentions upon. Be sure that the identity of the protagonist is made absolutely clear. I have encountered many scripts that inadvertently mislead the reader to recognize one character as the protagonist, when it is in fact another. This confuses the audience by creating a FALSE PROTAGONIST. The audience ends up hitching their wagons to the wrong horse, making them unable, and often unwilling to give their affection to the character to whom it rightfully belongs. If a story must open with characters other than the protagonist (like in *Star Wars*), it must be clear to the audience that these characters will not be the story's hero. This requires some skill on the part of the writer. One must know how to construct a scene from one point of view or another – or no one's point of view at all. In general, it is best to keep early appearances by non-protagonists short, so it becomes clear to the audience when the real protagonist takes center stage.

Beware of stories with ambiguous protagonists – that is, stories where the audience is left unsure who is supposed to be the lead. The audience needs a specific character to whom they can anchor their thoughts and emotions. While some story types can operate with two leads, such as romance or "buddy" films, generally the protagonist must be one person, not a group. *Star Wars, The Lord of the Rings,* and *The Matrix* are all stories containing groups of heroes, but the audience always knows which character amongst the group deserves their primary attention. These stories all clearly identify their protagonists from the start.

Along with a story's rules and protagonist, the setup must also establish any other information the audience must know before the story's conflict begins. *The Godfather* opens its story with a wedding reception where we meet every important character and learn how they fit into the family business. The setup of *Back to the Future* tells us about Hill Valley, the clock tower, Biff Tannen, the McFlys, and Doc Brown – all things the audience must know about before Marty gets stuck in 1955.

Stories are all about change. Audiences cannot understand the "after" without first experiencing the "before." So, the audience must be shown the protagonist's status quo as it exists before it is upset by the conflict. They should observe the protagonist's surroundings and how he or she operates within them. They should meet the other characters who occupy the story and see how the protagonist relates to them. If the main character has personal flaws or problems, they must be established here. If the hero has a drug addiction, marital problems, or an obnoxious rival, these are all problems that existed before the story began and are thus part of the status quo. In fact, any story-relevant information that existed before the movie began belongs to the status quo and should be given here.

The storyteller gets ten to fifteen minutes to fit all of this in. As soon as the inciting incident occurs, it becomes too late. Once the story starts moving, it becomes improper to halt forward progress just to explain things the audience should already know. Therefore, all necessary information must be given before conflict begins.

The key to a good setup is to establish all relevant information, but *only* the relevant information. Filling the setup with extra characters, situations, and information that hold no importance to later events will serve no purpose, no matter how amusing or interesting they might be. It may look really cool to put a cherry-red matchbox car on the chessboard alongside a silver Monopoly top hat, but they DO NOT BELONG THERE. Those pieces are irrelevant to the game and will only clutter up the board. Likewise, do not clutter your setup with irrelevant information. This not only slows down the sequence, but may mislead the audience to believe that this useless information holds importance. Later in the story, the audience will wonder what happened to that character they met in the setup, or why that early bit of information has never come back into play. The goal is to be efficient. Provide all the audience needs and nothing they do not.

THE INCITING INCIDENT

The setup sequence comes to a crashing halt with the arrival of the inciting incident. As mentioned in Chapter 4, the inciting incident is the moment the Story Problem invades the protagonist's world, disrupting the status quo and forcing the protagonist to take action. At this moment, the Story Spine forms and the plot officially begins.

In keeping with what was covered in Chapter 5, one should realize that the inciting incident is really nothing more than the story's first turning point. Like any other turning point, the inciting incident presents the protagonist with a problem that forces the setup sequence to end and prepares the actions the protagonist must take in the sequence to follow. However, as the event that launches the story's entire adventure, the inciting incident is the most significant turning point of the entire story. Without it, the Story Spine will never form and a story will not exist.

Some Story Problems arrive like a hammer blow. Others come on gradually. Because of this, writers can sometimes become confused over what specific moment qualifies as a story's inciting incident. In some stories, a problematic situation exists well before the story begins. Darth Vader's evil empire dominates the galaxy long before we meet Luke Skywalker. Lester Burnham's life has been miserable for years before the start of *American Beauty*. However, this does not mean the inciting incidents have already occurred. To "incite" means "to rouse to action." The inciting incident is not so much about the Story Problem itself, but rather the moment that motivates the protagonist to take action *against* the Problem. Three things must happen before the inciting incident has officially occurred.

First, the Story Problem must exist. Second, the protagonist must be aware of the Story Problem. Finally, the protagonist must decide to do something about it. Luke Skywalker starts his story well aware that the galaxy is ruled by an evil empire. However, he feels no need to do anything about it until he finds Princess Leia's hidden message. Lester Burnham is already painfully aware of his crummy life, but he is not motivated to change things until he lays eyes on his daughter's friend Angela.

The placement of the inciting incident is important. Audiences often complain when a movie takes too long to get moving. Most dramatists stress that the inciting incident should occur sometime between pages twelve and sixteen. Since one page of script roughly equals one minute of screen time, scripts that take longer than sixteen pages had better hope for patient audiences. Until the inciting incident sparks a conflict, the story has yet to begin. The audience is then left like a group of people sitting in a roller-coaster waiting for the ride to start. Make them wait too long and they will grow restless and complain.

A late inciting incident also harms a story by pushing important events later than they should occur. What should happen on page 30 now happens on page 45. What should occur sixty minutes into the film now happens near the film's end. This forces the rest of the story to play catch-up. I have read 120-page scripts where the Story Problem is not introduced until page 60! This amounts to an entire hour of boring setup, followed by only sixty minutes of actual story – a story far less satisfying now that it has been compressed into half a script.

Despite the dangers of a late inciting incident, this is still preferable to placing the inciting incident too early. Many insist that writers start the conflict as soon as possible. However, an inciting incident that occurs on page one or two will do even more damage than one that arrives on page thirty. When scripts launch their Spines too early, they invariably contract an illness known as "Perfect Stranger Syndrome." While these scripts may have complete Story Spines with heroes who take decisive action, the odd thing is that the audience will not CARE. No matter what the hero does, the audience feels emotionally distant. Why? The answer is simple. Which would you care more about? The problems of a friend or those of a stranger? Even the most generous of us care more for our friends. An early inciting incident forces the story to skip its setup. In doing so, the script eliminates the time in which the audience gets to know the protagonist and causes the story to start rolling while the protagonist is still a stranger. The audience will then sense no pressing need to care about story events because they have been given no reason to care about the persons they involve. To find success, a story's audience must care about the protagonist, root for his or her success, feel good when the protagonist wins, and fear when he or she is in danger. To do this, the writer must use the proper setup time to turn the protagonist into the audience's *friend*. Then, when disaster strikes, the audience is already on the protagonist's side. They care about the protagonist and will stick with the character to the story's end.

ACT 1, SEQUENCE 2...3...and the END of 1ST ACT TURNING POINT

As soon as the inciting incident occurs, the story starts moving. The protagonist recognizes the Story Problem, chooses a Story Goal, forms the Spine, and hooks the audience with the Major Dramatic Question. The action begins to unfold as outlined in Chapter 5. The protagonist takes his or her first course of action, an obstacle is encountered, a decision is made that creates a turning point, and the next sequence begins. Some first acts need only two sequences. Others may have three. It all depends on the scope and pace of the particular story.

Whether it contain two sequences or three, the first act must conclude with a Major Dramatic Turning Point that pushes the protagonist past a POINT OF NO RETURN. As the "end of the beginning," something must occur at the End of 1st Act Turning Point that forces the protagonist to cross some sort of *threshold*. Think of the threshold as a steel door the protagonist must pass through that immediately slams shut behind him or her, locking the protagonist into a new and unknown situation. Once the protagonist crosses the threshold, he or she cannot go back. Neo takes the red pill and is expelled from the Matrix. Ripley's crew brings a dangerous alien aboard the ship. Michael Corleone decides he will kill Virgil Sollozzo. Until this point, protagonists may have been able to back out of the situation, but not any more. They have allowed the steel door to slam behind them. This permanently entrenches them in the story conflict in such a way that the only remaining way out is to see the situation through to its bitter end, whether the protagonist likes it or not.

The End of 1st Act Turning Point does not only lock the hero into the situation, but it does double harm by making the situation *significantly worse.* Until now, the Story Problem has been rather simple. However, the End of 1st Act Turning Point adds a major COMPLICATION to the original problem. In *Back to the Future,* Marty McFly is stuck in the year 1955. This is problem enough, but Marty compounds his predicament at the end of the first act by inadvertently preventing his mother and father from meeting and falling in love. This turns Marty's situation from bad to much worse. He now cannot leave 1955 until he puts things right. Sometimes, the protagonist creates the complication by crossing the threshold willingly, as in *The Matrix* or *The Godfather.* Both Neo and Michael Corleone voluntarily step forward and choose to take on the danger to follow. Other times, the complication comes first, creating a situation that forces the protagonist to cross the threshold against his or her will. In *The Lord of the Rings,* Frodo's original task is to simply deliver the One Ring to Gandalf at the Prancing Pony Inn. However, Gandalf has been imprisoned. This complication forces Frodo to cross a point of no return and continue the ring's journey on his own even though he would much rather return home.

It should be noted that the complication merely adds a new layer to the existing Story Problem. It does not create a separate unrelated problem, add a new Story Goal, or do anything else to carry the story off its existing Spine. It merely takes what already exists and makes it worse. Marty McFly still needs to get back to 1985, only now he must get back to the 1985 where his parents remain happily married. Michael Corleone still wants to preserve the safety of his family, but now he must compromise his ethics and put himself in danger. In complicating the Story Problem, a good End of 1st Act Turning Point will complicate the entire Story Spine; conflict is now greater, the stakes are now higher, and the protagonist must take larger and riskier actions to continue the Path of Action. In doing so, the End of 1st Act Turning Point provides the story with a giant boost of development and escalation to propel it into the next act.

THE SECOND ACT

Many dramatists refer to a story's second act as the "Development Act" or the "Rising Action." However, the function of the second act is often misunderstood. There is a common misconception that the material contained in Acts 2A & 2B is nothing more than the connecting tissue that joins the story's beginning to its end. However, the second act is not just the "stuff in the middle." It does far more than string a story along until it reaches its end. Both Acts 2A & 2B carry out specific, independently dramatic functions as essential to a great cinematic story as the material contained in acts one and three.

Together, Acts 2A & 2B make up the bulk of a story's action. Because they are responsible for so much time, these acts must not only constantly develop and escalate the story situation, but provide some sort of additional structure to hold the audience's interest. This additional structure can be described quite simply: In Act 2A, the protagonist makes the situation worse by *creating a monster.* In Act 2B, the protagonist must *fight that monster.*

ACT 2A, SEQUENCE 1

The End of 1st Act Turning Point has just occurred, and the hero takes his or her first step across the threshold. In doing so, the protagonist enters a strange new world, one in which he or she may have never set foot had it not been for the complication that ends the first act.

In many stories, this literally means the protagonist must enter a new and unfamiliar place. Neo awakes in a post-apocalyptic world. Luke Skywalker takes his first journey any from home. Indiana Jones arrives in Cairo. Other times, this new territory is not a physical place, but an unfamiliar role the hero must now play. In *Shrek,* the first act ends with the titular ogre forced to take on the role of a knight. Shrek does not know how to be a knight. He does not want to be a knight. Yet, the situation has forced him into the role. In *The Godfather,* Michael Corleone begins his second act in the same house he has always lived, surrounded by the same family, only the role he plays within that family has dramatically changed. Some stories take the abstraction even further. In *The Sixth Sense,* Malcolm Crowe's new territory is Cole's mind. In *Alien,* it is the strange creature that has attached itself to Kane.

Most of Act 2A will focus upon how the protagonist deals with this new situation. Because of this, its first sequence behaves like a setup to the second act in which the audience learns about this new environment and observes how the protagonist tries to adapt. Though necessary to orientate the audience for later events, do not let this sequence continue for too long. Setup sequences generally lack the kind of active, conflict-oriented goals necessary to create tension and move the plot. Go too long without such material and the story will stagnate. Once all necessary exploration is performed, throw an obstacle in the hero's way to create a turning point that will push the hero into the next course of action.

ACT 2A, SEQUENCES 2...3...4...

After the second act setup has concluded, the protagonist must take action in response to the complication that ended the first act. The protagonist pursues a series of goals he or she believes will ameliorate the situation and ultimately bring it to an end. However, the curious thing is that no matter what goals the protagonist may pursue in Act 2A, his or her actions always inadvertently make the situation *worse.* In his or her honest attempts to make things better, the protagonist only aggravates things even more. These actions end up burying the protagonist deeper into the conflict and sets the stage for an even more dangerous complication to emerge at the end of the act. In short, in Act 2A, the protagonist *creates a monster.*

Think of the story of Dr. Frankenstein. Frankenstein wishes to bring the dead to life. He does this with the best of intentions. He believes if man can conquer death, there will be no limit to human achievement. Only things do not turn out as Frankenstein planned. His actions end up creating a monster – a monster who will eventually turn on him and threaten his life. Frankenstein's well-meaning efforts have ironically created his own doom.

In Act 2A, the protagonist makes the same mistake as Dr. Frankenstein. His or her efforts, while seemingly beneficial in the short term, end up leading the protagonist into a situation far more monstrous than the one before. In Act 2A of *Star Wars,* Luke and Obi-Wan take action to keep the Empire from finding the droids. In doing so, they accidentally deliver themselves right into the Empire's hands. In *Rocky,* the title character accepts a fight with Apollo Creed in the hope that it will bring him recognition and self-respect. But by the end of the act, Rocky realizes he has set himself up for nothing but humiliation. In *Die Hard,* John McClane does all he can to contact the police. But once the cops arrive, John learns that the authorities only make the situation worse.

Unfortunately, neither the protagonist nor the audience know that they are setting themselves on a path to disaster. This fact usually remains hidden until the Major Dramatic Turning Point that ends Act 2A.

THE MID-SECOND ACT TURNING POINT

The Mid-2nd Act Turning Point (or Midpoint) provides the story with its MONSTER MOMENT. Here, the seeds the protagonist has unwittingly sown through Act 2A spring to life and create an even more threatening complication. This monstrous new situation doubles the protagonist's danger and sets up the action that must occur in Act 2B. Depending on the needs of the particular story, the Monster Moment twists the story in one of three ways.

Type a: *The Out of the Blue* — Throughout Act 2A, the protagonist seems to be making all the right moves. In fact, he or she has found significant success. Only then, an unexpected development springs forth to flip the situation on its head and render all progress meaningless. Indiana Jones spends his Act 2A trying to locate the Ark of the Covenant before the Nazis can discover it themselves. Indy reaches success at the Midpoint,

only to find his enemies have him surrounded. Though it seems
Indy has done everything right, he has inadvertently put the Ark
right into the Nazis' hands. Likewise, John McClane finally
manages to contact the authorities at his Midpoint. Then, with
great irony, John realizes his actions have put him and the
hostages into more danger than before. This bitter irony is also
found at the Midpoint of *Star Wars*. Luke and Obi-Wan escape
Mos Eisley, and seem certain to reach the safety of Alderaan.
Only instead of Alderaan, they find the Death Star in its place.
After all their efforts to escape the Empire, they wind up right in
the belly of the beast.

Type b: *The Fool's Path* — In these stories, the monstrous
complication is not created by a sudden change or ironic twist,
but rather the cumulative mistakes made by the protagonist over
the course of Act 2A. The Midpoint provides an event which
causes the protagonists to realize the hole they have dug themselves into. *Back to the Future* finds its monster moment when
Marty notices his family photo has begun to disappear. Both he
and the audience now understand that Marty's meddling in the
past has created a paradox that threatens to wipe Marty out of
existence. Marty must now work fast to reverse the situation or
he will cease to be. The crew in *Alien* discover they have created
a monster (quite literally) when the alien creature bursts from
Kane's chest. The crew has no one to blame but themselves.
They allowed this to happen due to the poor decisions they
made throughout Act 2A. Now, there is a mon-ster aboard the
ship, threatening to kill them all.

Type c: *The Saving Grace* — In some stories, Act 2A puts the
protagonist through situations that make him or her well aware
of the increasingly dire situation even before the Midpoint
arrives. It takes Rocky Balboa only a few days before he regrets
accepting a fight with Apollo Creed. Frodo knows he has gotten

himself in way over his head as he continues his journey with the One Ring. Both protagonists are already certain they are doomed. In these cases, the Midpoint reverses the situation by offering the protagonist someone or something that could provide salvation. Rocky receives a shred of hope when Mick offers his help. Frodo's cause turns around when a band of heroes join his side. With the support of new allies, both heroes can now take on the monstrous situation and stand a fighting chance.

The Mid-2nd Act Turning Point provides a significant moment of change in the course of the plot. More importantly, the Midpoint also forces a significant change in the protagonist's behavior. In the story's first half, the protagonist typically behaves in a relatively passive or reactive manner towards the force of antagonism. He or she feels it is best to pursue the Story Goal by avoiding direct conflict. Indiana Jones tries to work in secret. John McClane prefers to run rather than fight. Luke and Obi-Wan do their best to stay hidden from Imperial forces. Conflict still arises of course, but this is always conflict the hero would rather avoid. The protagonist never goes out of his or her way to create conflict intentionally.

This all changes at the Mid-2nd Act Turning Point. The arrival of the monster moment causes the protagonist to realize his or her passive or reactive behavior will no longer work. The hero's efforts to avoid conflict have only managed to dig him or her into deeper trouble. Now, face-to-face with a monstrous situation of his or her own making, the hero has only one choice. In order to continue, the hero must FIGHT BACK.

The Midpoint event then transforms the hero into a "hero." No matter what attitude the protagonist may have had up to this point, the Midpoint forces him or her to rise above and take full responsibility for the story's outcome. The protagonist changes from passive to aggressive – from a character who wishes to avoid conflict to one willing and able to face conflict head-on. The Nazis have stolen the Ark. If Indy wants it back, he will have to chase them down and take it by force. John McClane cannot count on the police to fight for him. If he wants to survive, he will have to defeat the terrorists himself. Luke Skywalker can no longer avoid the Imperial forces. He is dead in their midst. The only way out is to grab a weapon and fight. So begins Round 2 of the fight, and this time the hero comes out swinging.

ACT 2B

The Midpoint has summoned a monster of the protagonist's own making. Now like Dr. Frankenstein, the newly-aggressive protagonist must fight and defeat that monster. Indy must get the Ark back. Ripley and her crew must get rid of the alien. Rocky must train like his life depends on it. In Act 2B, the protagonist must pursue specific goals that will overcome this situation and ultimately bring the conflict to an end.

Act 2B contains two to four more sequences in which this newly inten-sified struggle is carried out. Thanks to the Midpoint's forceful shove, these sequences contain more momentum than ever before. Events increase in urgency and actions hold greater importance as each turning point pushes the story forward with greater and greater intensity. The protagonist has declared war on the force of antagonism, creating bigger and more forceful clashes between the two sides.

However, as the protagonist's actions escalate, so do those of the force of antagonism. As the struggle develops, both sides put themselves on a path where they will eventually meet in an explosive battle to end Act 2B. The outcome of this battle will have a devastating effect upon the remain-ing story situation and create the story's third major dramatic turning point.

THE END of 2ND ACT TURNING POINT

Though the hero and force of antagonism have been in conflict throughout the story, the clash that ends Act 2B must be larger and more significant than any that has occurred before. This could be because the stakes have grown extremely high, because the Story Goal seems within reach, or possibly because this battle threatens to undo all progress the hero has made up to this point. Whatever the reason, Act 2B must end with an event that rivals only the Main Story Climax in its dramatic impact.

Like many concepts we have discussed, this battle could be literal or figurative. *The Matrix, The Bourne Identity,* and *Raiders of the Lost Ark* all end their second acts with intense action sequences. However, bullets and fists are not requirements for battle. Quite often, Act 2B ends with a battle of wills. *The Shawshank Redemption* ends its second act with a fight between Andy Dufrene's urge to prove his innocence and the Warden's desire to keep him enslaved. *Chinatown's* Act 2B ends with an intense standoff between Jake Gittes' will to uncover the truth and Mrs. Mulwray's refusal to give it. In even subtler drama, this can be an internal battle, caused by an event that forces the protagonist to question his or her own thoughts, emotions, morality, or mental state. *A Beautiful Mind* (2001) tells the story of a genius struggling with schizophrenia. Its Act 2B ends with the return of the protagonist's mental illness, throwing him into mental turmoil as he questions whom he can trust and what he can believe.

Structurally speaking, the storyteller creates this battle in order to end Act 2B with the maximum possible REVERSAL OF EMOTION. Like the rise and fall of a roller coaster, the audience experiences a burst of emotional excitement whenever the story situation suddenly changes from good to bad, bad to good, or bad to worse. Such abrupt shifts in emotion create an uncertainty that keeps the audience glued to their seats and mentally invested in the story's outcome. While every turning point should cause some sort of emotional reversal, this principle becomes especially important at the end of the second act. Just as a roller-coaster hurtles the fastest from its steepest drop, a good cinematic story requires an extreme emotional reversal at the end of Act 2B, so it may be thrown into its third and final act with the greatest possible momentum.

The protagonist may win the end-of-act battle, but more often than not, he or she loses. Traditionally, the outcome is dictated by how the writer intends to resolve the Story Spine at the movie's end. If the storyteller wishes to finish the film with an "up-ending" – that is, the movie concludes with the protagonist overcoming his or her Story Problem and achieving the Story Goal – logic generally dictates that the second act should end on a "down-beat." This means the protagonist must lose the end-of-second-act battle, resulting in an enormous setback. Conversely, if the movie will conclude with a "down-ending," meaning the hero will fail at the story's end, the second act should end in victory.

The reason for these alternating ups and downs relates back to the Major Dramatic Question. The protagonist's ultimate success or failure should always remain in doubt. If the hero ends the second act victorious, it will be no stretch of the audience's imagination to predict a victory at the final climax. This may answer the MDQ prematurely, weakening dramatic tension in the third act. On the other hand, if the second act ends with a terrible defeat, the question remains in doubt. Tension will increase and audience sympathy will reach a threshold as they wonder how the hero will find a way back from such a horrible loss.

As you may have already noticed, turning points operate in two parts. First, an obstacle blocks the protagonist's path. Then, the protagonist finds a new course of action that allows him or her to continue. This simple structure becomes far more pronounced at the Major Dramatic Turning Point that ends the second act. Instead of occurring in close tandem as they would in a regular turning point, these parts are executed as two separate, highly dramatic events. First, instead of a simple obstacle, the protagonist confronts the force of antagonism in the end-of-act battle. Due to the fact that it provides the most dramatic moment of the second act, this battle is referred to as the SECOND ACT CLIMAX. Win or lose, the outcome profoundly alters the landscape of the story situation. It may leave the protagonist at the heights of victory, or in the depths of despair. However, this does not last very long. The Second Act Climax is quickly followed by a second event, the THIRD ACT CATALYST, in which a new action or piece of information reverses the situation once more. The catalyst causes the hero to realize what must be done to finally overcome the conflict and claim the Story Goal once and for all. This in turn sparks the final course of action the hero will pursue in Act 3.

This two-part climax/catalyst can be executed in a variety of ways. However, four methods are most common.

1. **The Dark Moment**

A Dark Moment ends the second act with the hero suffering a terrible defeat. This setback is often so massive that it seems the hero has no choice but to throw in the towel. *The Matrix* ends its second act with its heroes devastated by betrayal. An attack has killed several of Neo's friends, and what is worse, Neo's mentor Morpheus has been taken prisoner. Neo knows that unless something is done, the antagonist will torture Morpheus until he confesses information which will spell humanity's defeat. It seems Neo's only choice is to euthanize his mentor before this can occur. Likewise, *Finding Nemo* ends it second act with Marlin finally reaching his son in Sydney. It seems a happy reunion is imminent – only he finds Nemo laying motionless, seemingly dead. Marlin turns back home in defeat.

Though the Dark Moment always ends its second act climax with the same result (defeat), the catalyst that follows allows two possible options.

a. *The Spark of Hope*

The end-of-act battle has left the protagonist in defeat. However, all is not lost. The defeat is followed by a new event or piece of information that gives the hero cause for hope. This hope may be a long shot or entail an incredible amount of risk, but it gives the hero one last chance to over-come defeat and seize victory in the end.

Neo is seconds away from pulling the plug on Morpheus. Suddenly, the gloom is reversed. Neo realizes he could rescue Morpheus rather than give in. This new option is incredibly risky, even bordering on suicide, but it gives Neo the shred of hope he needs to keep fighting. Neo throws himself back into the fray, setting up a course of action that will decide the story's fate once and for all. In the same way, Marlin turns back for home empty-handed. However, all is not lost. Nemo's death was only a ruse to allow his escape. Once realized, Marlin gets one last chance to reunite with his son and find a happy ending.

Out of all the ways to end the second act, the Dark/Spark typically provides the greatest reversal of emotion. First, the audience believes the situation is as hopeless as it can be. Then, the Spark reverses this emotion.

Because of its strong reversal, the Dark/Spark is used more often than any other type of End of 2nd Act Turning Point. Along with *The Matrix* and *Finding Nemo,* it is found in *Rocky* (Rocky realizes he will never defeat Apollo Creed/Rocky decides that if he can be the first to go the distance with Creed, that will be all the victory he needs), as well as *The Sixth Sense* (Malcolm Crowe tells Cole he does not believe him and will no longer be his doctor/Crowe finds evidence to change his mind). Incidentally, many writers try to force a Dark/Spark into stories where it does not belong. In fact, it has become so overused that some consider it cliché. The Dark/Spark is not appropriate for all stories. Do not automatically use it just because it seems to have the greatest payoff. Instead, look at your story and choose a second act ending that meets the specific needs of your plot. Adapt structure to story, not the other way around.

b. *The Nail in the Coffin*

This variation is typically found in stories with doomed or self-destructive protagonists who eventually meet sad or bittersweet ends, by way of a physical predicament (*Titanic*), or their own uncompromising behavior (*Raging Bull, Citizen Kane*). In this variation, there is no Spark of Hope to follow the Dark Moment. Instead, these protagonists compound their defeat by following it with a foolish action that sets up their eventual demise. In *Titanic,* Rose leaps from the lifeboat back onto the sinking ship. In *Raging Bull,* Jake LaMotta savagely beats his brother, losing the one ally who could have brought him salvation. With this action, the protagonist initiates a downward spiral of events that will continue through Act 3 and end with the protagonist's ultimate defeat.

2. The False Victory

Like the Dark/Spark, the False Victory also ends the second act on a downbeat, but does it in reverse fashion. In a False Victory, the protagonist wins the end-of-act battle. The protagonist, along with the audience, is given a brief emotional high. But then, something occurs to render the victory meaningless. The force of antagonism creates an enormous new obstacle that throws the outcome back into doubt. The hero must rise up once again and take on the even more dramatic battle that will make up Act 3.

Raiders of the Lost Ark provides a good example. Indiana Jones has reclaimed the Ark and escaped the Nazis. Now, on a ship back to America, it seems Indy has won. Only his enemies have not quit. They reemerge via submarine and steal the Ark yet again. This catalyst forces Indy to chase after the Nazis one more time, launching a battle that will decide a winner once and for all.

Like the Dark Moment, the False Victory also has a variation for use in stories that conclude on a down-ending. Stories with tragic heroes who fail in the end sometimes end the second act with a *False Hope*. The False Hope provides an alternating upbeat to the story's eventual down-ending through a dramatic event that fools the hero (and the audience) into thinking he or she will win out in the end. *American Beauty* ends its second act with Lester on top of the world. By giving a victory, but not the reversal that follows, the False Hope leaves the situation optimistic. For the moment, that is. Eventually, things turn sour in the third act as an unexpected series of mishaps send once certain victory tumbling downhill into defeat.

3. The Key Piece of the Puzzle

This type of End of 2nd Act Turning Point is commonly found in stories with a high element of mystery. Here, a vital piece of information has been kept hidden from the protagonist – and usually the audience as well – that once revealed, becomes a bombshell that alters the entire view of the situation. This information typically comes to light as a result of the protagonist achieving full or partial victory at the second act climax. Through the revelation that follows, the protagonist learns what he or she must now do to finally overcome the conflict and bring the story to an end.

Alien's second act climaxes with a battle between Ripley and the saboteur Ash. In the revelation that follows, Ripley learns that Ash brought the monster on board intentionally so their employer could turn it into a killing machine. Because of this, Ripley now knows the only remaining option is to destroy the ship and the monster with it. In *The Bourne Identity*, Jason

Bourne defeats an assassin sent by the antagonist, allowing him to finally discover who is trying to kill him and why. This allows Bourne to finally turn the tables and corner the antagonist in the third act. *Chinatown* provides the most famous example. Jake Gittes has long suspected Mrs. Mulwray of killing her own husband. He also suspects Mulwray of keeping her husband's mistress hostage so she may kill her as well. However, when Jake finally confronts Mrs. Mulwray, the ensuing battle reveals he could not be more wrong. Mrs. Mulwray's bombshell gives Jake the final piece of the puzzle, allowing him to solve the mystery and take proper action to set the world right again.

4. **The Launch of the Final Plan**

This is the simplest type of End of 2nd Act Turning Point and, depending on the story, may be the most obvious choice. Here, the heroes have overcome their end-of-act battle, for better or for worse, and have now devised an ultimate plan; one big effort they hope will finally defeat the Story Problem and bring things to a happy end. The third act catalyst occurs the moment this plan is set into motion. This is how *Back to the Future* launches its third act, as well as *Star Wars*. Though well-suited for action/adventure, the Final Plan's usage is not limited as such. In Act 2B of *The Godfather,* Michael Corleone is named successor to the Corleone crime family. Since the beginning, Michael has done all he can to protect his family from its enemies. However, he knows as soon as he takes power his enemies will sense weakness and attack. Because of this, Michael must devise a plan. The second act ends with the death of Michael's father, an event that prompts Michael to launch his attack upon the heads of the remaining Five Families, eliminating their threat once and for all.

Out of the four major varieties of End of 2nd Act Turning Points, the Final Plan generally starts the third act with the least momentum due to the general lack of an emotional reversal. However, it can still set into motion a tense, exciting third act as long as conflict continues to escalate and unexpected obstacles constantly arise to threaten the plan's success. Doc and Marty's plan in *Back to the Future* quickly falls apart with the arrival of the thunderstorm. The attack on the Death Star first falls short again and again. As time slips away, tension increases as it seems less and less likely that the plan will succeed.

THE THIRD ACT

The third and final act is commonly called the "Resolution Act." This means its content will ultimately resolve the Main Conflict, complete the Story Spine, and bring the narrative to a satisfactory end. A good third act begins with one or two sequences that continue to develop and escalate the situation in reaction to the turning point that ends the second act. This leads to a climactic sequence in which one side of the conflict is defeated, the Major Dramatic Question is answered, and the main story action is brought to an end. The narrative then concludes with a final resolution sequence in which the audience learns how the protagonist's ultimate success or failure has changed the protagonist's world from what it was when the story began. In all, the third act should wrap up the story in the most dramatic manner possible and give the audience an emotionally satisfying end.

ACT 3, SEQUENCE 1...2...

If the storyteller ends Act 2B with an effective End of 2nd Act Turning Point, the protagonist will enter the final act with a clear plan as to what must be done to finally overcome the force of antagonism and reach the Story Goal. The third act's opening sequence (or sequences, depending on how much further development is required to escalate the action to its final climax) follows the protagonist as he or she charges down this final road. Neo begins the attack to free Morpheus. Doc and Marty prepare the apparatus that will send Marty home. Jason Bourne hunts down Ted Conklin. Jake Gittes closes a trap on Noah Cross.

The story situation has grown to a fevered pitch. Thanks to the emotional reversal that ends Act 2B, the story's dramatic roller-coaster is now hurtling downhill. The stakes are at their highest, commitment is at its strongest, and conflict is nearing its peak. It is all or nothing time for the protagonist. The hero can either soar to victory, or go down in flames.

However, things do not go as planned. Another obstacle arises to reverse the situation and throw the plan into disarray. Agent Smith corners Neo. Noah Cross pulls a gun. A fallen tree branch pulls apart Doc's apparatus. The story has reached yet another turning point, one that sends the protagonist headlong into—

THE CLIMACTIC SEQUENCE & MAIN STORY CLIMAX

Throughout the story, the Path of Action has sent the protagonist twisting and turning down one road after another. With each development, the hero's options have become more difficult and the situation more and more treacherous. Now at this point, the protagonist's options have run out. He or she is left with no choice but to face the force of antagonism one-on-one in a fight for all the marbles. The entire Story Spine has been leading to this moment. The Story Goal is finally within reach – but, the force of antagonism is still in the way. And it will NOT back down.

This final confrontation reaches a peak at the MAIN STORY CLIMAX. The main story climax is the movie's biggest moment. As the final and most dramatically significant turning point of all, the main story climax provides an event in which one side of the conflict meets TOTAL VICTORY, and the other IRREVOCABLE DEFEAT, deciding the fate of the entire story in the process. As the story's big finish, the climactic event resolves the entire narrative with an action that finally answers the Major Dramatic Question, completes the Story Spine, and brings the story to a satisfying end.

Only one side of the conflict can be left standing in the end. If both the protagonist and the force of antagonism survive the event still capable of picking up the pieces and continuing onward, the movie will close with its conflict unresolved and its end inconclusive. Instead, the climax must be a deathmatch. Two sides go in, but only one comes out.

As always, the climax need not be a literal fight to the death. This simply means the winner must defeat his or her adversary in such a manner that it becomes impossible for the opponent to continue. Though some stories resolve their conflict by killing the protagonist or antagonist (*The Matrix, The Bourne Identity, Raiders of the Lost Ark*), in most cases, this death is figurative. Both Jake Gittes and Noah Cross survive the end of *Chinatown*, but Jake's hopes for justice have died. Rocky certainly does not kill Apollo Creed at the end of their fight. Rather, Rocky's moral victory "kills" the doubt and fear that has plagued him since the story's beginning. Nothing dies at the end of *Finding Nemo*, except for the threatening situation which had separated father and son.

Note that no presumptions are made that the hero will win the final battle. While a majority of stories indeed end with the protagonist in victory, there are plenty of stories where the hero puts his or her heart and soul on the line and still meets defeat (*Chinatown*, for example). It is also possible to end with a mixed outcome. The protagonist may achieve the Story Goal, or some portion of that goal, but for some reason, the final result falls short from being one hundred percent satisfactory. Perhaps the cost of victory turns out to be too high, or maybe with success comes pain, loss, or disappointment. This closes the film with an ambiguous or bittersweet end. Michael Corleone reaches his goal at the end of *The Godfather*, but does so at the cost of his soul. Both Lester Burnham and Captain Miller attain what they originally set out to achieve in *American Beauty* and *Saving Private Ryan*, but both die in the process.

Regardless of who wins or loses, the main story climax absolutely must provide a clear and conclusive answer to the Major Dramatic Question. The audience has stuck with the story from beginning to end because they want to know, "Will the hero achieve X?" The answer may be "yes," "no," or "yes, but-" but whatever the answer, it must be decisive. A conclusive ending makes the viewing experience feel worthwhile. It gives the long, winding narrative a sense of CLOSURE. Without closure, the audience will walk away upset or dissatisfied. I have encountered a number of scripts that not only fail to provide a suitable climax, but any climax at all. Instead, they have the gall to end with the words "TO BE CONTINUED." Audiences will not stand for this. They have just dedicated two hours of their lives to a story because they want to know how it ends. Instead, they have been cheated out of what they deserve. A good ending rewards the audience for sticking with the story to its end. Like the end of a great meal, the audience should leave with every appetite satisfied, not aching with resentment or hungry for more.

ACT 3, FINAL SEQUENCE – THE RESOLUTION SEQUENCE

After the climactic moment, the story proper comes to an end. The Main Conflict has been resolved, and the Major Dramatic Question answered. The ultimate goal has been reached and the Story Spine completed. Now, there seems to be nothing left to do but turn off the lights and head home. However, it would be premature to end the film right at this moment. From the beginning, the audience has watched, cared for, and invested their emotions in the protagonist's struggle. The audience has a natural desire to know what will come of the protagonist after all is said and done.

Because of this, every cinematic story must end with a FINAL RESOLUTION SEQUENCE. If the opening setup sequence gave the audience a "before" picture (the protagonist's world as it existed before conflict began), the final resolution sequence presents the "after," in which the audience learns how that world has changed as a result of the protagonist's struggle. Things may have changed for the better, or for the worse. Either way, the final resolution sequence wraps up the story in the same way it began – by presenting the *new* status quo.

In the final resolution of *Back to the Future,* we learn that Marty's actions have made his family happier and healthier, while turning Biff Tannen from a bully into a clown. In *Star Wars,* we see that Luke Skywalker has not only become a man, but an honored hero as well. In *Die Hard,* John, Holly, Sgt. Powell, and Argyle reunite and share the joy that comes from their victory. With these moments, the audience not only sees what has come of the protagonist, but gets an idea of how life will continue after the credits roll.

But how long should a resolution last? As long as the story needs it to and no more. The resolutions of *Rocky, Alien,* and *Chinatown* last only a few seconds. This is all the time required to show that Rocky Balboa has achieved happiness and self-respect, that Ripley is safe yet alone, and that Jake Gittes is crushed by the realization that corruption will always win.

Back to the Future, The Godfather, and *Finding Nemo* demand longer resolutions. These stories contain a number of additional subplots, character conflicts, and loose story threads that remain unresolved even after the main conflict has ended. The final resolution sequence gives the storyteller the opportunity to wrap up all loose bits and pieces before the credits roll, so the audience is not left with a feeling of unfinished business. In many cases, these are issues that by nature cannot be resolved until after the climax has occurred. Marty McFly cannot see how his actions have saved his parents' marriage until after he returns to 1985. Kay in *The Godfather* cannot realize what has come of the man she loves until after Michael's bloody revenge. The audience cannot see how Marlin's relationship with Nemo has changed until after they reunite. Like ripples in a pool of water, the final resolution shows how the results of the main story climax expand outward to impact every remaining area of the protagonist's life.

However, the final resolution must not be too long. The 2000 film *Cast Away,* though otherwise well-received, was criticized for its excessively long resolution. As the story of a man marooned on a desert island, *Cast Away* asks, "Will the hero get off the island?" But, once the hero escapes the island and returns home, the movie continues on for another twenty minutes, even though, for all intents and purposes, the story was over. Meanwhile, the audience grew restless as they checked their watches and eyed the exits, wondering why the credits would not roll. Once the Major Dramatic Question has been answered and the Story Spine completed, dramatic tension disappears. Continue too long in this state and the audience will grow bored. So wrap things up, wrap them up completely, and do it as soon as dramatically possible.

This concludes the 3-Act structure. All this information may seem like a lot to take in, but with a little observation and experience, these concepts become easy to spot and natural to understand. It will soon be impossible to watch any well-made film without recognizing its major sequences and turning points in action.

Now that you have a basic understanding of the machinations behind plot and structure, set them aside for the moment. Before going deeper into this area, we must address a subject of equal, if not even greater importance. Character.

CHAPTER 7
ON CHARACTER

Story comes from character. Not the other way around.

There seems to be two approaches to the Hollywood screenplay: those that begin with a great character and build their plots around it; and those that start from a "cool" concept and then throw in characters as an after-thought. While the latter type can provide a certain level of entertainment, the viewing experience is typically a mediocre one that quickly fades from the audience's memory. A cool concept may sell tickets, but those ticket holders will be disappointed without great characters to make the experience worthwhile. *Star Wars* spawned a host of sci-fi ripoffs. *Die Hard* did the same in the action genre. However, audiences never embraced these copy-cats as they did the originals. Why? Because the imitators merely stole the original's concept, while ignoring the fact that the originals were great because they were built around *great characters*. A concept may draw audiences in, but characters are what make them stick around for more.

Audiences experience cinematic stories by forming psychological attachments to the persons they see on the screen. They experience emotion and excitement by living through the actions of the characters. Unfortunately, this becomes difficult when characters are phony, dull, or flat as cardboard. Movies invented with the concept-first approach invariably wind up with weak, superficial characters. This is primarily because these characters are defined solely by the *function* they play in relation to an already-constructed plot. They are little more than hollow tools who exist for no other purpose than to connect the story's dots.

In a great movie, the plot is not in the driver's seat. Rather, the characters are in control. Characters cannot just stand around waiting for things to happen. Instead, they must be the ones advancing the plot through independent thought and action. Not because the script tells them to, but because they are driven to act by clear and understandable needs. Characters create story.

Remember that the Story Spine revolves around the protagonist and his or her needs. It is the protagonist's Story Problem, the protagonist's Story Goal, the protagonist's Path of Action... Without the protagonist, a Story Spine cannot exist. Without a Spine, a story cannot exist. So, if the entire Story Spine emerges from the needs of a single character, and the entire plot from the Story Spine, simple logic dictates that all plot originates from the wants and needs of that character. But, how does this happen? How exactly does a character create a plot?

It all starts by giving the character a strong INTERNAL NEED.

The internal need is some intangible thing missing from the protagonist's life. It is an emotional or psychological lack that prevents the protagonist from becoming a complete, emotionally satisfied human being. The protagonist may need self-worth (*Rocky*), to find his place in the universe (Luke in *Star Wars*), or to forgive himself for past failures (Dr. Malcolm Crowe in *The Sixth Sense*). Sometimes, the protagonist is aware of this need. More often, he or she is not. Usually this need is buried so deep inside the character that he or she does not even realize it exists. Regardless, this gaping, empty need becomes the subconscious drive behind the character's thoughts and deeds. The character cannot become happy and fulfilled until the need is met.

A good internal need must meet two requirements. First, the need must be authentically human. This means it must be something everyone can understand. We can all understand a need for safety, success, love, or self-worth. We recognize these needs because we want them for ourselves. Human beings share dozens of basic drives and urges. Picking one of them allows the audience to understand the internal need, and thus understand the character's behavior.

Second, the internal need must be strong enough to influence character behavior. A need is worth little to a story unless it motivates the character to act. The need makes itself physical through a character's observable traits, such as attitudes, opinions, and the actions the character is willing (or unwilling) to take. For example, Luke Skywalker's need to find his place in the universe causes him to be restless, impatient, and impulsive. Rocky Balboa's lack of self-worth makes him sad, bitter, and sensitive to criticism.

Now, here is the important part: Once the storyteller has given the character a strong internal need, he or she must place that character into a physical predicament that forces the character to PURSUE THAT NEED.

Think of yourself as the god of your story world. You created this world. You have absolute power over it and absolute control. As the creator, you know your protagonist down to the most intimate detail. You know his or her internal need, and as a benevolent god, you want the protagonist to receive this need so he or she can become a better, happier person. However, the storyteller-god cannot simply hand the character this need. This is not how the story universe works. Instead, the character must *earn it*.

Here is where plot comes into play. The storyteller-god manipulates the story universe to thrust the protagonist into a situation specifically designed to give the protagonist exactly what he or she needs. Rocky needs self-worth. So, the storyteller places him into a situation where he must become either a contender or a joke. Luke Skywalker needs to find his place in the universe. So, the storyteller puts him at the center of a galaxy-wide struggle that forces him to seek his destiny. Neo of *The Matrix* needs to believe in himself. So, Neo is placed into a predicament where humanity's entire fate hangs upon that belief. However, for this to work, the situation must be filled with conflict and danger. Most people are slow to act in real life. They become comfortable with the way things are, flaws and all, and grow unwilling to change. But, when the storyteller-god throws a Story Problem into the protagonist's life with all of its associated conflict, a proverbial gun is placed to the protagonist's head. The protagonist must take action whether he or she likes it or not. The physical events of the plot, with its various conflicts and goals, actually exist for no other purpose than to get the protagonist off his or her butt and send him or her down a path that will ultimately lead to what the character desperately needs.

To make this easier to understand, think of the supporting characters from the classic film *The Wizard of Oz*. The Scarecrow, Tin Man, and Lion come to the Wizard with obvious internal needs. The Scarecrow needs a brain. The Tin Man needs a heart. The Lion needs courage. However, the Wizard, like a storyteller-god, does not simply give these characters what they need. Instead, he demands they bring him the broom of the Wicked Witch. The Wizard sends them on an *adventure*. This is not just any adventure. This is an adventure specifically designed to put the characters into a predicament where they must find their internal needs all on their own in order to succeed. As soon as the quest begins, Dorothy is captured by the Witch. To rescue her, the Scarecrow, Tin Man, and Lion must summon the qualities they supposedly lack. The Scarecrow finds the brains to think up a plan. The Tin Man leads them on with loving emotion. The Lion musters the courage to face danger. It is the adventure itself that transforms the characters into better, stronger persons. In the end, the broom itself is meaningless. The physical goal was merely an excuse invented to send the characters down a path that eventually leads them to what they really need.

For the point of emphasis, I must make clear that the internal need is not the same as the Story Goal. They are separate, yet connected ambitions. The Story Goal is a tangible, real-world accomplishment that can only be achieved through physical action. To capture the killer, to save the farm, to win the big game. The protagonist is aware of this goal and takes willful steps to achieve it. In contrast, the internal need is an abstract emotional or psychological necessity tugging at the character under his or her surface that the character may be unaware of or resist. It can only be achieved through internal processes triggered by the struggles faced by the character in the outside world. Though Story Goal and internal need influence each other, they are two separate accomplishments that are reached individually. More on the relationship between need and Goal will be covered later this chapter.

Unfortunately, something within the protagonist prevents him or her from attaining the internal need. Standing in the way is a second internal force called the FATAL FLAW. The fatal flaw is a defect in a character's personality, point of view, or way of thinking that interferes with his or her ability to find happiness and success. Perhaps the character is selfish, or insensitive, or cowardly. Maybe he or she has no ambition, no confidence, or no self-control. This flaw has grown and festered within the protagonist for years, sometimes to the point where it seems the two are inseparable. Like the internal need, the protagonist is often unaware of this flaw, or if he or she is aware, the character is unwilling to recognize the harm it brings.

As long as the flaw exists, the protagonist will remain an incomplete person, doomed to fail at whatever he or she attempts. Doomed because the flaw not only creates problems in the character's internal life, but also interferes with any external efforts the character makes towards his or her physical goals. As the protagonist pursues the Path of Action, the flaw makes it difficult, or even impossible, to find success. Luke Skywalker is too immature. Marty McFly is too reckless. Michael Corleone is too passive. The flaw becomes a stumbling block that trips up the protagonist time and again. Because of the flaw, the character will never reach the Story Goal or internal need. Unless, that is, the character is willing to CHANGE.

CHARACTER CHANGE

In every cinematic story, events cause characters to grow and change. Who they were at the story's beginning is not who they are at its end. This is only natural. No human being, real or fictional, could possibly go through the extreme situations found in any cinematic story and not wind up transformed as a result.

If you look back on your own life, I wager the person you are today is very different from the person you used to be. In your youth, you may have been less responsible, more optimistic, less confident, or different in any number of ways. Most likely, your personal evolution did not occur slowly and gradually by its own accord. Instead, changes came in reaction to major, life-altering events; marriages and divorces, first jobs and first loves, births and deaths, heartbreaks and failures. The stresses and responsibilities of each new milestone forced you to reevaluate how you saw the world and your place within it. As your view of the world changed, so did your attitudes and behavior.

Cinematic stories revolve around major milestones in characters' lives. Quite often, these are the most significant, most difficult, most extreme experiences the characters will ever face. Given the severity of these situations, character change is not only inevitable, but mandatory.

This course of change is known as the CHARACTER ARC. Like the Story Spine, the character arc is a journey. But unlike a physical journey, the character arc is an invisible path of personal transformation a character undergoes as he or she struggles with a story's events. But, what must change about a character, and why?

Human beings tend to view people, both real and fictional, as a collection of qualities known as PERSONALITY TRAITS. If you were to give a purely non-physical description of a friend, you would be listing that person's traits. Perhaps you see your friend as quiet, intelligent, well-meaning, but prone to anger or jealousy. Or maybe your friend is confident, proud, energetic, but very poor at communication. Every person possesses an assortment of attitudes, behaviors, habits, and beliefs (both positive and negative in nature) that suggest how the person will behave in any given situation.

Characters, of course, should possess an equally rich collection of traits. Some traits are beneficial, such as Indiana Jones' bravery, Rocky's bumbling charm, or Frodo's pure heart. Other traits give no discernible benefit, yet cause no harm, like John McClane's sense of humor, Marty McFly's rockstar ambitions, or Ripley's fondness for cats. These traits typically do not change over the course of a story, simply because there is no need. They are found helpful or at least benign to the character's journey, and are thus retained.

Characters will also begin the story with a collection of *negative traits.* Though we usually consider a "negative trait" as anything socially undesirable about a person; such as rudeness, immaturity, or arrogance; in terms of story, a negative trait refers solely to behavioral qualities that interfere with the character's ability to reach his or her goals. Sometimes, these interfering traits are qualities considered to be good things. A character may struggle because he or she is too honest, too easy-going, or too trustful. In *The Godfather,* Michael Corleone's ability to protect his family is at first hampered by a sense of ethics he learned in college and the military. In relation to his Story Goal, Michael's ethics are a negative trait. Conversely, a character may have a host of socially undesirable qualities, yet these traits are not negative traits unless they specifically interfere with the character's ability to reach his or her goal. For example, Indiana Jones is quite arrogant. While arrogance is generally frowned upon by society, in terms of story, Indy's arrogance is a positive trait since it benefits him on many occasions during his quest.

Because they interfere with the protagonist's ability to reach his or her goals, negative traits must be overcome if the protagonist is ever to find success. Characters who do not will wind up failing in the end. This is seen in movies such as *Raging Bull* or *Citizen Kane*. Jake LaMotta ends his story a miserable failure because he is never able to put aside his jealous and self-destructive behavior. Charles Foster Kane of *Citizen Kane* winds up bitter and alone because he never learns to love others the way they love him.

As you can see, the ability to abandon negative traits in favor of more beneficial qualities becomes the key to a protagonist's ultimate success. However, characters cannot change like the flip of a switch. This would be unnatural. Most people are set in their ways and are thus resistant to change. Like an old tree stump anchored to the ground, it is going to take a lot of force to pull it from its roots. Story events must act as a slow, steady force pushing against the protagonist. The protagonist will resist at first, but eventually this force breaks his or her inertia and pushes the protagonist in the direction of change. Conflict is the key ingredient. When characters encounter story conflict, they are forced to act, react, and then evaluate the effectiveness of those actions. If characters struggle or fail, it tells them they must learn to do things differently. They realize they must change in order to survive. The cumulative experience forces characters to transform and adapt, slowly re-shaping themselves into persons more capable of overcoming their situations. Like how a lump of coal is transformed into a diamond, the constant heat and pressure of dramatic conflict slowly transforms the protagonist into something stronger, purer, and better. Now, with the negative traits wiped away, the protagonist is finally able to defeat the story's conflict and reach his or her goal.

This process is actually quite simple. Despite all the various negative traits a character may have, there is only one thing about the character that really needs to change. Fix that, and all other problems will disappear. A character's negative traits are all rooted in the same fatal flaw. Like how a massive crack at a stone's foundation will radiate upward until it appears as a spiderweb of tiny cracks on the surface, the character's deep-seeded fatal flaw is the source of everything that holds the character back. For example, if a character is unwilling to connect with others, this flaw will present itself as reclusiveness, loneliness, bitterness, and coarse behavior. If a character's flaw is a fear of taking chances, it will emerge as timidness, indecisiveness, or cowardice.

However, there is one peculiar thing about the fatal flaw. It is not rooted in anything real or physical within the characters' world. It is rather the result of an *incorrect belief* the character holds about that world. Because of this incorrect belief, the character willingly causes him or herself harm. In short, all of the internal difficulties characters encounter in the face of conflict are really the characters' OWN DAMN FAULT.

As any therapist will tell you, most psychological problems come not from a person's actual reality, but from a FALSE PERCEPTION of that reality. Negative past experiences cause people to develop certain false beliefs about themselves and the world. These beliefs then lead to harmful or self-defeating behavior. For example, a depressed person may withdraw socially because she honestly believes no one likes her. Someone suffering anxiety may panic under pressure because he has convinced himself that everything he does ends in failure. However, when viewed objectively, these beliefs turn out to be untrue. The woman has many people who like her. The man's past failures have actually been few and far between. The world is not as bad as these people have led themselves to believe. The goal of therapy is to change a person for the better by leading him or her away from such harmful misconceptions and toward healthier, more accurate views of the world. Once changed, self-defeating tendencies will slip away, and life's obstacles become easier to overcome.

Character change works in the same way. Fatal flaws originate from a deficiency in how characters perceive themselves or their world. *Casablanca*'s Rick acts with cold, self-centered detachment because he believes caring for others will only get him hurt. Neo is reluctant to become a hero because he honestly believes he is no one special. Indiana Jones is coarse and emotionally distant because he has been betrayed so many times that he has been led to believe people cannot be trusted. But, these problems are all in the characters' heads. Once story events force characters to see their world for what it really is, they will change their ways, abandon their negative traits, and clear a path to happiness and success.

Here then, at long last, is how the character arc works:

At the beginning of a story, the protagonist's ability is limited by a defective view of him or herself, or his or her world. When the protagonist encounters conflict, this defective view causes difficulty. Eventually, events force the protagonist to reevaluate and then CHANGE this view to a more positive, truthful perception of reality. Because of this change, the protagonist loses his or her negative traits, allowing him or her to overcome all obstacles and achieve the Story Goal.

As you may notice, the character arc and Story Spine are vitally connected. Character change cannot occur without the conflict provided by the Story Spine. At the same time, the Story Spine cannot reach completion until its protagonist undergoes personal change. Story Spine and character arc thus possess a symbiotic relationship where one cannot succeed without the other. The Spine and arc are not two separate threads traveling in unrelated directions. They are instead two pieces of the same whole, woven together like a piece of rope, providing mutual influence and support as they work together to reach a common end. A piece of rope gets its strength from its two braided threads working in cooperation. A story gains strength from the same principle.

We will use *Star Wars* to illustrate. Luke Skywalker starts the film with a need to find his place in the universe. To accomplish this, the storyteller puts Luke into a plot situation that will ultimately force Luke to reach his destiny as a hero and Jedi Knight. However, as the story begins, it seems unlikely that Luke could reach such a goal. He is hampered by a simple, immature view of the universe. This flawed perspective creates self-defeating traits, such as naïvete, passivity, impatience, and most importantly, a fear of leaving the protection of his guardians to strike out on his own.

Something must be thrust into Luke's life to begin his transformation. Luke encounters two droids, one of whom carries a secret message from Princess Leia. This makes Luke curious, however his immaturity prevents him from mustering the courage to investigate further. He even gives in to his Uncle's request to erase R2D2's memory and forget the whole matter. Because of this, the plot must intercede to push Luke onward. R2D2 runs away, forcing Luke to follow. This leads him to Obi-Wan Kenobi. Obi-Wan gives the wide-eyed boy his first taste of life outside of the farm with tales of Jedi and the Force. Luke is intrigued, especially at the mention of his father, but when asked to join Obi-Wan, Luke is reluctant. His immature view of the world prevents him from taking the next step.

Plot must intercede once again. Imperial soldiers kill Luke's family and destroy his home. Though Luke was previously stuck in his ways, this traumatic event pulls him up by the roots, forcing him to begin a journey which will lead to ultimate change. Luke has no choice but to join Obi-Wan and accept him as a mentor. Though Obi-Wan tries to rid Luke of his negative traits, Luke continues to cling to his flawed, immature views. He is still a boy hiding behind Obi-Wan, rather than a man with the confidence to take action on his own.

Plot events must again intervene to force Luke to change. When the Millennium Falcon is captured by the Death Star, Luke is separated from his mentor and put into a situation where he must take action or perish. Bolstered by what he has learned from Obi-Wan, Luke accepts his first real test of manhood by taking it upon himself to rescue Princess Leia. Through this action, Luke discovers he is capable of far more than what his fatal flaw has led him to believe. His perception of himself and his place within the universe begins to change.

However, one thing remains in the way of Luke's final transformation. He still feels dependent upon Obi-Wan. Obi-Wan must die if Luke is to reach his destiny. The plot intervenes once again to accomplish this. Now on his own, Luke must find the strength to overcome one last test of character. It is not until the film's climactic moment that Luke finally abandons the last shred of his old view of the universe, and fully surrenders himself to the way of the Force. Now fully transformed, the wiser and stronger Luke is able to find destroy the Death Star and claim his internal need.

Star Wars demonstrates a clear relationship between Story Spine and character arc. Plot events cause Luke to grow as a person. As Luke grows, he becomes more capable of taking actions necessary to advance the plot. Had Luke not changed, he would have been unable to overcome the obstacles he faced aboard the Death Star and during the final climax. Luke finds victory in the end only because the conflicts he faced forced him to challenge his flawed views and grow into a better, more capable human being. Because of this interwoven path, Luke achieves both his Story Goal and his internal need through the same course of action.

As seen here, Story Spine and character arc form the most perfect unity when the Spine's Story Goal and the arc's internal need are related in such a way that one can only be achieved by first reaching the other. Luke Skywalker finds his place in the universe (internal need) only after he defeats the Empire (Story Goal). Rocky Balboa achieves self-worth (internal need) by going the distance with Apollo Creed (Story Goal). This can also work in reverse. In *The Matrix,* Neo is able to defeat the Agents (Story Goal) by first learning to believe in himself (internal need). Which comes first will depend on the needs of the particular story. Either way, this cause-and-effect relationship should exist. It binds Spine and arc together, uniting the needs of both plot and character into a single whole.

REQUIREMENTS OF A GOOD PROTAGONIST

A good story demands a good protagonist. Good protagonists encourage the audience to climb into their heads and experience the story through them. If done well enough, the audience will feel as if they have entered the story in the protagonist's place and will respond to story events as if they were happening to themselves. This concept is known as AUDIENCE IDENTIFICATION.

Unfortunately, audiences will not identify with just anyone. The protagonist must be appealing enough that the audience will *want* to attach themselves to him or her. If the audience should reject the protagonist, they will never become fully invested in the story's events and all of the storyteller's efforts may come to naught. Many insist the only way to create audience identification is to make the protagonist a "likeable" person. However, this is a fallacy. Likeability is not an absolute prerequisite for audience identification. A character can have many traits the audience finds unlikable, yet still make a capable protagonist. Conversely, there are many very likeable characters who do not have what it takes to be a story's hero. What then are the necessary factors for audience-character identification?

1. The Protagonist Must be Humanly Relatable.

*"We do not need to 'like the people.' We need to
understand the people."*
- Dr. Lew Hunter, Screenwriting 434

Human beings the world over share the same psychology. There are thousands of small variations that make each of us unique, but generally, all of our brains work in the same way. We all react to similar situations in similar ways. We all smile when happy and cry when sad. Victories, setbacks, joys, and frustrations all bring about predictable responses, no matter to whom they occur. This sameness of mind helps us understand others. It is what makes us collectively "human."

If on the other hand we should encounter someone whose behavior does not align with what we have come to know and expect; if someone laughs when they should cry or shows anger at what should bring joy; we feel uncomfortable. This person is labeled as schizophrenic. In most cases, people try to avoid the schizophrenic since they are unable to understand or predict their behavior. Because they do not behave in the manner traditionally considered "human," these people appear frightening and alien.

To this point, if a character is to appeal to an audience, he or she must first behave in a manner the audience is used to seeing in other human beings. When the audience recognizes behavior, they can then understand the thoughts and emotions behind that behavior. This opens the door to a concept known as EMPATHY. Empathy is the ability to share in the emotions of another person as if they were your own. This is not to be confused with sympathy. Sympathy merely applies one's own emotions to another person's situation. Empathy, on the other hand, comes by way of putting oneself in another's shoes. Audiences feel empathy when they are able to see the story situation from the character's point of view and thus understand the character's thoughts and emotions as if they were their own.

However, empathy becomes impossible when the audience is unable to understand or relate to a character's behavior. They cannot share a character's thoughts if they cannot first comprehend them. This becomes most apparent when dealing with characters who are not physically human. For instance, if a protagonist is Zeebloxx, the four-armed Axturan warlord from the Andromeda galaxy, the audience will have a hard time empathizing with this character because they cannot understand the processes by which a four-armed Axturan thinks and feels. At best, Zeebloxx will seem distant and alien. At worst, he will be an inscrutable wall the audience will reject altogether. To solve this problem, the storyteller must give Zeebloxx some of the same behaviors and emotions we find in our fellow human beings. The character must be *humanized.* This gives the audience a way to connect with Zeebloxx and understand him. Recall from Chapter 3 how storytellers anthropomorphize non-human characters so audiences can connect to them as one of their own. The difference can be seen by comparing *Star Wars'* C3P0 to the HAL supercomputer from *2001: A Space Odyssey* (1968). While both are inhuman machines, one has been given a full range of emotions, making him as approachable as any human, while the other lacks all emotion, keeping him cold and alien. *Terminator 2* (1991) demonstrates both sides of this principle. The terminator cyborg starts the story emotionless and inhuman. The audience feels no connection to it until the protagonist teaches it some human behavior. Suddenly, the audience warms to the cyborg, eventually giving it the empathy it usually reserves for human beings.

It may seem obvious that characters must behave like human beings. However, I have read many scripts featuring protagonists who display unintentionally schizophrenic behavior. They act without proper motivation, display inappropriate emotion, and reason with fractured logic. Though human in form, they do not act as humans are expected to behave. Audiences will be unable to connect with these characters because they cannot make sense of their actions. Psychopaths and the mentally disturbed also make unrelatable protagonists because the audience is (hopefully) unable to empathize with their warped thinking. To identify with a character, the audience must first understand the character, and this all begins with behaviors to which they can relate.

2. The Protagonist Must be Worthy of the Audience's Interest

This one is a no-brainer. If the audience must spend two hours with a character, it ought to be someone interesting enough to hold their attention. Have you ever been at a party and gotten stuck talking to an absolute bore? Imagine if that continued for two hours. If a character is to gain the audience's affections, there must be something special about the character that makes him or her worthy of that honor.

This seems like common sense. Yet time and again, I find scripts that offer protagonists described as "an average 20-something," or "an average housewife," or "an average middle-aged man." Well, if there is nothing special about these people, why do they deserve their own movies? What makes the writer believe the audience will want to spend two hours of their lives with them? I dare you to find any successful film in which the hero is truly average. Marty McFly is not an average teenager. He is a reckless rock-star wannabe who hitches rides on the bumpers of passing cars. Rocky Balboa is not some average schmo. He is a two-bit slugger/professional thumbreaker who raises turtles and takes pride in his unbroken nose. John McClane may be billed as an average New York cop, but his wit, attitude, and perseverance make him anything but.

Dull, generic protagonists are usually the result of lazy writing. Writers are unwilling to put in the time and effort required to make the protagonist unique. If the writer cares so little about his or her protagonist, guess how much the audience will care in return? Some writers create generic protagonists on purpose under the misbelief that it will lead to greater audience identification. They think the audience will see these mundane bores as people "just like them." But, this is a bit of an insult, isn't it? No one wants to think of themselves as average. In fact, "average" people do not even exist. Everyone in the world is a unique individual, with his or her own special traits and abilities. The only problem is that one must often make an effort to get to know a person before his or her unique qualities begin to emerge. This is what storytellers must do. They must explore their protagonists, find what makes him or her special, and then put it on display for the audience to see. Anything short of this is simply laziness on the part of the writer.

A protagonist does not need to be as daring as Indiana Jones or as simple-minded as Forrest Gump to be special. All the protagonist needs is some uncommon quality or skill that sets him or her apart from the crowd. Dr. Malcolm Crowe of *The Sixth Sense* is set apart by a gift for dealing with children. *American Beauty*'s Lester Burnham is a raging teenager trapped in a 40 year-old's body. Ripley in *Alien* manages to be tougher than any of the roughnecks on her ship. Little differences, well-executed, can go a long way. After all, a storyteller cannot take any old character and slap on the label "hero." That character must deserve the title. A character first does this by being special. But being special is not enough in itself to turn a character into a hero. He or she must also meet a third qualification.

3. The Protagonist Must Be Worthy of the Audience's Respect

Sometimes a story demands its protagonist to display behavior considered antisocial, unethical, or unsympathetic. These protagonists tend to throw studios, producers, and sometimes even writers into a panic as they once again get hung up on the idea of likeability. However, being a nice person does not necessarily make a good protagonist. A character can be the sweetest person on earth yet still fail with an audience. What matters most is not that the audience likes the protagonist, but that they RESPECT the protagonist.

A worthiness for respect is the most essential quality a protagonist can have. A likeable personality may allow the audience to enjoy a character's company, but behavior the audience can respect is what turns that character into the story's hero. When a story begins, the audience naturally seeks out someone to latch onto as their guide. They seek a *leader*. People choose leaders based on qualities they respect. This could mean honesty, bravery, intelligence, trustworthiness, compassion, or any number of traits. When the audience sees such qualities in the protagonist, it points to the character as someone they can not only get behind, but *want* to follow. Give people a leader they can respect, and they will follow that person to hell and back.

On the other hand, a leader unworthy of respect will never gain support, no matter how nice or likeable that person may be.

How does one make a character respectable? First, the storyteller must give the character a set of admirable traits. This could include charm, skill, smarts, kindness, charisma, toughness, ingenuity... the list could go on and on. Second, the character must use these traits for purposes which the audience can morally approve. By some form of logic or another, the protagonist's actions must appear to be ethically "right." The audience will forgive, and even embrace a myriad of unsympathetic traits within the character as long as they can still approve of what the character does and how he or she does it. Indiana Jones has plenty of bad traits. He is arrogant and rude. He is a jerk to his friends. He takes selfish risks that put others in danger. Yet, audiences still love him. Why? Because they can respect him. They respect his bravery, his integrity, and the sacrifices he is willing to endure for the greater good. Jake Gittes of *Chinatown* first appears cynical and unsympathetic. However, the audience soon grows to respect Jake; for his intelligence, his guts, and because he sticks to his principles regardless of the consequences. This makes Jake a hero.

A protagonist can get away with socially unacceptable behavior as long as his or her actions continue to follow a CODE OF CONDUCT. A code of conduct is a set of personal guideline that recognizes a clear line between actions that are morally acceptable and those that are not. A code of conduct becomes especially important when the audience must retain respect for characters who break the law. Vito Corleone of *The Godfather* is the head of a criminal organization. This might label Vito as an immoral character. However, Vito operates his business within clear ethical boundaries the audience can respect. Vito protects rather than exploits. He supplies "harmless" activities, such as gambling and drinking, but refuses to deal in narcotics. He uses violence, but only when necessary to protect his community. Though Vito is surrounded by greed and corruption, he stands firm by his moral code. This makes Vito heroic. In the same way, a character can be a thief, a hitman, or a bank robber and still make a respectable protagonist as long as his or her code of conduct forbids actions the audience will find morally reprehensible. The thief does not steal from the poor. The hitman kills only those who deserve it. The bankrobber tries to avoid bloodshed, and so on.

While there are many ways for a protagonist to gain the audience's respect, writers should be aware that there are also many ways to lose it. Sometimes writers create protagonists who are weak-willed and pathetic in an attempt to foster sympathy. A helpless protagonist makes a poor leader. Eventually, the audience will reject this character in favor of someone more proactive. At other times, a writer allows the hero to make one stupid decision after another until the audience becomes certain they are being led by an idiot. With no respect for their leader, the audience will abandon the character, and the story with it. Sometimes a storyteller allows the protagonist to momentarily stray across moral boundaries and commit an action the audience cannot accept. Like a scandalized politician, one moral lapse can ruin an entire reputation. Codes of conduct act as barriers to protect the audience's respect. Step over them once and it may be difficult, or even impossible, to gain that respect back again.

THE ANTAGONIST

Though not all stories use a character as their force of antagonism, stories that do use an antagonist must treat this character with an importance second only to the protagonist itself. As the yin to the protagonist's yang, a good antagonist provides a story with a balanced conflict. Every time the protagonist pushes, there must be something pushing back.

A weak antagonist creates weak drama. If the antagonist is some weakling the protagonist can defeat at any time, the story will contain little dramatic tension. The antagonist must be a force equal to, or greater than the protagonist. In fact, the more powerful the antagonist the greater the drama. Darth Vader is far more powerful than Luke Skywalker. Apollo Creed is a far better fighter than Rocky Balboa. The CIA is nearly god-like compared to Jason Bourne. These David-versus-Goliath scenarios create uphill battles that put the hero's chances into the greatest doubt. If the hero must be superior to the antagonist in certain ways, the antagonist should have other advantages to balance the scales. Superman for instance has invincible strength. His nemesis Lex Luthor could never defeat him man-to-man. However, what Luthor lacks in strength, he makes up for in intelligence. This compensates for his weakness and returns the conflict to an even field.

There is often confusion over who or what can qualify as a story's antagonist. First of all, the antagonist must be a character – a real, physical being. This character must be present within the story and capable of taking actions that directly impact the plot. The antagonist cannot be an idea. It cannot be the environment or a location. It cannot be a person who makes no actual appearance within the story. It also cannot be a cosmic force, such as fate or "God" – unless God literally appears in physical form and takes actions that influence the story's events.

Second, the antagonist must *directly* and *willfully* oppose the protagonist's attempts to achieve the Story Goal. Indiana Jones wants to claim the Ark of the Covenant. Belloq wants it for himself. Neo wants freedom from the Matrix. Agent Smith would rather kill him than let that happen. Rocky Balboa wants to prove himself in his fight with Apollo. Apollo wants to humiliate Rocky by knocking him out. A character who merely causes trouble, but does not oppose the Story Goal cannot be the antagonist. This character is only a PEST. Pest characters provide the protagonist with additional difficulty, but they are not the story's real threat. Lieutenant Robinson is a pest in *Die Hard*. So is Golem in *The Lord of the Rings*. Do not mistake a pest for an antagonist. This will create a weak, one-sided conflict with no legitimate force threatening the hero's defeat.

In addition, many people refer to the antagonist as the "bad guy." However, this is misleading. The antagonist need not always be a bad person, just as the protagonist need not always be good. Evil and malice are not absolute requirements to oppose the protagonist. In *Fargo*, the unscrupulous protagonist Jerry Lundegaard is opposed by Chief Gunderson, the most morally upright character of the entire film. In *The Sixth Sense*, Dr. Malcolm Crowe is opposed by the little boy Cole. Malcolm wants to help Cole, yet Cole creates conflict by refusing Malcolm's efforts.

Even if the antagonist does "bad" things, the antagonist will rarely see him or herself as a bad person. Great antagonists believe their actions to be justified. In many cases, antagonists consider themselves the good guy. Darth Vader is trying to maintain peace by destroying dangerous insurgents. The monster in *Alien* kills for the sake of its own survival. Agent Smith sees humanity as a disease the world is better without. Belloq believes the Nazis to be a superior society who deserve to rule the world.

If both protagonist and antagonist are trying to accomplish what they consider right and proper, what then separates the two in the minds of the audience? What causes the audience to embrace one, yet oppose the other? Why cannot Hans Gruber be the story's hero? Or Apollo Creed? Or Darth Vader? The previous section established that in order to appeal to an audience, a story's hero must be humanly relatable, worthy of the audience's interest, and most importantly worthy of the audience's respect. The difference between hero and antagonist is that, of these three qualifications, only the second is required of the antagonist. (Note: I realize I may have opened a can of worms with my earlier reference to the concept of "good" antagonists found in films like *Fargo.* To avoid confusion, the rest of this section will use the word "antagonist" to refer to the villainous side of the conflict whom the audience is expected to reject. In the case of *Fargo,* this would be the immoral Jerry Lundegaard.)

Unlike the protagonist, the antagonist need not be humanly relatable. This quality is optional. The antagonist can be a monster, an alien, a psychopath, or a mindless robot. Inhuman antagonists frighten or unnerve the audience, all but ensuring the audience will attach their sympathies to the hero and not the villain. However, this is not to say an antagonist cannot demonstrate behavior to which the audience can understand and relate. *Die Hard, Rocky,* and *The Bourne Identity* all have very human antagonists. But just because the audience can understand the villain's behavior, this does not mean the audience will automatically support him or her. The key factor in a good antagonist is that while he or she may or may not be humanly relatable, the antagonist must absolutely NOT be worthy of the audience's respect.

If behavior the audience can respect is what turns a protagonist into a hero, then behavior unworthy of respect becomes the mark of a villain. In many stories, protagonist and antagonist are similar persons. Indiana Jones and Belloq are both globe-trotting archeologists. Rocky Balboa and Apollo Creed are both prizefighters. The American and German soldiers in *Saving Private Ryan* are all simple young men fighting for their respective countries. In these situations, often the only factor that separates the hero from the villain is that one side demonstrates behavior the audience can respect while the other side does not.

This does not mean the antagonist cannot have admirable traits. To the contrary, the antagonist can and should impress the audience with qualities such as intelligence, charisma, or strength of will. However, unlike the protagonist, the antagonist uses these gifts for purposes which the audience cannot morally approve. Hans Gruber is witty, charming, and brilliant. But rather than use these talents for society's benefit, Hans uses them to steal and kill. Darth Vader has strength and skill any leader would admire. However, Vader uses his abilities for tyranny and oppression.

Ironically, the more an audience admires the antagonist, the greater the reaction when the antagonist commits actions the audience must morally condemn. People talk of "villains we love to hate." This may sound like an oxymoron, but it is based on a simple principle. Think of the antagonist as someone you love and admire – who continually stabs you in the back. You like this person and wish they would act right, but he or she constantly hurts you in the worst possible ways. Betrayal by someone you dislike does not come as much of a shock. However, betrayal by someone you admire, such as Hans Gruber, stings on a personal level. Like a relationship with a cheating spouse, the audience constantly alternates between love and hate. They are drawn to the antagonist for his or her attractive qualities, and then repulsed as the antagonist commits actions the audience must condemn.

Finally, it should go without saying that an antagonist must be an active force in the development of the story. It is not enough for the villain to sit in his fortress, idly waiting for the hero to show up and fight. The antagonist must be out in the story world, taking strong, willful actions that impact the situation. Like the protagonist, the antagonist must pursue a goal. To rob Nakatomi Tower. To destroy the Rebel Army. To find the Ark so the Nazis may conquer the world. This goal must be at direct odds with the protagonist's goal. The Main Conflict of the Story Spine then arises as a result of these two goals colliding head-to-head.

However, the antagonist cannot set a goal unless he or she first has a problem. The antagonist must then take a set of actions to reach that goal. The antagonist encounters conflict along the way, and has stakes attached to success or failure. This should sound familiar. Like the protagonist, the antagonist has his or her own CHARACTER SPINE. And as you will see, the protagonist and antagonist are not alone in this matter.

CHARACTER SPINES

The whole time we have been discussing the Story Spine, we have really been talking about the *protagonist's spine.* As the story's central figure, the protagonist's problem, goal, path of action, conflict, and stakes become the story's main focus. However, to present a compelling, true to life world, a great story must be filled with supporting characters just as active and driven as the protagonist. Everybody must want something and be willing to take action to get it. The only way to accomplish this is to give *every* character his or her own personal spine.

One measuring stick for a great screenplay is how it uses its supporting characters. A poor screenplay treats supporting characters as little more than cogs in the story's machine. They seem to exist on planet earth for no other purpose than to help the protagonist get where he or she needs to go. However, if a story is to be filled with active, compelling, true-to-life persons, supporting characters cannot be treated as mere tools. Each one of them must be a unique individual with their own lives to live. They all have their own problems, goals, wants, and needs that continue to exist even after the characters disappear from the screen. A storyteller should think of each supporting character as the star of his or her *own movie,* a movie we only catch a glimpse of whenever he or she happens to cross paths with the protagonist. Because of this, every character needs a personal spine to motivate his or her actions. The protagonist has a spine. The antagonist has a spine. Supporting Character A has a spine. Supporting Character B has a spine. Minor Character #42 has a spine. Some of these spines are in line with the protagonist's. Some are in opposition. Others are completely tangential. Nevertheless, story events form as these various character spines collide and interact with that of the protagonist. Each sequence and scene is the result of an intersecting spiderweb of various conflicting wants and needs.

An antagonist is effective only when he or she acts according to a spine directly opposed to that of the protagonist. Darth Vader has a clear spine. Vader's problem: a rebel alliance threatens to overthrow his empire. Vader's goal: to find the rebel base and destroy it. From this, Vader pursues a path of action that begins with the capture of Princess Leia. Vader's conflict: Luke, Obi-Wan, and their allies are doing everything they can to stop him. Vader's stakes: if he wins, his power in the galaxy will be solidified; if he fails, his glorious empire may be thrown into ruin. If done well enough, it becomes possible to flip-flop the conflict and see the story from the antagonist's point of view. *Star Wars* could be the story of a general defending his kingdom against a band of traitors. *Die Hard* could be the story of a master criminal plagued by a rogue cop. *Alien* could be the tale of a misunderstood creature's battle for survival.

In every story there are also characters who assist the protagonist. However, just because two characters share the same side, it does not mean these characters are driven by the same wants and needs. In *The Matrix,* Neo is aided by his mentor Morpheus. Though Morpheus's main purpose within the story is to help Neo achieve his goal, Morpheus remains an independent force following his own personal course of action. Morpheus's Problem: machines have enslaved humanity. Morpheus's Goal: to defeat the machines by finding a savior known as "The One." He pursues his Path of Action by first finding Neo, whom he believes to be The One. Morpheus's Conflict: Neo refuses to believe he is The One. Morpheus's Stakes: either succeed and pave the way to humanity's salvation, or lose and abandon all hope for the future.

Morpheus's character spine is different from Neo's. This creates moments of conflict between Neo and his mentor, even though they are on the same side. Here we see something very important about the relationship between characters and drama. When taken individually, each character spine helps bring a story to life by filling it with active, goal-oriented individuals. But, whenever two or more characters interact, the differences in their unique spines will create conflict. It does not matter whether the characters are friends, enemies, or otherwise. The places where their spines fail to match will create conflict between them. Thus, the interaction between various character spines becomes the SOURCE OF DRAMATIC CONFLICT.

Therefore, to create consistent drama, every character must be motivated by clear factors unique to each individual. Even when two characters share the same goal, conflict will still emerge from other differences within their spines, such as each character's personal stakes or how each character wishes to pursue their paths of action. As you will read in Chapter 9, conflict is necessary in every scene to maintain dramatic tension. Well developed, spine-driven characters allow this to happen, no matter what the situation. A story will never have a dull moment as long as two characters have spines in conflict.

Any character, major to minor, can add to the story's richness and complexity with a clear and distinct character spine. Before Rocky Balboa gets his big break against Apollo Creed, he works as an enforcer for a sleazy loan shark named Tony Gazzo. Objectively, Gazzo's scenes have been put into the film as little more than an excuse to demonstrate a different side of Rocky's character. However, these scenes must be kept dramatic. So, Gazzo needs a character spine that conflicts with Rocky. Gazzo's problem: the people who owe him money are not paying up. Gazzo's goal: to get his money. His path: he sends Rocky to break these deadbeats' thumbs. His conflict: Rocky is going easy on these bums. His stakes: if he succeeds, he will get his money; if he fails, he will lose respect as a loan shark. Gazzo does not exist merely as a tool for the sake of Rocky's character. He has a whole world of his own in which Rocky plays only a small part. This suggests a wider and more expansive story universe that goes beyond the edges of the frame, giving the story a sense of depth which was not previously there.

Even the smallest moments can be made dramatic through the use of conflicting spines. *Chinatown* contains a scene where Jake Gittes must look up recent land sales at the Hall of Records. This material could have been rather dull, but the storyteller keeps things dramatic with the addition of a snotty file clerk who: dislikes that Gittes is bothering him (problem), and tries to make Gittes go away (goal) by being arrogant and rude (path of action). Only Gittes does not go away (conflict), threatening the clerk's peace and quiet (stakes). *Chinatown* is a shining example of a film that remains constantly entertaining by simply recognizing every character's wants and needs, no matter how minor that character may be. Whether it be a file clerk, an orange farmer, or a little old lady, every moment is kept memorable through clear and well-executed character spines.

DIMENSIONS AND DEVELOPMENT

Characters with little screen time can get by with only a character spine to explain their behavior. More prevalent characters require additional effort if the audience is to accept them as authentic human beings. The audience needs to see these characters in multiple DIMENSIONS.

A dimension is a "side" to a character's personality. If a character is "one-dimensional," this means the audience never sees the character demonstrate anything but a single set of behaviors. These characters can usually be summed up in one or two words. The "angry cop." A "worried mother." The "jealous girlfriend." Since the whole of their existence is generalized by a glib little label, these characters have no choice but to become stereotypes. Stereotypes create fraudulent characters because they are based on the notion that a single quality can make up the totality of a person's being. Stereotypes do not exist in real life. No one defines their entire existence under a single label. Every person's life is filled with many other aspects that communicate a wider sense of who they are and how they see the world. Audiences cannot connect with one-dimensional characters because they are caricatures rather than authentically relatable human beings.

Thankfully, most writers avoid stereotype by taking their characters beyond one dimension. They present multiple sides of a character's personality, giving a more well-rounded impression of who that person is and how he or she differs from everyone else. The angry cop who is also quite affectionate to his family and has trouble with his weight due to a penchant for junk food. The worried mother who married for money and struggles with her phony social life. The jealous girlfriend with overbearing parents and a mountain of credit card debt.

However, while more authentic than stereotype, these expanded characters remain completely superficial. The physical details about a person; their appearance, their occupation, their physical behavior, their friends and family; do not make up character, but simply *characterization*. Characterization goes only skin-deep. When the audience's knowledge of a character is limited to superficial details, that character remains only two-dimensional. While adequate for minor supporting roles, two-dimensional characters will never have what it takes to fully connect with audiences since there is nothing to help the audience understand these people on a deeper, more emotional level.

"One-dimensional" and "two-dimensional" are terms borrowed from geometry. If curious why take a look at this diagram:

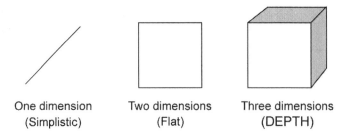

One dimension   Two dimensions   Three dimensions
(Simplistic)   (Flat)   (DEPTH)

When storytellers limit themselves to characterization, characters remain "flat." They are all surface, with nothing underneath. The audience has no choice but to remain emotionally distant from these characters since there is no way to empathize with a person until we can understand his or her behavior on a deeper, more intimate level.

Great characters require DEPTH. Like an iceberg, characterization is only the tip that peeks over the waterline. The majority of character lies hidden underneath, deep down in the unseen needs and flaws that operate under the surface. As soon as the audience catches a glimpse of these depths, the character crosses into the third dimension.

There are two parts to the human persona: a person's physically observable behavior, and the *deeper psychology* that causes that behavior. Behavior must come from somewhere. There are deeper reasons that explain why people do what they do. Authentic character behavior must be rooted in this deeper psychology. This is where the internal need lies. This is also the source of the fatal flaw. Without a window into a character's unseen needs and impulses, the audience will never be able to truly understand the character, leaving him or her a distant mystery, or even worse, a hollow, inauthentic shell.

Character development begins by exploring this psychology. The storyteller should not only identify the character's need and flaw, but figure out how this specific need and flaw came to be. Everything about a person originates from events in his or her past. Pinpoint the root of the problem and then trace how it has grown to influence the ways the character thinks and behaves in the present.

The next step is to figure out how this deeper psychology can manifest itself through physical behavior. The audience can only understand a character based upon what they can see or hear. The storyteller may know a character's inner life down to the most intimate detail, but unless he or she can communicate this information through physically observable evidence, it will never get passed along to the audience. External characterization is all about finding ways to make a character's internal influences understandable through action and behavior. When done properly, characterization can become a window into the character's soul.

However, this can be tricky. Authentic characters, just like persons in real life, rarely behave like open books. There are two sides to any person. The person they really are, and the person they choose to show the world. Most of the time, the two are not one and the same. Human beings tend to hide their true selves behind a social front. This allows them to get what they need while protecting their vulnerable inner selves. Some of the deeper psychology may shine through the facade, but for the most part it remains hidden. How then can a storyteller communicate deeper character without running counter to this natural instinct? Once again, conflict comes to the rescue.

In times of stress, a person's social mask begins to slip. Pretenses fall away, leaving only the raw human underneath. When characters experience conflict, the stress and anxiety of the situation forces their true natures to emerge. A character may act tough, but what happens when he faces real danger? Does he rise to the occasion or run away? A character may act as if she cares only for herself, but what happens when she encounters someone in real need? Does she refuse to help, or does she show she has a heart after all? The heat of conflict forces the two sides of a character's person to stand in stark relief. By seeing a character's true self in contrast with the front they show the world, the audience receives a fuller understanding of the character, both inside and out. Frodo of *The Lord of the Rings* may seem like a foolish dreamer, but when in danger, he reveals himself to be as stout-hearted as any warrior. John McClane is stubborn and petty towards Holly, but when their lives are threatened, all he can think about is how much he wants to see her again. Rocky Balboa likes to put on a tough front, but when pressed, he reveals vulnerability under his surface.

As you can see, conflict reveals *contradictions* within character. Contradictions are an important part of character psychology. Deep down, every human being is a complex tangle of wants, needs, hopes, and fears. Unfortunately, these impulses rarely agree. Take for example a normal college student. This student wants to have fun and enjoy college while she can, but at the same time she knows she must work hard and study. She feels pressure to live up to her parents' expectations, but she also wants to follow her own dreams. She needs money, yet cannot spare the time to get a job. There are many attractive boys on campus, yet she feels the need to stay loyal to her boyfriend back home. She enjoys the independence of adult-hood, yet misses the coddling she received as a child.

Contradiction rule our lives. Every day we must strike a delicate balance amongst our dozens of conflicting wants and needs. We want love, but want to avoid heartbreak. We want success, but fear failure. We need attention, yet value privacy. The choices we make on a daily basis are a continuous series of compromises based upon what needs are best fulfilled at each particular moment.

Because of these contradictions, characters face conflict from within as well as without. Luke Skywalker wants to strike out into the world, yet feels the need to fulfill his duty at home. He wants to be treated as an adult, but recognizes his youth and inexperience. He wants to learn about his father, but is warned to ignore the urge. Every decision Luke makes is the result of an internal battle between his conflicting desires. Story events pull him this way and that, forcing him to choose which impulse to follow at each particular moment. Even when events cause Luke to abandon one desire in favor of another, there remains a lingering regret over the need left behind.

How far must a storyteller go when it comes to dimensionalizing each character? It all depends on how important the character is to the story. The cinematic storyteller has neither the screen time nor the necessity to fully develop every character into three dimensions. So, minor characters like the file clerk in *Chinatown* need only a character spine. Gazzo in *Rocky* requires only a couple extra personality traits to keep him from falling into stereotype. Major characters require far more attention so the audience may better understand who they are and what causes them to take action.

The protagonist, of course, needs the most work of all. A story can get by with a less than stellar supporting cast as long as its audience can surrender their hearts and minds to the protagonist. This psychological bond can only be achieved once the storyteller has given the audience enough to understand a protagonist's thoughts and emotions as well as their own. Start with a character whom the audience can identify and respect, and everything else will follow from there. A great story begins with a great character.

CHAPTER 8
PLOT PROGRESSION

When it comes to plot, it is not enough to simply move the protagonist from one structural guidepost to the next. The plot must advance with sufficient dramatic action to keep the audience engaged. This demands constant *conflict* and *change*. PLOT PROGRESSION refers to the specific methods the storyteller employs to advance the narrative from turning point to turning point. This chapter gives the basic knowledge necessary to accomplish this task in the most dramatically effective manner possible.

THE TWO TYPES OF STORY

The first and most elementary step is to identify what type of story you are trying to create. Those working in the film industry tend to lump all screenplays into two vague categories: "plot-driven" and "character-driven." Unfortunately, these labels are of little help to the screenwriter. This is firstly because neither group has ever been conclusively defined. What makes a story "character-driven" as opposed to "plot-driven" is completely open to interpretation. To what degree must a story's characters outweigh its plot, or vice versa, to qualify as one or the other?

The entire argument turns out to be pointless. EVERY cinematic story is driven by plot. At the same time, EVERY cinematic story is also driven by character. As long as at some point one event causes the next to follow, a plot moves the story. At the same time, every story requires character action to make those events occur. To judge a story as having more of one than the other is absurd. Every story requires both in equal degrees.

However, this two-category system does not entirely miss the mark. All cinematic stories can be divided into two groups. However, the criteria must be redefined. Rather than rely on some imaginary ratio between plot and character, cinematic narratives are better defined with one simple question:

Who (or what) controls the story's action?

From where does the story action originate? What incites the protagonist to act? There could be two possible sources: an *external force* that causes the outside world to act upon the protagonist, or an *internal force* that causes the protagonist to act upon the world. In short, who acts first? Does the universe challenge the protagonist, or does the protagonist challenge the universe?

This concept is best understood by first recognizing the parallel between storytelling and its sister art philosophy. As introduced in Chapter 2, humanity invented storytelling as a means to make sense of the world around it. Philosophy was developed for the same purpose. A *philosophy* is any set of ideas that attempts to explain the nature of the universe through non-scientific means. When used broadly, philosophy includes religious ideologies, since religion explains the universe through the existence of a higher power.

Throughout history, all philosophies have fallen into two general camps: theist and human-centric. Theist philosophies believe the universe to be controlled by a higher power, whether this power be a god, spirits, fate, karma, or even "The Force." The higher power exerts a constant influence over daily life. This creates a world where events are largely outside of the individual's control. Individuals can do their best to gain the favor of this power, but it is ultimately up to the power to decide whom to aid and whom to punish.

In contrast, human-centric philosophies either disavow the existence of a higher power, or assume if one does exist it does not take a hand in daily events. Instead, these philosophies consider human beings to be the center of their own universe. People have total control over their lives. Success or failure depends solely upon the actions each individual is willing or unwilling to take. Though this view grants the individual maximum personal freedom, the downside is a lack of any kind of cosmic order. When in trouble, individuals have no one to count on but themselves.

The two methods philosophy used to explain the universe find distinct parallels in the way we tell our stories. This is not to suggest a storyteller's personal belief system should have bearing on how he or she constructs a plot, or that either story type specifically implies any theological or ideological connotation. The human mind has simply followed the same paths to reach separate destinations. In the first story type, the hero lives in a universe where events are largely outside of his or her control. External forces invade the hero's life, forcing him or her to react. (Stories where the Universe Challenges Man/Woman.) In the second, the hero is capable of controlling his or her own destiny. The hero takes action by his or her own volition in an attempt to create change. (Stories where Man/Woman Challenges the Universe.)

STORY TYPE 1: UNIVERSE CHALLENGES MAN/WOMAN

When someone calls a story "plot-driven," what they usually mean is that the story is driven by *antagonism*. The story begins with an antagonistic force invading the protagonist's life. This creates a threatening situation. The protagonist did not ask for this situation, nor does he or she want it. Nevertheless, the hero is forced to take action.

To put things simply, the "villain" strikes first. The hero's life is relatively stable until someone blows up a bridge, kidnaps a friend, tries to foreclose on the family farm, or something to that effect. The hero did not start the fight. The fight has come to him or her. John McClane is attending an office party. Indiana Jones is teaching a class. Luke Skywalker is doing his daily chores. Then suddenly, life-changing problems are dropped in their laps.

Once it arrives, outside antagonism becomes the story's driving force. The protagonist must react as he or she is bombarded by neverending surprises, misfortunes, and dangers from forces outside of his or her control. As in the theist philosophies, the protagonist is at the mercy of the story's higher power. Like Homer's *Odyssey* or the Biblical story of Job, the storyteller-god creates tests for the hero by manipulating people and events against him or her. The storyteller-god challenges the protagonist to prove his or her worth by smiting the hero with one misfortune after another.

"Snakes. It HAD to be snakes."

Like Homer's hero Odysseus, *Raiders of the Lost Ark* forces Indiana Jones to prove himself against a hellish array of physical trials. No matter what Indy does, his storyteller-god finds new cruelties to inflict upon him. Even before Indy reaches his Midpoint, he faces a steady barrage of scheming Nazis, vicious thugs, and sword-wielding maniacs who seem to fall from the sky simply to make life hell. But this all seems behind Indy once he finds the Ark's hiding place at the Well of Souls. Now, all he needs to do is go into the Well and get the Ark. Sounds easy, right?

Wrong. The Well just *happens* to be filled with SNAKES! The one thing Indy fears most. A critical viewer would have to wonder how thousands of poisonous snakes happened to wind up in a sealed-off chamber in the middle of the inhospitable desert. The reason is simple. The storyteller-god put them there just to make Indy's job as hard as possible!

Okay, so Indy survives the chamber of snakes and finds the Ark. All there is left to do is get the Ark to the surface and Indy can be on his way. Easy, right? Wrong. Belloq and his Nazi friends just *happen* to be waiting outside. Indy's storyteller-god has screwed him over again. Now, the Nazis take the Ark, and seal he and Marian inside the tomb.

Luckily, Indy proves his worth yet again and manages to escape. Now, if he can steal a plane, he and Marian can get to safety. Easy, right? Wrong. The biggest, meanest German of the whole camp just *happens* to spot Indy and corners him into a fight. But, the storyteller-god still thinks it is going too easy on Indy. So, the pilot just happens to fall dead on the controls, the hatch just happens to trap Marian inside, and the plane's wing just happens to tear open a fuel truck, spilling an ocean of gasoline that threatens to explode any minute. Despite Indy's efforts, outside forces continue to turn his situation from difficult to nearly impossible. How will Indy ever escape this time?

As seen here, antagonism-driven stories tend to promote a certain degree of fantasy. Events are highly exaggerated and often occur by little more than dramatic coincidence. This is perfectly acceptable, and often encouraged, as long as the storyteller backs up these contrivances with reasonable logic. It is reasonable that Belloq should discover Indy at the worst possible moment. After all, Belloq's camp is located less than a mile away. It is reasonable to assume snakes would breed in a cool, dark tomb. The storyteller then takes this basic logic and stretches it to extreme fantasy.

STORY TYPE 2: MAN/WOMAN CHALLENGES UNIVERSE

When many hear the term "character-driven," they picture stories made of slow, talky scenes that lack sufficient action. However, these stories hold just as much potential for action as any other. The truth is, when people say character-driven, what they are really trying to say is *protagonism-driven*. Unlike antagonism-driven stories, where the hero must constantly react to events outside of his or her control, protagonism-driven stories put the hero in the driver's seat. Instead of change coming to the hero, it is the hero who creates the change. Rather than being attacked, the protagonist always makes the first move.

An antagonism-driven story begins with the hero in a more or less acceptable status quo. At the inciting incident, an outside force disrupts the status quo by changing the situation for the worse. The hero must then react to this change with willful attempts to set the world right again. In a protagonism-driven story, the situation is reversed. A problem does not interrupt the status quo. Instead, the problem *is* the status quo. The protagonist considers the conditions of his or her world unacceptable from the start. Maybe the protagonist is trapped in an abusive relationship. Perhaps the protagonist dislikes the quality of his or her life. Maybe he or she is angry about the conditions of society. Whatever the case, the protagonist is fed up. The inciting incident occurs the moment the protagonist decides to DO SOMETHING about it. This decision is voluntary, through no outside influence. The hero takes action because he or she *wants* to take action. The story then unfolds through a series of willful efforts made by the protagonist to change his or her world for the better. Like the human-centric philosophies, these protagonists realize their world is what they choose to make of it. There is no higher power to dispense justice. No benevolent force to lend them a hand. If they want happiness and success, they must rise up and claim what they want with their own blood, sweat, and tears.

Protagonism-driven stories also differ in the nature of their conflict. In antagonism-driven stories, forces actively wish to destroy the protagonist. In contrast, protagonism-driven stories contain foes who are merely compelled to *resist* the hero. The protagonist is trying to create change. However, the hero's opponents do not want things to change. They support the current status quo and do not want to see it altered. To them, the protagonist is a troublemaker. They then resist the protagonist's actions in an effort to keep things as they have always been.

Take a look at *American Beauty*. Lester Burnham begins his story quite unhappy with life. He feels imprisoned by a thankless job, an unsatisfying home life, and a grave disappointment over what he has become. This all changes when the sight of his daughter's friend Angela awakens within Lester the carnal desire he has not felt in years. Angela does nothing to physically force Lester to take action. He takes action by choice. Lester single-handedly challenges his universe with a desire to take control and regain the freedom of his youth. Naturally, Lester's rebellion meets resistance; from his boss, his daughter, and especially his wife. Lester's wife is the dominant force in the household and wants to keep it that way. Conflict occurs as Lester pushes against the status quo. Fueled by nothing but sheer will, Lester drive the story forward with his attempts to create real and permanent change.

Protagonism-driven stories generally lack the kind of dramatic contrivances found in antagonism-driven stories, thereby creating worlds much closer to objective reality. This makes them best suited for straight drama. However, protagonism-driven stories can also be found in comedy (*Sideways, Clerks, Coming to America*), romance (*Jerry Maguire*), historical/biographical films (*Dances With Wolves, Lawrence of Arabia*), and rise-and-fall narratives driven by greed or ambition (*Scarface*). This form also works well for social issue films (*Erin Brockovich*), or stories of troubled protagonists undone by their own flaws (*Raging Bull*). Genres further removed from reality such as action, sci-fi, or horror will rarely, if ever, have a protagonism-driven narrative since these genres generally require some form of outside antagonism or dramatic coincidence. In fact, it is difficult to find any commercial blockbusters driven by protagonism. One could argue that antagonism-driven films are more commercially successful because they give audiences the fantasy of a pleasant, ordered universe, while protagonism-driven films tend to reflect the flaws of everyday life. However, when done well, protagonism-driven films have the potential to connect with audiences on a far more personal level. These stories usually get more attention at award season, since they provide an opportunity for far more emotional truth than a hundred genre blockbusters.

MIXED STORY TYPES

It is not uncommon for stories in one category to borrow traits from the other when necessary. These are usually special cases in which an abnormality in plot or character requires the narrative to momentarily diverge from its type. Once again, structure must conform to the needs of the story, not the other way around.

Rocky begins as a typical protagonism-driven story. Rocky's problem is that he feels like a "bum," a pathetic loser who has never accomplished anything in life. His goal is to transform his life into something he can be proud of. For the most part, Rocky pursues this goal through his own volition. He tries to impress Adrian and fights with Mick for some respect. However, the story's most essential plot point requires outside intervention. Rocky ultimately reaches his goal by going the distance with the Heavyweight Champion of the World. In a purely protagonism-driven story, Rocky would have to accomplish everything on his own, meaning he would have to be the one to challenge Apollo to a fight. This would have been implausible for both plot and character. First of all, Rocky would never be so bold. Even if he were, such a request would only get him laughed at. So, the hand of the storyteller-god must momentarily appear to manipulate the situation in Rocky's favor. Apollo Creed (the force of antagonism) chooses Rocky as his next opponent. An outside power intercedes in the situation. This shift is temporary, however. Once this plot problem has been solved, *Rocky* reverts to a protagonism-driven story in which the title character is the sole driving force.

While *Rocky* requires a mixed story type to solve an abnormality in plot, *Forrest Gump* demands one due to character. *Forrest Gump* is the story of a simple-minded man experiencing the ups and downs of life while pursuing the woman he loves. This suggests a protagonism-driven story. However, since *Gump*'s protagonist is such a docile and innocent character, it becomes implausible that he should go out of his way to create the conflict his story requires. Since Forrest is unable to go to the conflict, the conflict must come to him; through historical events, through war, and through the actions of others. Though its Spine is protagonism-driven, *Forrest Gump* must use outside antagonism to advance the situation.

BASIC PLOT DEVICES

Regardless of what drives the story, antagonism or protagonism, the story's plot must constantly maintain dramatic tension through events that provide CONFLICT and CHANGE. Though the narrative follows a clear and simple path from one turning point to the next, the situation must continue to appear exciting and unpredictable to the viewer.

Great plot progression is about controlled chaos – the illusion of unpredictability, underpinned by clear, logical order. To the viewer, events may seem to be spinning out of hand, but in reality the storyteller has everything planned out and under control. No matter how crazy or chaotic the protagonist's path may seem, the audience should be able to look back upon the story and realize every event was necessary and logical in order to get the hero from where he or she was at the beginning to where he or she wound up at the story's end. The storyteller maintains this sense of constant conflict and change through the use of certain DRAMATIC CONTRIVANCES.

Though the word is often given negative connotations, to "contrive" simply means to invent creatively. A dramatic contrivance is any event the storyteller dreams up to alter the story situation. In essence, a story is nothing but a collection of contrivances. Events deserve criticism only when they become *overly*-contrived, meaning the situation has been manipulated beyond the realm of plausibility. Dramatic contrivances specifically designed to develop plot are called PLOT DEVICES. Though the storyteller has dozens of such devices at his or her disposal (far more than can be covered in this book), three basic devices are most common: OBSTACLES, COMPLICATIONS, and REVERSALS. These simple plot devices are explained below, followed by two of the more advanced devices, FORCED DECISIONS and DILEMMAS.

1. OBSTACLES

Obstacles are the simplest and most frequently used plot device. We have already discussed how major obstacles are used to create turning points within the sequence method. However, smaller, more easily defeated obstacles can be used in any scene to provide a source for constant conflict and change. As previously defined, an obstacle is any person, thing, or event that creates conflict by interfering with the pursuit of a goal. They create change by forcing a character to alter course and take unexpected new actions. An obstacle could be anything; a locked door, a flooded road, a stubborn coworker, a room full of ninjas. In Act 2A of *Raiders of the Lost Ark,* Marian is stuffed into a laundry basket and kidnapped. Indy's attempts to rescue her are then made difficult by a series of obstacles: crowded streets, Nazi agents, a scimitar-wielding maniac, and the confusion created by dozens of people carrying baskets identical to the one which hides Marian. Indy's simple and straightforward course of action is made to appear chaotic and unpredictable by the addition of these conflict-inducing devices.

2. COMPLICATIONS

Complications behave like time-delayed obstacles. While obstacles create problems in the here and now, complications set up problems that will arise in the future. When Ted Conklin summons three assassins to find and kill Jason Bourne in *The Bourne Identity,* this creates a complication, not an obstacle. Bourne is not under immediate threat. However, the audience knows these men will eventually find Bourne and put him in danger. Complications are like ticking time bombs. The audience realizes a threat is coming, but is not allowed to know how or when it will occur.

Sometimes characters are aware of the complication. This creates a ticking clock scenario where characters must act quickly before the complication sets in. At other times, the audience learns of the complication, but the characters do not. In *The Matrix,* the Cypher character creates a complication when he agrees to betray Neo and his friends to Agent Smith. The audience knows this betrayal is coming, but the heroes remain in the dark. This creates suspense. The audience knows danger is on its way, but can only watch as the characters walk into a trap. (More on suspense and ticking clocks will be covered in Chapter 10.)

3. REVERSALS

A reversal (or reversal of fortune) is an event that suddenly and unexpectedly flips the situation 180-degrees. What was once very good swiftly turns very bad. What was once doomed is suddenly filled with hope. Common scenarios include a sudden betrayal (Ash attacks Ripley in *Alien*), the antagonist's unexpected arrival (Belloq and the Nazis appear outside the Well of Souls), or a last-minute rescue (Han Solo saves Luke at the climax of *Star Wars*). The reversal can be the most dramatically powerful of plot devices. Not only do they come as a surprise, but they also trigger a major reversal of emotions. This makes them well suited for use at a story's most important turning points.

Though reversals can be exciting and unexpected, the storyteller must make certain they are logical in retrospect. Many films have had their credibility ruined by implausible twists and last-second rescues where salvation seems to materialize from thin air. The audience considers this cheating. There is even a name for it: "deus ex machina," named after an overly-contrived device used in early Greek drama where a god would appear at the end of a story to magically set things right. Yes, the storyteller-god can make anything happen, but his or her hand must stay hidden behind a sense of logic if the audience is to accept the contrivance as possible.

FORCED DECISIONS

As mentioned in Chapter 4, human beings naturally seek the path of least resistance. If an easier, less risky option is available, we will choose it. Why take on more risk than we have to? Why expel more energy than needed? This is called common sense.

However, the path of least resistance creates weak drama. A good story requires its characters to get into increasingly more difficult and dangerous situations. Here, the storyteller faces a conundrum. How can he or she force characters into risky situations when everything in the characters' nature tells them to run the other way? The storyteller cannot force characters to go against human nature, or else the action will appear manipulated or overly-contrived. The story must always appear to advance based on logic and reason. How then does a storyteller make characters do what common sense tells them not to?

A skilled storyteller finds a clever solution. He or she can push characters down the most dramatically exciting path, while still maintaining the plausibility of character actions by creating FORCED DECISIONS.

Chapter 5 made frequent reference to characters making decisions. At every turning point, characters must choose a new course of action. However, in a well-written story, this never amounts to much of a choice. Instead, the situation has been manipulated in such a way that there exists only *one* reasonable path open to the protagonist – a path that leads to more risk and more danger. While there may seem to be other options, those paths are blocked by obstacles or reasons which make the path unwise. The character must then take the difficult road because it is the only road available.

In a great cinematic story, there is no such thing as FREE WILL. While there may be the illusion of free will, the plot eliminates a character's right to practice it. The actions characters take are not done by preference, not because the characters want to take those actions, but because the story situation has left them no other choice. They have been painted into a corner, leaving them only one way out.

When Luke and Obi Wan first encounter the Death Star, the story requires them to go inside the fortress so Luke might eventually rescue Princess Leia. However, at this point, the heroes have no reason to go on board. Even if they did, it would be suicide. Common sense tells them the best option is to get away from the Death Star as quickly as possible. Only the path of least resistance is eliminated when a tractor beam locks onto their ship. The heroes are forced onto the Death Star whether they like it or not. In the same way, Marty McFly does not willingly choose to jump into the DeLorean and travel back to 1955. Instead, he is forced to use the machine as his only means to escape Libyan terrorists. Ripley does not want to destroy the ship at the end of *Alien*. She does so because it is her last remaining option. The best story actions are those one would be crazy to take in any other circumstance. Would a sane man jump off a skyscraper with nothing but a firehose tied around his waist? Of course not. Unless an FBI helicopter was coming to kill him and there was no place to run or hide. So, John McClane jumps off the building. John McClane's insane act becomes completely reasonable due to the circumstance.

To force a decision, the storyteller should consider all options currently available to the hero, and then create obstacles to block all but the intended path. If a character has an easier option, but chooses not to take it, there should be a legitimate reason. John McClane is being shot at by an FBI helicopter. Can he run to the stairwell? No. The helicopter blocks his way. Can he hide? Not for long. Can he reason with them? These trigger happy g-men do not seem reasonable. Can he wait it out? No. Hans is going to blow the roof at any second. John has only one remaining option. Jump off the roof.

No other options. Multiple options dilute dramatic tension. The more a character has, the more chances he or she has to meet success. There is little risk in failure since the character can always double back and try the next one. On the other hand, if a character has only one option, and a very risky one at that, the character is forced to put all the dramatic eggs in one basket. This maximizes dramatic tension by creating a situation where disaster will occur should that action fail.

Sometimes, a character goes against better judgment and takes a riskier path even when an easier one exists. This can be good or bad, depending on whether it is intentional on the part of the storyteller, or merely the result of poor oversight. If a character takes a foolish action just because the storyteller did not consider common sense; such as when a horror movie victim flees upstairs when he or she could have just as easily ran out the front door, or if the hero risks his or her life in a fight against the villain when he or she could have simply called the police; it creates a LOGICAL HOLE. Logical holes are bad. They damage the story's integrity and make characters look stupid by association. The audience will question the action, turning them from viewers into critics and taking them out of the story. But, sometimes storytellers want characters to ignore easier paths intentionally. In this case, the storyteller must provide an explanation why. Perhaps the character wishes to prove him or herself. Perhaps they see a greater reward in greater risk. Maybe they are crazy. Either way, before a character takes a risky action, the storyteller must make sure all logical holes are filled. He or she must provide evidence to explain why the more sensible option was not taken.

In action sequences, forced decisions must come at their most fast and furious. The most tense and exciting sequences occur when the storyteller first strips the hero of any advantages he or she may have, and then throw disadvantages in the hero's way. This puts the hero in maximum danger, forcing him or her to take riskier and riskier actions as the sequence develops.

As *Die Hard* approaches its climax, John McClane has two things to his advantage: a machine gun and the element of surprise. John could easily ambush Hans and end the conflict in the blink of an eye. However, this would make a very disappointing climax. So, the storytellers create the necessary tension by first stripping away John's advantages. He has a machine gun but only two bullets. This throws the situation into doubt. How can John win with such meager resources?

With advantages eliminated, action sequences then develop through a series of slowly building disadvantages that make the hero's only available path less and less desirable. Observe how difficulty escalates in the underground cavern sequence of *The Lord of the Rings: The Fellowship of the Ring* as the heroes try to escape the Balrog. The heroes begin with no advantages. They cannot fight the Balrog. They can only run. This forces them to cross a narrow, broken strip of rock suspended over a bottomless chasm. Though difficult already, the situation gets worse as goblin archers are added to the mix. On top of this, the strip of rock starts to collapse. At this point, common sense would tell them to turn back. But this path is blocked as well when the Balrog arrives. Things started bad and have grown progressively worse. Now, the heroes are forced into a corner where they must do the unthinkable – confront the Balrog head-on.

THE DILEMMA

The rule of forced decisions does have one exception. Quite often, the most dramatic moments occur when the hero DOES have a choice between two or more options. However, these are both options the hero does not want. This is a DILEMMA – a forced choice between two undesired outcomes.

You're damned if you do, and you're damned if you don't. No matter what the hero chooses, he or she loses.

Indiana Jones faces a dilemma when he threatens to destroy the Ark of the Covenant with a rocket, only to have Belloq call his bluff. If Indy pulls the trigger, he will thwart the villain's plan, but he and Marian will be immediately killed for the offense. If he does not destroy the Ark, he and Marian will survive, but his enemies will continue unopposed. *In Saving Private Ryan,* Captain Miller faces an ethical dilemma when he must decide what to do with a captured German. No matter what he decides, he will lose the respect of his men.

These are both no-win situations. While a usual forced story decision leaves some hope that its new path may make things better, dilemmas put characters into situations they know can only become worse. The hero must then choose the lesser of two evils. Quite often, the fate of the entire story hangs upon this decision. Choose right and victory may still be possible. Choose wrong and all may be lost.

We see this quite well by taking another look at the End of 2nd Act Turning Point of *The Matrix*. Morpheus has been captured. Given time, the antagonist will hack into Morpheus's brain and retrieve a code that will doom all of humanity. Neo must choose. Kill his mentor or condemn the human cause. Neo chooses the lesser of two evils. However, just as he is about to pull the plug on Morpheus, Neo realizes this dilemma has a third option. He could try to rescue Morpheus. This option is no more appealing than the other two. He and Trinity against a building full of agents is an act of suicide. Furthermore, Morpheus will still surrender the code if they do not reach him in time. All three options are undesirable, yet Neo must decide. The story's entire fate hinges upon whether Neo chose correctly.

Like the reversal, dilemmas are among the most powerful tools at the storyteller's disposal. As such, they should be used sparingly since overuse results in overkill. Anything of power loses its ability to shock and surprise if seen too often. Therefore, save your big bombs for when the story needs them the most, such as the end of the second act or the third act climactic sequence.

DEVELOPING THE PLOT: THE PUSH/PULL METHOD

The protagonist and antagonist share a unique and dynamic relationship. The storyteller can take advantage of this relationship to create a tense and exciting plot through a simple method called the PUSH/PULL. Though not ideal for every story (such as stories without an antagonist), some variation on this method can often be the ideal way to provide the plot with constantly escalating conflict and change.

First, imagine an old-fashioned railroad handcar. For those who have never seen one, a handcar is a platform on rails with a lever at its center resembling a see-saw. Two persons would ride atop the platform, one on each side of the lever. The pair take turns pushing and pulling on the lever, with each push propelling the car further down the tracks. The harder they push, the faster it goes.

Now, imagine your story as that handcar, and your protagonist and antagonist as the persons on each side. The protagonist pushes, then the antagonist. With each alternating effort, the story moves further down its track.

This may be a cute image, but how does this apply to plot progression? As mentioned before, the most dramatic of stories are those where protagonist and antagonist have completely spines in direct opposition. Because of this unity of opposites, every action taken by one becomes a direct THREAT to the other. Every time one side pushes forward, it also *pushes against* his or her opponent. Whenever threatened by one's push, the other must retaliate by pushing back.

The plot then develops into an epic shoving match of attack and retaliation. When one party takes action towards his or her goal, it creates an obstacle in the way of the second party. To overcome this obstacle, the second party must take an action of his or her own. A bigger action. This counter-action then becomes a counter-threat to the first party, forcing him or her to escalate with another, even bigger action. Actions then grow in force and severity as both protagonist and antagonist try to outdo, and ultimately eliminate their opponent so he or she no longer blocks the way.

Like sumo wrestlers, the two sides must shove at each other until one is completely thrown from the ring.

The plot of *Die Hard* is built on a constant push and pull between John McClane and Hans Gruber. Hans makes the first push towards his goal by invading Nakatomi Tower. However, this action is a threat to John. If John wishes to survive, he must do something to fight back. So, John pulls the fire alarm. Hans senses someone pushing against him and feels threatened. So he pushes back by canceling the alarm and sending a gunman after John. Hans' retaliation puts John in even greater danger. So, John must take a bigger action, one stronger than the last. He kills the gunman, steals his radio, and tries to contact the police. This action makes John an even bigger threat to Hans. Hans' first reaction did not solve the problem, so Hans must one-up himself and send three men this time, not just to find John, but kill him. This action once again forces an even bigger reaction from John. To survive this threat, John must escape down an elevator shaft and hide in the ventilation. This move is yet again met by a counter-move. Hans' men track John down and try to trap him like a rat. Luckily, John gets out of this situation. However, another event soon occurs to continue this alternating escalation. This shoving match endures through the second act and ultimately to the main story climax, where one last push finally eliminates Hans and allows John to reach his Story Goal.

Actions in a push/pull are never random. Though every push occurs in reaction to the one that preceded it, this conflict should never send the plot off of each characters' spine. Like a game of chess, both sides remain dead-set on their ultimate goals, but must make every move in reaction to the preceding move of their opponent.

The push/pull also creates great action sequences when used at a faster pace. Check out the final climactic sequence of The Matrix. Agent Smith's goal is to kill Neo. Neo's goal is to escape. Every action Neo takes to escape is immediately met with a counter-action to stop him. Each new obstacle forces Neo to react with a new course of action, only to be threatened by an even stronger reaction from Agent Smith. Neo is an unstoppable force. Agent Smith is an immovable object. Actions escalate until one side finally pushes the other over the brink and destroys him for good.

CHAPTER 9
SCENE CONSTRUCTION

"Scene" is the most widely-known term in all of moviemaking. But what exactly is a scene, and how are they used? Technically speaking, a scene is any unit of action that takes place in a single location over a single unbroken length of time. This means if two characters are having a conversation indoors, in the middle of which they step outside, the action indoors would be one scene, and the action outdoors a second. In the same way, if the characters stay in the same location, but at one point the action jumps ahead by five minutes, this would be treated as two separate scenes, divided by the break in time.

However, scenes are far more than isolated chunks of action and dialogue. Scenes are the units through which the story is physically executed. The Spine gives a story its form, but scenes give it substance. There is no part of a cinematic story that is not carried out within the boundaries of a scene. Like the cells in a living organism, scenes are the small, interconnected parts through which the story lives, breathes, grows, and develops.

Though the term itself originated in the theater, the concept of a story told exclusively through segmented pieces of time and space is the invention of cinema. This was a practical development rather than a creative one. To save time and money, movies are shot out of sequence. To accommodate this, a script must be broken into clearly defined units of action that can be shot separately, and then later stitched back together through editing.

Though production crews may treat a movie as a loose collection of bits and pieces, it is dangerous for a cinematic storyteller to think in the same way. Beginning screenwriters are commonly afflicted with "scene-itis," a disease that causes them to fix all their attentions on the pieces and forget about the whole. The result is a script that may have some good individual moments, but fails to come together to tell an effective story.

A cinematic story is a single entity. Just as the human body is more than a collection of organs, just as a machine is more than a collection of components, and just as a symphony is more than a collection of instruments, the whole of the cinematic story is greater than the sum of its parts. The story is a single functioning unit, not a confederacy of scenes. No scene exists for its own sake. They are not separate or self-contained. The action of any scene is merely part of one continuously developing line of action, an unbroken narrative river that flows steadily from a story's beginning to its end. Despite what the formatting on a shooting script might suggest, the cinematic narrative does not start and stop with each new 'INT.', 'EXT.', or 'CUT TO'. These breaks are just arbitrary marking points established for the sake of production. Each scene is simply the natural continuation of all that has occurred before it, and the source of everything to follow.

A prose writer has little problem creating a narrative that unfolds as one continuous whole. Screenwriters, unfortunately, must create stories that achieve this state while meeting the production's demand for short, shootable pieces. How then can a storyteller fulfill cinema's practical needs, while at the same time maintain this one long, fluid state? Once again, structure provides a solution.

THE SCENE & STRUCTURE

The cinematic structure is crystalline in nature. The closer we examine it, the more we find the same patterns repeating again and again. The overall narrative is composed of a series of acts. Acts are composed of a series of story sequences. Story sequences are themselves composed of a series of individual scenes. The scenes within a sequence are never random in their content. Just as the content of each story sequence serves to develop the main Story Spine, the action contained in every scene must serve to develop the spine of the sequence it exists within. Each scene acts as a single step in the protagonist's pursuit of the sequence goal, with one setting up the next through cause-and-effect, inevitably moving the sequence forward to its logical end.

Here we see the thread which connects all story structure. Each scene works to support and develop its sequence spine. Each sequence spine, in turn, works to support and develop the main Story Spine. Thus, every scene is directly connected to the Story Spine. Each is a link in one continuous chain. If a particular scene does not contain events that support and develop its sequence, and therefore the Story Spine, that scene will work *against* the story and be counterproductive to its development. Because of this, we establish the first rule of scene construction.

Rule #1: Every scene must be relevant to the Story Spine.

Since every piece must support the whole, any action that does not relate to the Story Spine will be superfluous and therefore meaningless to the story. Not only will it add nothing to story development, but will in fact distract from it. Irrelevant scenes undo a story's cohesion by muddying the clarity of action with meaningless side trips and distractions. It does not matter how entertaining or original these scenes may be. If they have nothing to do with the Story Spine, they have nothing to do with the story, and should not be included.

As previously established, a cinematic narrative must be in a state of constant development. Every event adds upon those which preceded it, causing the situation to CHANGE. This is a scene's essential structural purpose: to provide physical events that cause the story situation to undergo continual change.

Rule #2: Every scene must cause a change in the story situation.

Something must *happen* in a scene to move the story forward. If the situation remains exactly the same at the end of a scene as it was at its start, that scene has had no effect upon the narrative. One must question why it is there at all.

Every scene requires a FUNCTION. Simply put, the function is the reason the scene is in the film. It is the job the scene performs to move the story forward. If one removed a scene from a film, the audience should be able to sense that something was missing. There is a hole in the story's development that the missing scene's function was meant to fill. On the other hand, a scene without a function can be removed and no one would be able to tell the difference. Therefore, a scene without a function is inessential to the story and does little more than waste time.

A scene's material; its action, its dialogue, its visuals; exist to achieve the scene's function by leading to a MOMENT OF CHANGE. The moment of change behaves like the scene's climax. It is an event that alters the course of the story, thereby meeting the function and setting up the action that must occur in the scene to follow. Once reached, the scene has completed its duty and must come to an end.

But, how does a writer do this? How can a scene fulfill a preconceived function without appearing manipulated or overly-contrived? As previously established, the best drama is achieved by giving characters goals they must pursue through willful action. A good scene meets its function by the same principle. Just as characters pursue more immediate sequence goals to get them one step closer to the main Story Goal, in every scene characters pursue an even smaller, even more immediate SCENE GOAL. A scene goal is some accomplishment the character wishes to achieve within the boundaries of that one scene. Doing so will get him or her closer to the sequence goal. These goals are usually something simple: to win an argument, to learn information, to find the car keys, etc. Just as sequence goals break up the protagonist's mission into more manageable units, individual scene goals take the process even further, into a series of even smaller and more discrete steps. By pursuing a scene goal, characters cause change to occur, thereby reaching a scene's function through natural and necessary action.

Characters have only one goal per scene. They pursue this goal until a change in the situation makes further pursuit unnecessary. However, one must realize that the scene goal is only what a character wishes to accomplish in a scene. The actual outcome (that is, the moment of change) does not always align with this desire. This is mostly due to conflict. Every character that populates a scene wants something different. They all have their *own* scene goals. It is through the conflict between these differing goals that the scene moves to its moment of change and advances the story. Goal-oriented behavior is the impetus for story change, whether characters meet victory, failure, or something in between.

To illustrate how these concepts work together, let us invent a story sequence in which a police detective must capture a suspect. To reach this sequence goal, the detective must take a series of smaller steps. Each step becomes the action of an individual scene.

Scene #1: Before the detective can catch the suspect, he must first learn the suspect's whereabouts. So, in the first scene, the detective questions a witness. The detective's scene goal is to convince the witness to cooperate. When the detective meets this goal, it creates a moment of change. The detective's situation is now different from when he began. With this accomplished, the detective moves on to–

Scene #2: Using the information received in Scene 1, the detective arrives at the suspect's hiding place. The detective has a new scene goal: to spot the suspect. A second moment of change occurs when he sees the suspect enter the building. This event sets up the action that will occur in–

Scene #3: The detective follows the suspect into the building. His new scene goal: to arrest the suspect. However, the suspect sees him coming and runs for it. This time, the detective does not find the result he had hoped for. Conflict has created a moment of change the detective did not want. This alters the situation and leads the action into–

Scene #4: The detective chases the suspect through a warehouse. Because of the previous moment of change, the detective has a new goal: to catch the suspect before he gets away. But, before this can happen, conflict causes another moment of change. The suspect pulls a gun and shoots, allowing him to escape into an alley.

Scene #5: The situation has changed from a chase into a shootout. This sets up yet another scene goal: to disarm the suspect without getting shot. Actions taken by both sides lead to yet another moment of change. The suspect runs out of ammo and the detective tackles him. With this event, the detective finally reaches the goal he set out to achieve four scenes previously.

This sequence is made of five individual scenes, with five individual scene goals. However, every scene is connected. Each exists as a smaller step the detective must take to reach his larger sequence goal. Each moment of change may have seemed to send events down an unpredictable path, yet everything was designed toward a predetermined end that completed the sequence and advanced the Story Spine.

From this example, we can see that the spine model repeats itself not only on the sequence level, but also within each individual scene. Characters begin each scene with a smaller, more specific problem and a smaller, more specific goal. The characters take action within the scene to reach that goal. They experience conflict in that pursuit, and have stakes attached to success or failure. Win or lose, the moment of change resolves the situation. Like a mini-turning point, the change brings the pursuit of the current scene goal to an end, and sets up the course of action characters must pursue in the next.

As with anything that follows the spine model, conflict is a necessary component. Conflict keeps a scene dramatic, and thus interesting to the audience. In fact, conflict is so important to a scene it becomes the third rule of scene construction:

Rule #3: Every scene must contain conflict.

By every scene, I mean *every single* scene, no matter how small or short-lived. If you want to hold an audience's attention for every moment, every moment must be dramatic. Once again, conflict is drama's only source. Should any scene lack conflict, whatever its content may be, tension will slack and excitement will cool, creating a dramatic dead spot in the story's development.

Scene conflict can come from countless sources. The most obvious is characters with opposing goals. However, to create the most suitable conflict, each character's scene goal must be an *active* goal. Active goals are those that require willful, physical effort to achieve. For example, in our scene where the detective questions a witness, the detective has an active goal: to convince the witness to give information. This requires effort. He must ask probing questions backed up with force and persistence. However, for suitable conflict, the witness must have a scene goal capable of providing adequate resistance. A poor way to do this would be to say the witness wishes "to not answer questions." This goal is inactive. One cannot actively "not" do something. To do nothing requires zero physical effort. Inactive goals create weak and one-sided conflicts since there is nothing pushing against the other character's efforts. Instead, the witness should wish "to deceive the detective," or "to get the detective to leave her alone." These goals are physical accomplishments that require willful effort to achieve. Now, the scene contains two characters actively pushing each other in opposing directions. The action is dramatic, bringing the scene to life.

Though conflicting goals are the best way to create conflict, this is not always a viable option. Sometimes all of the characters wish to achieve the same goal in cooperation. However, just because everyone is on the same side, this does not mean conflict cannot exist. Conflict must merely come from another source. Sometimes characters can conflict over the manner which they wish to achieve the goal. Let us say two little boys both want a cookie from the cookie jar. The first boy wishes to ask for permission first. The second boy is sure mother will say no, and wants to take the cookie without asking. Though they share a mutual goal, their conflicting stances dramatize the scene.

At other times, conflict can be found in differences in *character*. There could be a conflict of personalities (one character finds the other irritating), a conflict of opinions (one person's point of view runs counter to that of another), or a conflict of understanding (one character is confused by another's intentions). Please mind this does not mean a scene can get by with petty, irrelevant bickering. Bickering is pointless conflict for the mere sake of conflict which serves no purpose to advance the story. Conflict must be orientated around scene goals. Friction arises from differences in each character's method of pursuit. In *Star Wars*, R2D2 and C3P0 may argue a lot, but their disagreements are always relevant to the problem at hand.

Even when a character is alone, conflict must still exist. No matter what the situation, something must exist to provide difficulty. This could be the environment (it is too hot, too windy, too dark), an object (a car that will not start, a footstool to trip over, a sandwich that falls apart the moment one takes a bite), or even the character's own body (a pair of shaking hands, a sneezing fit, sweat in one's eyes). Barring that, conflict can come from within the character's own self as he or she struggles with opposing desires or internal contradictions (a young man is angry at his girlfriend, yet is dying to give her a call; a recovering alcoholic struggling with the urge to break his sobriety). As you can see, the possibilities for conflict are endless. So, there is no excuse for a scene without it. If there is no obvious source of conflict, invent one. Even the slightest addition will improve a scene greatly.

Conflict can do far more than keep a scene interesting. When used properly, it is a versatile tool that can cure just about any problem scene construction can present. Some scenes, burdened by their functions, must manipulate action or spell out information in a way that, if done too straightforward, may appear phony or overly-contrived. The storyteller's hand then becomes too obvious, pulling the audience from the story's illusion of reality. If the storyteller wants the scene to do what it needs to do while keeping the audience wrapped up in its events, the storyteller must hide these manipulations. Through something distracting. Something dramatic. Something the audience cannot take their eyes off. Through conflict.

Conflict can act as a *mask* to hide a scene's contrivances. Just like a magician's sleight of hand, the storyteller draws the audience's attention to one hand so they do not notice the trickery he or she pulls with the other. Using conflict, the storyteller keeps the audience so wrapped up in drama that they do not notice any manipulation that occurs under the surface. Anything that occurs in the scene, no matter how contrived, will simply seem to be a natural and understandable outcome of the conflict at hand.

Take as an example the scene in *Die Hard* between John McClane and the limo driver Argyle. The intended purpose of this scene is to communicate John's backstory: his failing marriage, his problems with Holly, and the reason he has come to Los Angeles. However, if John were to simply blurt out this information, it would not only feel phony, but out of character, since John is supposed to be a man who does not like to share his feelings. So, the scene's function is achieved behind a mask of conflict. Argyle wants conversation, but John does not. Argyle fights through John's resistance and forces him to give the information the audience needs to hear. The audience does not notice that this information has been served to them on a silver plate because it seems to be nothing more than the natural outcome of two personalities in conflict.

Chinatown unravels its mysteries in the same way. Certain essential clues must be revealed to the audience at certain points for the narrative to advance. However, it would appear contrived, not to mention boring, if this information were simply dumped into the audience's lap. Instead, *Chinatown* gives this information through a series of dangerous and conflict-filled situations. The audience is not simply told that a portion of the water supply is being dumped into the ocean at night. Instead, they learn this when Jake Gittes is swept up in the flow of the runoff and nearly drowns. The audience is not simply handed proof that the Water Department is lying about irrigated orange groves. Instead, Jake nearly gets his head blown off making the discovery. Every dry and potentially dull piece of information is given to the audience through an exciting event. The audience absorbs this information while swept up in the drama.

STRUCTURE WITHIN THE SCENE

Remember how cinematic stories are best served when executed in a three-part structure. Great scenes share this trait. A well-structured scene also follows a three-part form with a clear beginning, middle, and end.

Here is how it works. Characters enter a scene with certain scene goals in mind. These goals inevitably collide with those of others, inciting the scene's conflict (providing the scene's "inciting moment," if you will). This begins the scene's "first act" in which the characters pursue their respective goals in the face of this conflict. But, before long, something occurs to alter the situation. This moment is called a SCENE BEAT. Like a tiny turning point, scene beats turn the course of the scene's conflict in a new direction. However, unlike a regular turning point, each characters' scene goal remains the same. Instead, the scene beat merely provides an event that alters *how* those goals are pursued. While the context of the conflict remains the same, the characters' method of approach to the conflict must change.

This begins the scene's "second act." The characters continue to chase their individual goals, but now do so in reaction to the development caused by the first scene beat. Eventually, the conflict reaches a head, leading to a second scene beat. This second beat is more influential than the first. While the first beat merely altered the manner of the conflict, the second beat provides a moment that finally tips the scales in favor of one side or the other. This decisive event leads into the scene's "third act," in which the scene conflict is carried to a resolution, and the scene reaches its moment of change.

When it comes to three-part scene structure, there are few better films for study than Joel & Ethan Cohen's *Fargo*. Rarely a scene goes by in this Academy Award-winning screenplay that does not turn on two strong, identifiable beats. Let us take a look at its opening scene to demonstrate.

Jerry Lundegaard, the story's morally bankrupt anti-hero, arrives at a bar to meet two hired goons, Carl and Gaear. Jerry's scene goal is to finalize a scheme where Carl and Gaear will kidnap Jerry's wife Jean in order to scam ransom money from his father-in-law. However, there is a hiccup in the plan. The scene encounters its first beat when Carl announces that he and Gaear are not yet on board. They do not yet understand the plan. In fact, they do not think it makes any sense at all. Jerry must now alter his actions in order to reach his scene goal. He sits down and tries to convince the pair that the plan will work. Eventually, Carl grows tired of arguing and gives in. This action provides a second scene beat that tips the scales in Jerry's favor. Carl and Gaear accept the job, creating the moment of change.

You may notice that the "third act" of this scene (everything after Carl gives in) last for only a few seconds. This is not unusual. Unlike the three acts of the main story structure, scene acts have no predetermined length or ratio of time that must pass between beats. A scene act can last for any amount of time, from a few seconds to several minutes. The only requirement is that there must be at least *some* time separating the scene's major structural moments. The first scene beat cannot be immediately followed by the second, nor should the second scene beat be immediately followed by the scene's end. Without time separating these events, the scene will not appear to have all three acts. The absolute minimum is to follow each beat with a pause lasting a few seconds so the characters (and the audience) can momentarily digest how the situation has changed. Though slight, this pause will constitute one of the scene's acts.

Scene beats typically occur by one, or a combination of, the following events:

1. *A Change in Strategy*

A change in strategy brings variety to a scene's conflict. Scenes become monotonous when characters stick to the same behavior from beginning to end. If a certain approach meets difficulty, it is only natural for a character to try something new. This is something we all do in real life. If we have a problem with a person, our first impulse might be to yell. However, this strategy may not work. So, we try something else. We stop yelling and try to reason with the person, or beg, or appeal to emotion. If that does not work either, we may change strategy yet again.

A change in strategy is most useful whenever the scene conflict reaches a *stalemate* – that is, the conflict becomes locked into a situation where neither side can make any more progress through their current methods. Jerry and Carl reach a stalemate at the end of their second scene act. Both can continue to argue, but it would do neither of them any more good. So, Carl changes strategy. Rather than continue to question Jerry's plan, he shrugs his shoulders and accepts him for his word.

2. *A Shift in Power*

Every conflict is a battle, and in battle one side is always winning and the other losing. If the tug-of-war is not moving one way or the other, the conflict seems to stand still.

A shift in power occurs when an action reverses which side holds the upper hand. This keeps the outcome unpredictable and thus more dramatic. Though useful in any conflict, shifts in power become especially important in chases or fights. First the hero is winning the battle, then favor suddenly switches to the villain's side. Another shift may then occur, once again giving the hero the upper hand. This back and forth keeps the audience on the edge of their seats since they have no idea how the conflict will turn out.

3. *A Revelation of New Information*

New information can create a scene beat when that information forces characters to reconsider how they must pursue their scene goal. The reveal could be something previously unknown to the character, something unknown to the audience, or most commonly, both. The characters must then pause, reevaluate the situation, and then choose the best way to continue.

4. A Situation-Changing Action

This beat works the same as a revelation of information, only it is the result of physical action. If Character A pulls a gun on Character B, this action changes the landscape of the conflict. Both sides must reevaluate the best way to continue the pursuit of their goals. Likewise, if a character bursts into tears, if someone trips and falls, if a gust of wind blows a note from a character's hand, these actions can all turn a scene by forcing characters to alter their behavior.

5. An Addition or Subtraction

A beat can also occur when someone or something enters or exits the scene, as long as it significantly alters the situation. The hero's ally may come to the rescue, or conversely leave the hero to fend for him or herself. A character may discover an important object, or throw a key item out the window. Such changes, be they large or small, can dramatically impact the conflict and turn the tide of the battle.

6. An Outside Interruption

Sometimes a conflict can turn on something as simple as a momentary distraction. Someone enters the room, the phone rings, a gunshot is heard... An interruption gives characters an opportunity to pause, rethink their strategy, and restart the conflict anew. This can be useful to break a stalemate. It is even more useful should a storyteller wish to leave a conflict unresolved so it may be continued at a later time. Early in *Die Hard,* John and Holly's marital argument gets shelved when a coworker interrupts at the second beat with news from outside. This forces the scene to end with its conflict up in the air so it may linger for the rest of the film.

To see these scene beats in action, let us return to *Fargo* with a selection of scenes from the late first act. (If you have not yet viewed *Fargo*, I suggest you become familiar with it before reading on.)

1.   Jerry meets with his father-in-law Wade, planning to trick him out of a large loan under the guise of a phony investment deal. The scene meets its first beat when Wade asks Jerry what kind of finder's fee he wants for bringing him this deal (a reveal of information). It turns out Wade has misunderstood Jerry's intentions and wants to invest in the deal himself. Jerry then tries to persuade Wade to loan him the money directly. Wade refuses. The argument reaches a stalemate, causing Wade to put his foot down (a change in strategy). This seals the conflict. Jerry has no choice but to back down. Winner of the conflict: Wade.

2.   A frustrated Jerry returns to his car to find the windshield covered in ice (the inciting moment). The scene's conflict is Jerry vs. the ice. Though short, this scene still contains three acts. In the first, Jerry attempts to clear his windshield with an icescraper. However, frustration builds and Jerry throws the scraper in a fit of anger (a change in strategy). This new strategy of course does not help. So, Jerry must pick up the scraper and start again (another change in strategy). Winner: the ice.

3.   Jerry's wife Jean watches television in her living room. She sees Carl approach her back door wearing a ski mask (the inciting moment). At first, Jean's only reaction is curiosity. Then, Carl smashes the glass (a situation-changing action). Jean runs. Gaear grabs her. Jean bites Gaear's hand (a shift in power), allowing her to flee upstairs. Winner: Jean.

4.   Jean locks herself in the bathroom and tries to use the phone. But, the phone is yanked from her grasp (a shift in power). Because of this, Jean must search for a new plan. Carl and Gaear bust open the door, only to find what seems to be an empty room (reveal of information). Assuming Jean escaped through the window, Carl takes off after her. Winner: Jean (for the moment).

5.   Gaear stays in the bathroom. He hears a noise (inciting moment). Jean jumps from her hiding place behind the shower curtain (a combination of action/revelation of information). She runs and falls down the stairs (another situation-changing action). Jean is knocked unconscious, allowing the goons to capture her. Winners: Carl & Gaear. (Though there is no break in time or location between this scene and the previous, there is a slight pause in action to indicate a new scene action has begun. More on this will be explained in the following section.)

6.   Carl & Gaear drive down a deserted highway with Jean tied up in the back. Suddenly, a state trooper appears in their rearview and signals for them to pull over (inciting moment). Carl & Gaear's goal: get rid of the trooper. Carl's first strategy is to bribe the trooper. However, this does not work. The trooper then hears Jean whimper (an action), forcing Gaear to shoot him in the head (a change in strategy). In doing so, Gaear resolves the scene's conflict. Winner: Carl & Gaear.

7.   With the trooper dead, Carl and Gaear have a new goal: hide the body before it can be seen. However, a pair of headlights appear in the distance (the inciting moment). As the car passes, its occupants see the dead trooper (a shift in power) and speed away (an action). This beat forces Gaear to chase after them. Winner: the witnesses.

8.   The chase. Gaear's goal: catch the witnesses. However, the taillights of the witnesses' car suddenly disappear (a subtraction). Gaear fears he has lost them, until he sees the car overturned in a ditch (reveal of new information). Gaear stops the car. Winner: Gaear.

9.   Gaear exits his car. His goal: kill the witnesses. One witness climbs from the overturned car and runs (an action). Gaear takes aim and shoots him (another action). With no more conflict opposing Gaear, he kills the helpless second witness and ends the scene. Winner: Gaear.

You may notice some scenes contain a short setup before the arrival of an inciting moment, while others begin with their conflict already engaged.

Some scenes do not require their inciting moment to be shown since the conflict has already been set up by the preceding moment of change. Storytellers should opt for this approach whenever possible. It provides the sequence with momentum and allows the scene to begin with dramatic tension already present.

SUPER-SCENES

The more that occurs within a scene, the harder it becomes to maintain clear structure. Because of this, most scenes find clarity by giving characters only one goal per scene, creating only one line of conflict, resulting in one moment of change. This simple goal/conflict/moment of change structure creates a singular UNIT OF ACTION. In our earlier sequence with the detective and the suspect, the action was laid out in the traditional manner with five individual scenes, with one unit of action per scene. But, what if the storyteller does not want to execute this sequence as five separate scenes? What if he or she believes it will be more exciting to execute this material as one continuous stream of action with no breaks in between? This would create a SUPER-SCENE.

A super-scene is a collection of individual units of action played out end-to-end with no pauses or breaks in between. Since the action does not move to a new location after each moment of change or leap forward in time, this would be technically considered a single scene – but only on paper. A super-scene, with its various individual units of action, continues to behave as a group of separate scenes. The only difference is that the action remains continuous in time and place.

If our detective sequence were a super-scene, the detective would begin just as before, with his attempt to learn the suspect's whereabouts. Only this time, the witness simply points across the room. The detective need not journey to a new location to continue his sequence. He simply transitions to his next goal without a break in time or place. What was formerly treated as a separate scene becomes a "unit" within the super-scene.

Likewise, when the suspect sees the detective and runs, this moment of change forces the detective to transition to his next scene goal, just as it did before, even though action remains in the same time and location.

As this super-scene unfolds, its units continue to follow the simple goal/conflict/moment of change structure, one by one in linear fashion, as they did before as a series of separate scenes. The characters continue to pursue one scene goal at a time until their actions cause a moment of change. This change forces characters to drop their former scene goal and adopt a new one, beginning the next unit of action. Structurally, there is virtually no difference between a super-scene and a group of consecutive individual scenes except for the fact that, rather than cut to a new location after each moment of change, everything flows together in one seamless piece.

Super-scenes can help writers maintain focus and structure in complicated situations that require very long scenes with multiple units of action. *Fargo* contains a brief super-scene when Jean hides in the bathroom. Carl and Gaear break down the door, but find the bathroom empty. They think Jean has escaped, creating a moment of change. However, the action must stay in the bathroom. To accommodate the lack of a break in time or place, there is a brief moment of calm, indicating the transition to a new scene unit. Then, Jean jumps from behind the shower curtain, launching a new line of action with its new conflict.

Each unit within a super-scene will continue to contain three scene acts. Though not absolutely necessary, a perfectly structured super-scene will take the Dramatic Rule of Threes even further by containing three scene units, with three scene acts apiece. For longer super-scenes, six or nine units are best.

Though super-scenes can provide escalating excitement and momentum, they can be unwieldy to execute since it is often difficult to create the clear breaks between units the audience with a sense of structural form. However, some simple tricks can be employed to indicate when one unit has ended and the next is about to begin.

- Move characters to another area of the location. For instance, if a scene takes place in a restaurant, have the characters leave their table and move toward the restrooms at a break. Though unbroken in time, this move will imply the beginning of a new scene unit.
- Create an artificial break through aesthetic means. A well-planned camera move, sound effect, or even a meaningful moment of silence can work to divide the scene into separate units.
- Bridge the units with an action that shifts the audience's attention from the outgoing scene goal to the new one. Doing so will turn the audience's focus in the same way as the break between two normal scenes.
- Briefly cut away to an outside action. This will literally divide the action into separate scenes, even though the action of the super-scene will remain continuous from its previous segment.

MICRO-SCENES

Scene structure can also become a problem whenever storytellers use PARALLEL ACTION. Parallel action is the practice of rapidly cutting back and forth between multiple locations to suggest simultaneous events. This is often used to create excitement or suspense, such as in the climactic sequence of *The Matrix*. Neo's battle with Agent Smith is shown in alternation with the attack on Morpheus's ship. This parallel action suggests that the two events are connected and interdependent. Neo must act fast to save not only himself, but his friends as well.

Because of its quick pace, parallel action sequences are composed of slivers of scenes instead of full and complete units. In this case, the best structure is achieved by dividing the intercut scenes into their separate scene acts, and then alternating from one scene to the other at each beat. What appears to the audience as six short scenes is actually two regular scenes with their scene acts woven together like a shuffled deck of cards. Though this is an area where the storyteller finds a great deal of wiggle room, a perfectly structured parallel action sequence will also follow the Dramatic Rule of Threes. A sequence that intercuts two locations should consist of six segments, or twelve segments, or even eighteen segments for longer sequences. If cross-cutting between three locations, the sequence should ideally consist of nine or eighteen segments. Often, finding the best structure is just simple math.

WRITING THE SCENE

Scenes must be written with EFFICIENCY. The best scenes strive to accomplish the greatest amount of impact in the shortest amount of time. Keep scenes brief and memorable. Do not waste time with trivial details unless this information is significant to plot, theme, or character. Recall from Chapter 3 how a cinematic story is told through the constant communication of information from storyteller to audience. Each new piece builds upon all previous to advance the scene in one continuous stream. The use of the word "stream" is not accidental. Just as a stream of water will flow forward at a constant rate, the action of a scene must always advance. This leads to the fourth rule of scene construction:

Rule #4: Scenes must constantly move forward.

If a scene does not constantly progress, the situation will stagnate. Thus, everything seen or heard should advance the audience's comprehension of the narrative and move the scene to its natural end. Information can only do this when it provides the audience with something both NEW and RELEVANT to the situation. Anything that does not amounts to NONINFORMATION. Noninformation is superfluous material that has no significance to the story. It is empty filler that does nothing but slow the scene down. Any actions, visuals, or dialogue that do not communicate anything new and useful, are extraneous to the scene and should be eliminated. Instead, everything contained in a scene, large or small, should create a tightly-packed string of atoms that sends a constant stream of important information the audience's way. There should be no gaps, no filler, no useless noninformation to slow things down.

Take note that information must be both *new* and relevant. Re-telling the audience something they already know will also amount to noninformation. If you have a scene where a character is chased through a shopping mall, do not follow that scene with the character giving a friend a play-by-play on how he was just chased through the shopping mall. If the audience already knows something, do not waste their time by telling them again. This is like hearing the same joke twice. It is not funny the second time around.

Action within a scene should not dawdle. Your scene has a function. Your characters have goals. Go after them both with drive and focus, and waste no time along the way. Long lead-ins are unnecessary. Start the scene as close to its inciting moment as possible, or better yet, begin with the conflict already underway. As soon as the scene reaches its moment of change, bring it to an end. Since the function has been achieved, there is no more reason to stick around. Writing a good scene is like guerrilla warfare. Attack at the best moment, make the most impact in the shortest amount of time, and once the objective is achieved, get the heck out of there.

CHAPTER 10
MANAGING YOUR INFORMATION:
A RETURN TO THE ATOMS

Storytelling is all about communication. A writer may have a Spine, characters, and the action of a plot, but without the ability to communicate these elements dramatically, the story will never be fully enjoyed or understood. The manner which one gives story information is just as important as the information itself.

The previous chapter concluded with a brief return to the notion of story atoms. Every action, image, or sound should be used to advance the story with new and relevant information. However, a great cinematic story requires more from its storyteller than to simply lay out information one piece at a time like a mason with a pile of bricks. Such a strategy may communicate the facts of the narrative, but those facts will provide little excitement. The storyteller's goal is not just to tell a story, but to communicate that story in a manner the audience finds stimulating, exhilarating, and emotionally engaging from beginning to end. A great story is worth little if it cannot grab its audience and never let go.

Thus, the art of story*telling*. A storyteller's true skill lies in the CREATIVE CONTROL OF INFORMATION – knowing what information to GIVE, what information to WITHHOLD, and knowing the right time to do either one. The same story can be executed in many different ways with many different results, all depending on how the storyteller chooses to communicate his or her information. A great storyteller must be like a riverboat gambler. His or her cards are out on the table, but he or she must know when to flip each card over to reveal what is underneath. An amateur will reveal too much, too soon, and end up losing the game. An expert knows to keep things hidden until just the right moment. In other words, great storytellers get the most out of the audience's experience by controlling at all times what the audience knows, what they do not know, and most importantly, what they *want* to know. Great storytelling keeps people in the dark and then creates pleasure by turning on a light.

STRINGING YOUR ATOMS

Recall from Chapter 3 how every single thing seen or heard in a cinematic narrative can be thought of as an atom of information projected from storyteller to audience. It is by the accumulation of these atoms that the audience comprehends a story's events and finds their larger meaning. The easiest and most common way to deliver information is to give it to the audience plainly and directly. If the audience sees Erica walk across the room, this communicates "Erica walked across the room." If Tim says "I'm sick and cannot come to work," the audience is told "Tim says he is sick and cannot come to work." If a car explodes, it literally tells us "that car just exploded." We will call this type of information NEUTRAL ATOMS (or n-atoms, for short). They are "neutral" because their information can be taken at face value, and will rarely require any kind of mental or emotional activity on the part of the viewer to understand. The audience simply absorbs the information and processes it away.

Because it is so simple, easy, and direct, most of any story's information will be given neutrally. However, a story told exclusively through neutral atoms will be intolerably dull. This is because neutral atoms require no involvement on the part of the viewer. There is no drama or intrigue about the information. It is simply dumped into the audience's laps whether they asked for it or not. This is known as *spoon-feeding*. And, as anyone who has ever tried to spoon-feed an infant will know, half of the time the receiver will not be interested in what you have to give.

If the audience is to become involved in a story, they must first want what the storyteller has to give. They must consider information valuable. People do not place high value on things that come easy. We only value that which requires effort. Diamonds are expensive only because they are so difficult to find. If they were scattered all over the ground, they would be as worthless as gravel. Information is the same way. The only way to get the audience to care about important story information is to make them put some sort of effort into getting it.

Think back to your school days. Which type of lesson did you find more engaging? A lecture where the teacher droned on and on while you were expected to sit and listen? Or an interactive lesson where the teacher encouraged participation through questions and answers? Which method kept your interest? Which helped you learn? Which made you *want* to learn? A great storyteller, like a great teacher, seizes the audience's interest by turning the story into an *interactive experience.* The audience becomes involved in the story because the storyteller encourages them to participate. Just like a school teacher, the storyteller does this by leading the audience to ASK QUESTIONS, and then guiding them to FIND ANSWERS.

The term *dramatic tension* has been used throughout this book. Now comes the time for an official definition. Dramatic tension is a state of mental anxiety that exists within an audience when, and only when, they have questions in their minds that remain unanswered. Will the hero achieve X? Will he or she make it in time? What is the antagonist planning? Will it stop the hero? The bigger the question, the greater the anxiety.

By setting up questions and delaying the answers, storytellers feed off of the audience's natural need for *cognitive closure.*

Cognitive closure is a phenomenon created by the human mind when it encounters situations where information remains incomplete. When confronted by an ambiguous situation, people have the natural desire to find the information that allows everything to make sense. Some people have such a strong need for closure that they are unable to relax until this state is achieved. Storytellers can take advantage of this need to keep audiences hooked.

Along with neutral atoms, the storyteller has two additional types of information that can be used to achieve this interactive state: Q-ATOMS: pieces of information that cause the audience to ask questions; and A-ATOMS: information that answers an existing question. Observe how the three previous examples of neutral atoms become more dramatic once altered to encourage the audience to ask questions. If Erica walks across the room, but we do not know for what reason; if rather than call in sick to work, Tim simply does not show up; if the car explodes, but we do not know why; the audience now has cause to wonder. Tension exists. This tension will continue until these questions find their answers.

When an answer is found, the tension is released. This release is an enjoyable experience known as the PLEASURE OF DISCOVERY. The audience feels satisfied because they have reached cognitive closure. A great movie experience comes from the constant alternation between tension and release, from anxiety to pleasure. Spoon-feeding creates a dull story experience because it disallows the pleasure of discovery. The audience receives information, but no satisfaction from it.

However, there is a potential downside. Once tension disappears, the audience may lose interest. To counter this, the storyteller must keep the audience's minds chasing after something new. Have you ever watched a cat play with a dangling string? As long as the string is kept out of reach, the cat remains fascinated. But as soon as the cat is given the string, it loses all interest. So, with each answer, the storyteller must provide new questions to keep the audience involved.

Another unexpected problem comes from the fact that the audience will try to predict the outcome of every event. While the storyteller desires such a high level of involvement, dramatic tension will completely disappear if the audience figures things out too early. Because of this, the storyteller must always stay one step ahead. Keep answers unpredictable. Confound or reverse expectations whenever possible. Answers should be surprising, yet plausible. They must make perfect sense, but not in the sense the audience expects.

Three basic guidelines help ensure that story information is delivered with the greatest dramatic impact. First, never give the audience plot information until the story requires them to know it. When spies are sent on missions, they are kept on a "need to know basis." This means the spy is given only the information he or she needs to complete the task and nothing more. All other information is withheld until a situation arises that requires the spy to learn more. Audiences should be dealt with in the same way. When the audience knows too much, too soon, it spoils the adventure. Delay important information until the story reaches a point where the audience must absolutely know it in order to continue. If, for example, we have a story about a small town school teacher who turns out to be a former assassin, do not ruin the surprise by revealing this secret before the appropriate time. Instead, keep the audience in the dark until the moment when this revelation will have its greatest impact.

Second, do not give important story information until you have created in the audience a *desire to know* that information. Dumping key information in the audience's lap will have little dramatic impact. Instead, lead the audience to ask questions first. A shadowy figure is following the schoolteacher. Why? The teacher keeps a sniper rifle under his bed. Why? Now that the audience has questions, they genuinely want to know what secrets the story hides. Good storytelling is about keeping the audience hungry. Hungry for what you have to give.

Finally, once the audience has a question, delay giving the answer for as long as the story allows. Dangle that string for as long as you can get away with it. The longer a question remains, the more tension that will build. If you celebrated Christmas as a child, you should remember how those presents under the tree used to drive you nuts. You knew there was something good inside, but you were not yet allowed to know what it was. Now, remember the amazing emotional release you felt Christmas morning when that mystery was finally revealed. Quite often, great drama is more about the question than the answer. The story teases the audience with a secret, and then lets them squirm with the desire to know.

But, how much time is appropriate between a Q and an A? The storyteller has to know when to give. Hold out too long and the audience may grow frustrated and lose interest. The ideal amount of delay is usually proportional to the importance of the information. The build-up should match the payoff. For example, *Die Hard* contains a short scene where a security guard notices something resembling a hockey puck roll around the corner and stop at his feet. Both the audience and the guard take a moment to wonder what it is. Then, it explodes. The hockey puck grenade is only a small piece of information, so it requires only a few seconds of delay. In comparison, the audience is left to wonder for nearly an hour before they learn the final step of Hans' master plan. The larger the revelation, the longer the build-up. Without it, the information would have lost significant impact.

CINEMATIC ALGEBRA

In a way, story information is like mathematics. Neutral atoms work like simple addition. ($2+2=4$, $5+1=6$, $7+8=15$) The audience is given one piece of information and then another. They combine those pieces to form a logical conclusion.

Questions and answers turn storytelling into something more like algebra. ($6-x=2$, $3x+4=7$, $2x-3=y+1$) Hopefully, you recall from your school days that algebraic equations are made of two elements: constants and variables. Constants are numbers whose values are definitely known. The number 2 means exactly 2. No more, no less. A variable (x or y) is also a number. However, this is a number whose value is *unknown*. x is a mystery value. Solving an algebraic equation is solving a mystery. One wishes to identify the missing value so the whole equation will *make sense.*

Dramatic tension works in the same manner. There are constants (information the audience definitely knows) and variables (information that remains unknown). The audience knows the main character is a school teacher. They also know he keeps a sniper rifle under his bed. These are the constants. But at the moment, the equation does not make sense. The value that connects these facts remains missing. This becomes the scene's *x-factor.* Just as algebra is more challenging than addition, scenes with unknown information force the audience to become more involved. They become engaged in the situation because they want things to make sense. They want to solve for *x*.

THE STORYTELLER'S ATOMIC TOOLKIT

Dramatic tension comes in three forms: MYSTERY, SURPRISE, and SUSPENSE. Each generates its own form of tension based upon the type of questions raised and the mental activity required from the viewer to find the answers.

MYSTERY

mystery: n. 1. Something unexplained or secret. 2. A story involving unknown persons, facts, etc.

Simply put, a mystery is a puzzle with a missing piece. All the facts of the situation exist, however the most important of these facts is purposely hidden, leaving the audience unable to see the picture as a whole. The result is CURIOSITY. The audience sees the available information, realizes there is something missing, and feels the urge to learn more. They want to find the missing piece so everything will make sense.

Storytellers create mystery by hinting at key information – but only enough to arouse interest. Everything else is withheld. For example, midway through the first act of *Die Hard,* the audience is repeatedly shown a large truck approaching Nakatomi Tower. Nothing else is explained. Each time the audience sees the truck, they wonder, what is in the truck? Why is the truck important? This arouses curiosity. Tension builds until the truck's doors finally open to reveal Hans and his henchmen inside. Because of the mystery, this moment has far greater dramatic impact than it would had the storytellers shown the contents of the truck right away.

Both *The Matrix* and *The Bourne Identity* have first acts powered almost entirely by mystery. Curious events occur to the protagonists, but neither the protagonist nor the audience fully understand the events or why they occur. The audience becomes hooked – not by what they know, but by what they want to know.

Mysteries have the quality of being "known, yet unknown." The facts of the story already exist. Only the storyteller has not yet chosen to reveal all of these facts to the audience. Though we may not fully understand all that occurs in the first act of *The Matrix*, Morpheus, Trinity, and the Agents clearly do. The facts are known to them, yet kept unknown from the audience. When Hans Gruber is told it will be impossible to break through the seventh lock of Nakatomi's vault, his only response is a mysterious smile. Hans already knows what he will do, yet this information is kept hidden from the audience. The story has secrets. The audience becomes involved because they want to know those secrets as well.

The bigger a mystery's x-factor, the longer it should be allowed to grow. Plant the seeds for major revelations early, and then build upon that initial curiosity as the story advances. Though the final phase of Hans' plan was kept hidden until the end of the second act, its mystery was established well before this time. From the opening moments of Hans' invasion, the audience sees men working on the top floor. They hear Hans make several references to the roof. They discover a bag full of detonators. This all begs questions. Why the roof, and why all the detonators? Little by little, the mystery evolves. Because the audience has been led to wonder and keep wondering, the payoff builds to epic proportions. The audience gets the maximum pleasure of discovery as they look back to the beginning and find the cognitive closure that allows everything to finally make sense.

A skilled storyteller can use mystery to dramatize even the simplest bits of information. Act 2A of *The Matrix* needs to give the audience lots of minor details so they may understand later events. However, as said before, information should not be given to the audience until the audience has a desire to know. So, *The Matrix* first generates curiosity through a simple trick of dialogue. Characters constantly make casual references to things such as "Zion," "The Oracle," or a "squiddy." Neither Neo nor the audience know the meaning of these words, so they become curious and ask questions. Dramatic tension is set up by one line of dialogue, and released with the next. The audience becomes receptive to this information because a momentary mystery has created a desire to know.

SURPRISE

surprise: v. 1. to come on suddenly or unexpectedly. 2. to attack without warning.

Surprise works in exact opposite manner as mystery. While mystery slowly nurtures the audience's interest by hinting at important information, surprise abruptly seizes attention by throwing information into the audience's face without warning. Basically, the storyteller leads the audience into an ambush. The storyteller withholds all clues, and then drops a bomb on their heads.

To illustrate the difference, let us imagine a scene from a horror film. We begin with the hero seemingly alone. Only later, we discover there is a monster in the closet. If mystery is used, the hero would first appear to be alone. Then, he or she hears a noise from the closet. This makes the hero, and the audience, wish to creep closer and closer to the closet, building tension until the noise's source is revealed. If, on the other hand, the storyteller uses surprise, no evidence would be given to suggest that the hero is anything but safe and sound. No noises. No hints. Both the hero and audience are lulled into a false sense of security. Then, without warning, the monster attacks.

The audience reacts to surprise with SHOCK. They are thrown aback, momentarily disorientated as they scramble to understand the sudden onslaught of information. Like mystery, surprise raises questions. However, these questions are far more immediate. The audience asks, "What just happened?" "How did it happen?" or "Why did it happen just now?" Since information is given suddenly with no rationalization to back it up, the audience is compelled to ask questions to get back on solid ground. The opening combat sequence from *Saving Private Ryan* is filled with shocking events. Drastic changes occur in the blink of an eye, sending the audience scrambling to keep up with the scene. Such confusion excites the audience, encouraging them to seek out more information.

Though a surprise comes on like an ambush, its information must be plausible in retrospect. The audience seeks the how and why of the event, so the storyteller had better follow things up with a suitable explanation. Fail to do so, and a logical hole will exist. *Die Hard* contains a shocking moment at its Mid-2nd Act Turning Point. Sgt. Powell strolls back to his squad car in a moment of peace and quiet. Everything seems fine. Then, a dead body comes crashing through his windshield. This is a huge surprise. Neither Powell nor the audience saw it coming. But, for the surprise to make sense, the storyteller must back it up with evidence. So, the initial shock is followed by a shot of John McClane looking down on Powell through a broken window. John threw the body. This answers the audience's questions and solves the dramatic equation.

A surprise is like an explosion. Powerful, yet short-lived. If someone jumps at you from the dark and yells "boo!" you become emotionally excited – but only until you discover there is nothing to fear. Likewise, a cinematic shock lasts only as long as it takes for the audience to regain their senses. Once the shock has worn off, tension fades. For this reason, surprise should not be a storyteller's primary tool. A story with nothing but surprises will become less and less shocking as the audience becomes desensitized to the device. Eventually, the audience will come to expect surprises, undermining their effect. Therefore, use surprises sparingly, reserving them for moments when a sudden reveal will have the most dramatic impact.

SUSPENSE

suspense: n. 1. a state of uncertainty. 2. the growing excitement felt while awaiting a climax.

Suspense can provide a story with more tension than any other dramatic device. It takes the curiosity of mystery and combines it with the intense anxiety of surprise. The key difference however is that while mystery causes the audience to ask questions about that which already exists (the past), and surprise about that which has just happened (the present), suspense causes the audience to ask questions about that which has *yet to occur.* Suspense is all about the uncertainty of the future. What will happen? How will the hero escape? Will he or she make it in time? An important situation hangs in the balance, causing the audience to wonder and worry about its potential *outcome.*

Let us return to our monster movie. With mystery, the audience receives clues that something is in the closet, but the identity of that something is kept unknown. With surprise, the audience receives no information until the monster attacks. Suspense operates quite differently. With suspense, the audience is allowed to see the monster ahead of time. The audience knows it is in the closet, but the hero does not. This makes the audience wonder what will happen. At the same time, they become afraid. Afraid of what *might* happen. The result is FEARFUL ANTICIPATION. This creates an anxiety in the audience that causes them to proceed with one eye open and one eye closed until the fateful moment arrives.

Suspense is something we encounter in daily life. When we are waiting to hear back from the doctor. When we are running late for work. When we have urgent news, but cannot reach the person who needs to hear it. Any time there is an important situation where the outcome remains in doubt, suspense will exist.

Creating dramatic suspense is relatively simple. The storyteller sets up an uncertain situation, and then delays giving the audience its result. However, suspense cannot exist unless there is first something at stake. The audience has no reason to worry about an outcome unless there are significant consequences attached. At its best, suspense puts the hero into situations where the worst seems all but inevitable: Luke Skywalker's X-wing has Darth Vader on its tail. What will happen? Indiana Jones has been sealed inside the Well of Souls. Can he escape? Vito Corleone is left unguarded at the hospital. Can Michael save him? Because the audience fears the possible consequences, they have a vested emotional interest in learning the result.

Suspense comes in two varieties: STANDARD and HEIGHTENED. With standard suspense, both the characters and audience are fully aware of the situation at hand. Suspense exists simply because the outcome remains up in the air. The hero and villain are fighting it out. Who will win? The protagonist races to save a friend from danger. Will she make it? The hero's team is down by three runs in the bottom of the ninth. Can they still win?

Standard suspense can be intensified with the addition of a TICKING CLOCK. In a ticking clock scenario, a character has a goal he or she absolutely must achieve, but a very short amount of time to do so. The character must not only overcome the obstacle in his or her way, but must do so before time runs out. As the seconds slip away, the situation becomes more and more urgent as it seems less and less likely that the character will succeed. In *Back to the Future,* Doc and Marty have only minutes to execute their plan before lightning strikes at exactly 12:05 AM. In *Alien,* Ripley has only ten minutes to reach the escape pod before the ship explodes. However, a ticking clock need not be so literal. Often, it is not known how much time the hero has left. All one knows is that the hero must act quickly or disaster will occur. In *Die Hard,* the audience knows John McClane must get off the roof before Hans sets off the explosives, but they do not know exactly when this will happen. In the climactic sequence of *The Matrix,* Neo must escape Agent Smith before Sentinals destroy Morpheus's ship, but we do not know how much time Neo has. Since disaster could strike at any moment, the situation feels all the more urgent.

Heightened suspense, in contrast, takes the audience's anxiety and gives it an extra twist. Whereas standard suspense allows both the characters and audience to be fully aware of the threatening situation, heightened suspense gives this information to the audience but *not* to the character. The audience is given what is known as PRIVILEGED INFORMATION. They know something vitally important that the character does not. As a result of this ignorance, the character is put in danger. The audience feels increased anxiety because they realize danger is coming the characters' way, but know they can do nothing to stop it. The audience can only watch and worry as the character walks into a trap.

One of *Die Hard*'s most intense moments occurs when John McClane meets Hans Gruber face-to-face for the first time. Only John does not know this man is Hans. The audience, on the other hand, knows full well and begins to panic as John not only befriends Hans, but hands him a gun. In *The Matrix,* the audience knows that Cypher has made a deal with Agent Smith to betray the heroes. They are then shown Cypher contacting Smith moments before Neo and Morpheus meet the Oracle. The audience knows ahead of time that an ambush is coming, causing them to experience anxiety as they wonder when it will occur and what will be the result.

Ironically, heightened suspense gives an audience its intense pleasure through a feeling of helplessness. Burdened by privileged information, the audience feels the urge to help the character. They want to yell out, "Look out!" or "Get out of there!" But of course, they can do nothing. This is known as a CASSANDRA COMPLEX. In mythology, Cassandra was the beautiful daughter of the king of Troy. The god Apollo became smitten with her and gave her the gift of prophesy to persuade her to be his bride. When Cassandra rejected his proposal, Apollo cursed Cassandra so no one would ever believe her visions. Cassandra continued to foresee disasters, accidents, death and destruction, but could never persuade anyone to stop them from happening. Cassandra eventually went mad from her helplessness. She could only stand and watch as the citizens of Troy wheeled the giant wooden horse through the city gates that she knew would bring their doom. This in a nutshell is what heightened suspense is all about. The audience sees danger coming yet can do nothing to stop it. Like Cassandra, their foresight drives them mad.

However, heightened suspense can only work if the audience first *cares* about the character under threat. If the audience is not emotionally attached to the character, they will have little cause to fear for the character's welfare. Thus, audience-character identification is a prerequisite for great suspense. When the audience identifies with the character under threat, it creates a *dilemma* in the audience's minds. They are torn between their desire to know the outcome and their compassion for the character who may come to harm.

As with mystery, the longer a situation remains in suspense, the greater the anxiety. Every additional moment is meant to torture the audience with desire. But also like mystery, the storyteller must know when to give. Once again, the appropriate amount of time is relative the importance of the conflict at hand. Most pieces of suspense need not last longer than a single scene or a short length of time within the scene. However, a major outcome can be built up by a piece of suspense that lasts an entire story sequence, or even an entire act. Many great third acts, including some of those seen in our study films, reach their climaxes through one long line of suspense, culminating in an event that seems all the more dramatic due to the amount of time the audience has been left to wait and wonder.

STORY PACE AND MOMENTUM

Pace is defined as the speed of progress. On the level of plot, pace is dictated by the rate at which new, situation-changing events occur. In individual scenes, this is decided by how quickly the scene advances by giving the audience new information. Momentum, on the other hand, is the sensation created when one event leads to the next through cause-and-effect. This refers not only to causality between scenes, but also how well questions lead to answers which then lead to more questions. Together, pace and momentum give the audience the sensation of being on board a moving train. Things are constantly moving forward, and at a dramatically satisfying speed.

A good pace needs consistency. The story should advance at a steady rate with the only change being a gradual increase in tempo as the narrative progresses. Good momentum depends on connectivity. In a great story, everything feels connected. One story atom naturally leads to the next, giving the narrative a sense of unstoppable forward inertia like a boulder rolling down a mountainside. Lack of consistency or connectivity gives the audience a jarring, stop-and-go experience. This is as unpleasant as it would be to ride on an erratically moving train. Whether the story moves slow and leisurely or fast and furious, pace and momentum should remain steady throughout.

There is always the question of a story's appropriate pace. Proper pace varies a good deal by genre. Action, adventure, and comedy must move very quickly, while other genres are allowed to take their time. A psychological thriller, for instance, must use a more deliberate pace due to its high reliance on suspense. A character drama can develop slower still, with plenty of room allowed to explore character and theme. The general rule of thumb is that a story's pace should move as swiftly as possible without sacrificing the details necessary for the audience to understand and enjoy the narrative. Pack your story atoms tight and move quickly from one to the next. No filler. No wasted time. Any pace that goes slower than needed is a recipe for boredom. The human mind is excited by movement. A lack of movement equals a lack of interest. So, keep events moving swiftly.

However, while moving too slow can cause boredom, moving too fast can damage a script even more. Some developing writers create storylines so convoluted that events must move at a breakneck speed just to fit everything in. Such a hurtling, stumbling pace forces important elements to fall by the wayside. The first casualty is character. With no breathing room, no time is allowed for the material the audience needs to understand and identify with the people who occupy the story. The second loss is comprehensibility. When a story moves too fast, the writer often neglects to give the audience everything it need to understand its events. With no time to explain, the audience is left in the dust. An ideal pace should move quickly, yet still take the time necessary to ensure that the audience has everything it needs to fully understand and enjoy the narrative.

Some things to remember:
- Avoid wasting time with irrelevant events or information. If any part of the story does not either advance the story or communicate something the audience must know, it only slows down the script.
- Every action, image, or piece of speech should move scenes forward. Storytellers should offer their audience a tightly packed string of atoms, not one or two pieces of information separated by filler.
- Avoid repeating information the audience already knows.
- Less talk, more action. Talk slows down a scene. Action communicates much more, much faster.
- Get in and out of scenes quickly. Do not waste time with a slow lead-in, or stick around after the action has finished. Join a scene with its conflict already in progress. Once resolved, bring the scene to an end.
- Avoid "shoe leather."

Shoe leather is a term used by film editors for the time wasted watching actors walk from one side of the room to the other. Unless something eventful happens along the way, this movement does nothing but eat up time. In screenwriting terms, shoe leather means any unnecessary step in a set of actions that can be implied rather than shown. If we learn a character must fly to Chicago for an important event, it is unnecessary to show him or her arriving at the airport, getting on the plane, the plane taking off, the plane landing, the character getting her bags, etc, etc, etc. Just cut to the character in Chicago. The audience does not need to see every little moment, unless something significant occurs along the way.

EXPOSITION

Exposition (also called expository information) is information that must be communicated ahead of time so the audience may understand future events. It is background information that may explain past occurrences (called *backstory*), describe how something works, or tell the audience what to expect. Like soldiers being briefed for an upcoming mission, exposition lays out the how, what, and why of the situation so the audience is caught up on information that characters already know.

Unlike regular story information, exposition is inactive in nature. It does little or nothing to advance the story situation through change. Rather, it is "old" information, based on things which already exist or events that have already occurred. This inactive nature can make exposition dull and dramatically static unless properly handled. While necessary for most stories to function, exposition is often the bane of the amateur screenplay. When performed in a clumsy, overt manner, it only works to highlight the contrived artificiality that proper storytelling strives to hide.

The worst way to give background information is through BALD EXPOSITION. Bald exposition is communication that makes no attempt to appear natural within the context of the scene. It is forced upon the audience in such a blunt, overt manner that the storyteller might as well yell it right in the audience's face. For example, here is how NOT to give exposition:

> "As you well know, my grandfather was an oil tycoon who founded our city in 1902. Being the youngest of four brothers, and the only one unmarried, I have always resented being kept from the family business..."

Dialogue such as this is the worst kind of spoon-feeding. This character behaves as if he were reading from an encyclopedia. It is completely unnatural for any human (with the possible exception of Forrest Gump) to spill out personal information unless they are put into a situation where they feel logically motivated to do so. Storytellers need to find ways to give story information while maintaining the illusion of natural behavior. Bald exposition ignores the latter need by forcing characters to announce information for no purpose other than so the audience can hear it. This sounds phony and artificial, causing the audience to roll their eyes in derision.

Just as bad are writers who give exposition through "info dumps." An info dump occurs when a writer chooses to spill out huge chunks of exposition all at once just to get it out of the way. Watch the opening sequence of the 1999 movie *The Mummy* for an example of one of the worst ways to handle exposition. The film opens with a six-minute info dump that spoonfeeds every insignificant bit of backstory, boring the audience stiff before they meet any characters or experience any relevant conflict. Not only does this open the movie in the dullest way possible, it spoils the fun by ruining any sort of curiosity or surprise that might have come from withholding this infor-mation until later. Info dumps are usually a sign of laziness or desperation from a writer who cannot think of a better way to give information. Some try to hide an info dump by disguising it as a TV news broadcast or in the headlines of a newspaper, but such transparent devices are hardly an improvement.

Exposition is best given when the audience does not *realize* it is exposition. Good exposition must be HIDDEN. Rather than shove important information into the audience's face, good writers allow the audience to absorb it while distracted by other material.

The best way to hide exposition is through conflict. As mentioned last chapter, conflict can act as a mask to hide a scene's true intentions. A relevant conflict will grab the audience's attentions and dramatize any exposition slipped in along the way. *The Bourne Identity* gives its background information on the Treadstone project through a series of arguments between the antagonist Ted Conklin and his supervisor Ward Abbot. These scenes do not seem to be about the exposition, but rather the conflict between two characters who cannot stand the sight of each other. While the audience is absorbed in the conflict, the storyteller slips them all the information they need along the way. Conflicts can be designed for the sole purpose of dramatizing important exposition. In *Star Wars,* everything we learn about Han Solo's backstory comes in response to either Luke's rude comments or Greedo sticking a gun in his face. By challenging Han with conflict, the character is given a legitimate reason to explain who he is and what he does. Thus, all exposition remains natural to the situation at hand.

At its best, exposition should be given through dialogue in a casual, "throwaway" manner, stated only because it happens to be relevant to the situation at hand. *Back to the Future* contains a scene where Marty's mother gives the entire backstory on her courtship with Marty's father. However, she gives this information only to criticize Marty's relationship with his girlfriend Jennifer. While the scene is outwardly about Marty and Jennifer, the situation provides a logical excuse to communicate this exposition in a natural, unobtrusive way.

Whenever possible, give exposition through visuals rather than words. Visuals allow far more efficient communication and can be subtly folded into a scene without distraction. In *Back to the Future,* the audience learns nearly everything they need about Doc Brown by a simple dolly across his home and belongings. In *Chinatown,* we learn of the lengthy relationship between Hollis Mulwray and Noah Cross through a handful of photographs. One look at Rocky Balboa's apartment tells us mountains about this character and background.

In some cases, exposition is too complicated to be communicated with a simple visual or offhand remark. Some elements require entire paragraphs of explanation. Here scenes always risk devolving into info dumps. One way to prevent this is to keep exposition conversational. Instead of a long, dull speech, give the exposition through back-and-forth interaction, with a little conflict thrown in along the way. For example, if we have a story about the theft of the world-famous Hope Diamond, the audience must first learn about the diamond and its infamous curse. Rather than give a long lecture, the information is better given like so:

Boss: You guys aint gonna steal me just any diamond. We're
    going after the most valuable diamond in the world.

Mugsy: You mean the *Hope Diamond*?? Are you crazy?

Bugsy: I thought that thing was cursed.

Boss: What are you, scared?

Bugsy: Everyone who's ever had it has wound up dead. So yeah, maybe
    I am!

However, sometimes this is not possible. Some information is so complicated that it does require a lecture. In these cases, keep things visual. When
Morpheus finally explains the Matrix, he is forced to talk for minutes on
end. This could have easily turned into an info dump. However, the storytellers avoid this by illustrating Morpheus's words with a series of images
that cannot help but grab the audience's fascination. They learn the exposition not so much by Morpheus's words, but by actively exploring this
new world with their own eyes. This keeps the scene active and the audience
dramatically involved.

Unfortunately, not all expository speeches can be matched with such
visual counterparts. Sometimes merely illustrating the speaker's words will
be dull, redundant, or even impossible. If exposition does not have a natural
visual complement, the storyteller should invent one. Humphrey Bogart,
facing a scene where he had to give two pages of expository dialogue on
his 1943 film *Sahara,* famously quipped that the director had better put two
elephants – let's say, "having amorous relations" – behind him, because
that would be the only way the scene would be interesting. Bogart was
being facetious of course, but he had the right idea. If dull, expository
dialogue is an absolute necessity, liven it up by communicating it alongside
an interesting visual or action. The human mind has the ability to multi-
task. We can receive one set of information with our ears, while absorbing
another with our eyes, with no loss in between. The master of the house
can explain the servants' duties while those servants are distracted by his
alluring wife. A character can give his backstory while recklessly weaving
his Porsche through traffic. Two lawyers can discuss the big case while
courtside at the NBA playoffs. Layering visual and auditory information
in this manner is not only more efficient storytelling, but can provide the
spoonful of sugar that helps the expository medicine go down.

INFO PLANTS

While exposition is "old information" the audience must know to continue, an info plant is a piece of vital information slipped into the narrative that does not at first seem to have any immediate use. Info plants are "sleeper information." While seemingly trivial at the moment, this is information that must be set up in order to allow a later event to occur. The storyteller "plants" the facts early so they may "pay off" later. For example, a storyteller establishes in passing that the protagonist has asthma. This seems like nothing more than a minor character detail which is soon forgotten. That is, until the hero must run for his life and is felled by an asthmatic attack. What at first seemed to be of minimal importance is revealed to have major significance to later events. The sleeper information comes back into play with a vengeance.

This process of PLANT-AND-PAYOFF helps give a story a sense of cohesion. Audiences do not like it when characters pull solutions from thin air or when it seems the storyteller makes things up as he or she goes along. Audiences enjoy the feeling that everything is connected, that every moment reflects back to what has occurred before. Quite often the most enjoyable experience comes when the audience realizes everything has been set up from the start, wrapped up in a tight little package.

This requires a great deal of deftness. The storyteller must plant information in a way that makes future events possible, while not being so overt that the audience will see the payoff coming. Like exposition, a plant is best established in a subtle, throw-away manner, ideally through conflict or action relevant to the scene. This way, the information is planted in the audience's mind without drawing attention to itself.

To illustrate, *Chinatown* invisibly plants two key pieces of information that, while insignificant at the moment, become crucial to the story much later. When Jake Gittes pays his first visit to the Mulwray home, he watches the Japanese gardener remove dead grass from around a koi pond. Jake also notices something shiny in the pond, but forgets it when interrupted by Mrs. Mulwray. Though the audience does not realize it, both pieces of infor-mation are plants. Though meaningless at the moment, they explode like landmines later in the story.

Jake learns that Hollis Mulwray has been killed. However, the circum-stances are mysterious. Hollis Mulwray died with salt water in his lungs, but the place where he supposedly drowned was filled with fresh water. It is not until Jake pays a second visit to the Mulwray home that the plants reveal their meaning. Jake realizes that the grass dies around the koi pond because it is filled with *salt water*. Looking closer, he finds the shiny object to be a pair of eyeglasses – a pair just like Hollis Mulwray's. The answer to the mystery has been under right Jake's nose the entire time. Hollis was drowned in his own backyard and then moved to look like an accident. The plant gives credence to the payoff.

Many beginners find plant-and-payoff difficult. This is often because they fail to realize the device's true purpose. Plant-and-payoff is not some-thing applied superficially just to spice up the narrative. Nor should it be used to appear clever. Plant and payoff is a marvelous tool that can over-come problems encountered while constructing a plot. When used properly, planted information provides plausible ways to get storytellers around a story's various jams and dead ends. The storyteller does not do this by thinking ahead, but by working *backwards*.

BACK-PLANTING

Often, in the course of constructing a plot, writers end up painting them-selves into a corner. The characters are put into situations where the only solution would be manipulative or overly-contrived. Sometimes, the only way out of the predicament is to go BACK to an earlier moment in the story and plant information to provide a plausible solution.

A perfect analogy can be found in of all places the 1989 comedy *Bill & Ted's Excellent Adventure*. Bill and Ted are two boneheaded teenagers caught up in an adventure through time and space. The pair does not have much smarts to help them with their problems, but they do have – a time machine. Whenever the pair faces an insurmountable obstacle, such as a locked door or when cornered by a policeman, they find a simple solution. All they do is make a mental note to use the time machine at a later date to travel a few days into the past and set up a solution they may use in the present. So, when confronted by a locked door, the heroes decide they will later use the time machine to steal the key and hide it under a rock. When cornered by a policeman, they decide to go into the past to rig a bucket that will fall on the policeman's head. By deciding to alter the past, Bill and Ted create instant solutions in the present. Now Bill and Ted look under the rock and find the key already placed underneath. They look up, and see the bucket has already been set up to fall on the policeman's head. With the ability to rewrite their own past, Bill and Ted can find logical ways to get around any problem in the future.

Back-planting solves story problems in the same way. It is the writer's time machine. Whenever a plotline is stuck, the writer can travel back to an earlier point in the story and add information to set up a proper solution.

To see this storytelling time machine in action, let us take a look at how back-planting may have been used in two of our study films, *Back to the Future* and *Die Hard*. (Note: These examples are hypothetical for the point of illustration. I have no first-hand knowledge on how these scenes were actually written. These are merely two possible ways back-planting may be been used.)

In *Back to the Future*, Marty is stuck in the year 1955 because the Delorian has no more plutonium to generate the 1.21 gigawatts of power necessary to send him home. The storytellers decided a lightning bolt could be used to generate the power. However, this solution creates an even bigger problem: How is it possible for Doc and Marty know when lightning will strike?

While writing *Die Hard*, the storyteller decided it would be great fun to force John McClane to run barefoot over broken glass. This would not only make John's mission harder, but set up a scene where McClane has a serious, character-revealing talk with Sgt. Powell while pulling the glass from his feet. But there is a problem: Why on earth would John McClane be barefoot?

Back to the Future found a clever solution. Marty, with his knowledge of the future, could somehow know of an exact time and place where lightning will strike. To make this plausible, the storytellers traveled BACK to the story's opening act and added an innocuous scene where a pushy old lady solicits funds to fix the clock tower – a tower that was struck by lightning in 1955. Marty even receives a flier that gives the exact time and date. The flier is a plant. The audience thinks little of it until much later, when Marty reaches into his pocket and finds it still there. With this tiny alteration, the storytellers create an elegant solution to unstick the stymied plot.

Die Hard's problem took a little more thought. It would make no sense for John to take off his shoes and socks while running for his life. The only reasonable scenario would be if John removed them before the terrorists invade. So, the writer traveled back to the first act and had John take off his shoes. But why would he do this? Why would John McClane go barefoot at a fancy corporate party? John is supposed to be a tough guy. He would not remove his shoes no matter how bad his feet might hurt. Again, the storyteller needed to plant a reason. So, the writer traveled even further into the past, all the way back to the opening scene, and planted a seemingly insignificant line of dialogue to set this up. A fellow traveler sees how tense John is and tells him the best way to relieve stress is to take off your shoes and socks and "make fists with your toes."

Play the action forward and everything makes sense. The traveler gives John advice. John is unlucky enough to try this advice as the terrorists invade. Therefore, John is still barefoot when he must escape over broken glass. As a result, John inadvertently forces Sgt. Powell to reveal his darkest secret to distract him from the pain of digging the glass from his feet. The storyteller traveled all the way back to Scene 1 to make Scene 154 work.

DOUBLE-PRONGED PLANTS

A big question remains. What is the best way to plant information without it looking like a plant? How can one keep the audience from recognizing the setup and predicting the result? The most effective and dramatically satisfying method is to hide the information's true purpose through a DOUBLE-PRONGED PLANT.

A double-pronged plant masks a piece of information's true purpose by setting it up as something that seems relevant to a completely unrelated situation – and *only* that situation. The audience does not suspect any type of set up because they believe the information has only one use. Then, a situation arises later in the story that reveals the plant to have a second and far more important purpose.

Once again, *Die Hard* provides two stellar examples. Before its inciting incident, *Die Hard* revolves around John's marital problems with Holly. John and Holly's relationship is in trouble. In fact, they are on the brink of divorce. To prove this, the storytellers provide two pieces of information. First, John learns that Holly is no longer calling herself by her married name. She has returned to her maiden name Gennaro. Second, when Holly hears that John has not yet bothered to call home, she is so upset at the insensitive lout that she turns over the family portrait behind her desk. At the moment, both pieces of information seem to have no meaning other than the obvious. They are simply the expressions of a troubled marriage. However, as soon as the Main Conflict begins, both are revealed to have much greater significance.

Early drafts of *Die Hard* no doubt struggled with a problem: What is to keep Hans from realizing that Holly is John's wife? Hans interacts with Holly. He even takes over her office. Hans is not a stupid man, so something must prevent him from putting the pieces together.

The storytellers solve this problem with a double-pronged plant. Holly's use of her maiden name is not in the story just to cause friction between her and John. It is a contrivance that also allows her to hide her identity. The plot also needs a way for Hans to eventually connect the dots. This is where the second double-pronged plant comes into play. Holly's turned-over photograph is not just an expression of her anger. It is a ticking time-bomb that allows the later event to occur. Eventually, Hans discovers the photograph, shattering Holly's anonymity and putting her in danger for the film's final act. Double-pronged plants pull off the ultimate in audience sleight-of-hand. The audience never realizes the plants have a second use because the information is so expertly disguised by their first.

ALTERNATIVE METHODS OF COMMUNICATION

FLASHBACKS AND DREAM SEQUENCES

Flashbacks and dream sequences are found by the truckload in amateur screenplays. In professional scripts, there are very few. This is because unskilled writers typically use these devices as cheap shortcuts to spoon-feed information that could be better given through more traditional methods.

It is one thing if a storyteller uses flashbacks or dream sequences to create a narrative that unfolds through their intentional and repeated use, such as *Memento* (2000), *The Usual Suspects* (1995), *Vanilla Sky* (2001), or to a lesser extent, *American Beauty*. It is an entirely different case should a writer tack on a single flashback or dream sequence because he or she cannot think of a better way to communicate a piece of information. This is clumsy and artless, amounting to little more than a fancy method of bald exposition. Do not take shortcuts with information that can be given more dramatically through action or character. These are the most effective roads, and must always be pursued first. Take alternative paths only when the story presents legitimate cause for a nontraditional solution.

If these devices must be used, the storyteller must realize that flashbacks and dream sequences are still part of the plot structure as a whole. They are not a timeout from the story. They behave just like any other scene and must follow the same rules. Their content must advance the story. They require conflict to drive their action and a function to justify their existence. Like any other scene, they exist within a story sequence, and must work to support the sequence's spine. Fail to do all this and the flashback or dream will distract from the plot rather than develop it. It will create an awkward dead spot in an otherwise cohesive narrative.

VOICEOVER

Like flashbacks or dream sequences, voiceover is frequently criticized as a tool of lazy writing. However, voiceover does not necessarily deserve this reputation. *Apocalypse Now* (1979), *Trainspotting* (1996), and *Election* (1999), all use voiceover from beginning to end, and all three were nominated for Academy Awards. The fact is, voiceover can either improve a story or detract from it. It all depends on the purpose for which the voiceover is used.

If voiceover is simply used to spoon-feed information to the audience; information that could be given more dramatically through action, visuals, or character; then yes, that voiceover is the work of a lazy writer. The storyteller has chosen to narrate information rather than put in the hard work necessary to dramatize it through physical action. The audience prefers to see the story unfold with their own eyes, not to be told about it like in a children's book. Some writers do both, narrating the action while the audience sees it on screen. However, this is both unnecessary and redundant. If the audience can see the action, they do not need to be told about it as well.

Voiceover is justified only when it provides an additional layer of meaning, one that actions, visuals, and sound cannot supply on their own. Good voiceover elevates a story by adding subtext, counterpoint, irony, commentary, or criticism to what is already seen or heard. For example, if a story uses voiceover to communicate a character's inner thoughts, but those thoughts contradict the character's actions, the conflict between the two allows the audience to see dimensions to the character that would not have been obvious through actions alone. A satirical comedy can use voiceover for ironic counterpoint. A drama can have characters comment on the situation in retrospect to provide dual perspectives to the story's events. Voiceover can also establish a specific emotional tone, such as the storybook motif found in *The Royal Tenenbaums* (2001) or the feeling of crisis and paranoia in *Fight Club* (1999).

When used properly, voiceover can also help solve problems with plot or character. *Apocalypse Now* had a problem with its plot. It needed to develop a relationship between its protagonist and antagonist, but wanted to keep the antagonist hidden until the third act. Voiceover provides a compromise. The protagonist narrates the antagonist's story as he reads his dossier. This seems natural and unobtrusive since it makes perfect sense that the protagonist would learn about the man he has been sent to kill. The voiceover not only allows the audience to learn about the absent antagonist, but forms a bond between hero and villain, even though the two sides have yet to meet. *Trainspotting* has a problem with character identification. Its protagonist is a heroin addict; one who lies, cheats, and steals to get his next fix. In most cases, it would be difficult, or even impossible to convince the audience to get behind such a person. Voiceover fixes the problem by putting the audience inside the protagonist's head. By hearing his thoughts and emo-tions, the audience is led to not only understand the protagonist's behavior, but sympathize with him and his actions.

Despite its potential benefits, voiceover should still be a tool of last resort. It should be used only when actions, visuals, sound, or speech cannot do the job on their own, and never in their place. If voiceover must be used for exposition, do so sparingly. *American Beauty* provides a perfect example. Its voiceover is used only at its beginning and in brief segments at the end of each act. This strategy works to support the story's most important structural moments without distracting from the narrative itself.

CHAPTER 11
WORDS, WORDS, WORDS...

Polonius: What do you read, my lord?
Hamlet: Words, words, words...
– Hamlet, Act ii scene ii

Cinema is not a literary medium. Its storytelling is not made of words. It is a medium of sight and sound that overwhelms its audience with a world that looks and feels as real as their own. Cinema creates a sensory experience for which words often need not apply.

However, a screenplay must be made of words. Black type on a white page. The storyteller may originate the sights and sounds of a cinematic story within his or her imagination, but unlike the painter or musician, a screenwriter cannot bring his or her vision directly into the world. Dozens, if not hundreds of other talented persons are required to complete what the storyteller has begun. Since it is impossible for the storyteller to communicate his or her vision to each person directly, the best the storyteller can hope to do is take the actions, images, and sounds as they exist in his or her imagination and record them as accurately as possible into a SCRIPT.

Here we see the screenwriter's conundrum. He or she must record a visual and auditory medium into an explicitly non-visual or auditory form. Some call a script the blueprint for a film, but this is not exactly so. A screenplay is in fact the film itself, *transcribed* into a different form. A script is to a finished film as what a compact disc is to a piece of music. A compact disc does not contain actual sound. If one holds a CD to their ear, nothing is heard. What the CD contains is the original music, transcribed into a code that can be stored in physical form. It is not until the disc is put into a stereo that its material is de-coded back into the music as it was originally heard. Likewise, a screenplay is a movie's storage medium. The actions, visuals, and sounds that make up the eventual cinematic experience begin inside the writer's head. The writer must then take this sensory material and transcribe it into a different form – into written words. There, on the printed page, the movie lays dormant until a team of professionals translate its words back into the actions, images, and sounds as they originally existed inside the writer's head.

The word "translate" is key. The writer must make sure his or her intentions are accurately re-interpreted when read. If ideas are communicated poorly, much of the writer's original vision may end up lost in translation. Thus, how the screenwriter uses his or her words becomes extremely important. The best-written script must record its content with enough clarity to recreate its story within a reader's mind exactly as it began in the storyteller's imagination with no loss or confusion in between.

However, this is no easy task. Words are often a poor substitute for the sensory experiences they describe. Furthermore, a screenplay must follow certain formal rules that limit how its story is recorded on the page. The challenge then is to use language that maintains cinema's sensory impact while conforming to the limitations of its written form. All this must be accomplished through the use of three elements: 1. Description, 2. Action, and 3. Dialogue.

DESCRIPTION

> *"It is a matter of words, perhaps, but words are*
> *important... If you cannot say what you mean, you will*
> *never mean what you say." - The Last Emperor (1987)*

Description is the written passages that tell the reader how to imagine the scene. They communicate what the audience will see and what they will hear (with the exception of speech). Though this may seem elementary, one thing must be made clear.

You are not writing a book! You are not a novelist! A novelist has the freedom to pen long, sprawling paragraphs that describe every detail. The screenwriter does not. Screenplay description must be kept simple, direct, and efficient. A screenplay should read at a pace brisk enough for its action to carry itself out in the reader's mind at the same speed it is expected to occur on screen. Unnecessarily detailed description slows down the read, making what should seem quick and exciting appear sluggish and dull. This fools the reader into believing the story moves at a far slower pace than it actually should.

Not only is a literary style counterproductive, it is completely unnecessary. A novel must go to great lengths to describe every detail because its written words are its audience's only source of information. The cinematic audience, on the other hand, gets information from a multitude of sources. The director, cinematographer, designers, and performers all use their talents to enhance and expand upon the writer's words. Because of this, screenwriters need only focus upon matters of story and leave the details to the other artists. Description should therefore be limited to the information necessary to understand the situation and advance the plot. The screenwriter should not waste time describing every piece of furniture in the room, how the sunlight filters through the curtains, or the color of the walls, unless these details are specifically relevant to the development of characters or plot. If not relevant, the description is nothing but noninformation that will clutter up the read.

Give description in a clean, direct style. Avoid being overly intellectual, poetic, or ornate. These are styles for a novelist. Pretty prose will ultimately mean nothing. All that matters is what ends up on the screen.

Words should be chosen carefully. Being clear and specific will promote the most accurate visualization. A young woman may be described as "attractive," but this generic term does little for the imagination. What kind of attractive is she? Is she pretty? Lovely? Cute? Stunning? How about handsome, shapely, statuesque, alluring, or sultry? Each communicates a different and more specific meaning. The English language is blessed with one of the most extensive vocabularies in the world. Make good use of it. Choose words and phrases with clear and solid meaning. Vague language allows ambiguity, which leaves the reader to make his or her own assumptions – assumptions that may not be in line with the writer's intent. The more specific the language, the more effective the communication.

Grammar should be simple and concise. Sentences should require little effort to read. You do not want to force readers to slow down to simply grasp your meaning. The most streamlined of sentences will lack any unnecessary words. Think of yourself as a sharpshooter and your words as ammunition. A novelist may be able to waste words like a machine gun, but a screenwriter should hit the target in one shot. Description should be a bullet of information, put right into the reader's brain. Cause maximum impact with minimal language.

Remember that description can only include what the audience *sees* or *hears.* Anything else will come to waste. Consider this example:

INT HARDY KITCHEN-MORNING

FRANK HARDY is an 8th generation Hardy, and has lived in Hardytown, California his entire life. His family founded Hardytown. He served two tours with the Marines in Iraq, and carried out missions in other parts of the world. His wife SAMANTHA is in her early thirties. She is from Memphis, Tennessee and teaches fourth grade. Their daughter TANYA is 16 years old and boy crazy. TIM is eight. It is Tuesday morning, the first day of April. The four are finishing breakfast at the kitchen table.

It is all well and good that the writer created so many details for his characters, but unfortunately THE AUDIENCE WILL NEVER RECEIVE ANY OF THIS INFORMATION! All they will see is a simple, nondescript family sitting around a simple, nondescript breakfast table.

Filmmakers have a saying: "If it is not on the screen, IT DOESN'T EXIST." Anything that cannot be shot by a camera or recorded by a microphone is called an UNFILMMABLE. Details such as a character's backstory, thoughts or emotions, who is related to whom, how characters prefer their peanut butter sandwiches, or what they did last summer vacation will all be lost on the page unless the writer can communicate them with words and visuals that can be shot, recorded, and put on the screen. There is no way the audience will know Frank Hardy was in the Marines unless the writer provides evidence the audience can see or hear. There is no way to know the daughter is boy-crazy unless we see her engaging in such behavior. The audience will never know it is the first day of April unless they see some evidence to the fact or someone states this information out loud.

Unfilmmables also include internal processes that are not accompanied by physical action. It is not enough to write, "Bob is sad," or "Susan gets an idea." The audience can only recognize thoughts and emotions when they manifest themselves through observable behavior. Instead of just being "sad," Bob could "slump his shoulders as he drags himself to the nearest seat." Instead of just stating that Susan gets an idea, the event must be made physical, as in "Susan suddenly perks up and grabs a pen." Do not assume the audience will "get it." Instead, ask yourself, "How will the audience KNOW?"

ACTION

While description gives the background of a scene (how an object looks, the atmosphere of the location, the way people and things impinge upon the senses), action passages communicate everything that physically *happens* in the scene. If it moves or changes it belongs to action.

Action passages are given within the same paragraphs as description and should follow the same guidelines for clear, efficient communication. On top of this, good action passages should incite a specific and proper visualization that allows the reader to see the action exactly as it is meant to occur on screen. Seek language that triggers the imagination. Words should suggest the same energy and emotion viewers will experience when they see the action with their own eyes. Which is better? "Susan trips and falls" or, "Susan stumbles, wheels about, and hits the pavement with a thud"? Both describe the same action, but only one makes the reader feel the impact of the action as if they had seen it actually happen.

Verb choice proves an essential part of this. Here are some grammatical guidelines to help ensure that actions are communicated in the strongest manner possible.

- Use verbs that convey a sense of physical activity. Try to avoid the verb "is." "Is" is a form of "to be," and it takes no physical effort to "be" anything. Rather than, "Mary is at the table," use "Mary sits at the table." Instead of "Frank is angry," say "Frank becomes angry," or even better, give Frank physical actions that imply his emotion.

- Avoid generic verbs. "Ed runs down the street," is generic. Verbs like stride, trot, sprint, or gallop allow the reader to visualize the action with far greater specificity. The more specific the verb, the more meaning the action will communicate.

- Always write movies in the present tense, and never the past or future. No matter when a movie was made or what time period it depicts, what we see on the screen is occurring THIS VERY SECOND and should be written that way.

- Also, avoid the present progressive tense. This means phrases such as "Bob is sitting," "Maria is running," or "Tom is walking." The addition of the inactive "is" implies passivity. Instead, stick to the present active tense: "Bob sits," "Maria runs," "Tom walks."

Sentence construction can also influence visualization. English teachers state that one should write with an *active voice* rather than a *passive* one. This means words should be ordered so the sentence's subject (the noun preceding the verb) is the person or thing performing the verb's action ("Sarah kicks the ball"), rather than the person or thing being acted upon ("The ball is kicked by Sarah"). However, in screenwriting, the storyteller can use the active and passive voice interchangeably to communicate how the action is meant to be visualized. "Sarah kicks the ball" implies that the focus of the shot will be on Sarah. "The ball is kicked by Sarah," suggests that the camera will begin on the ball, which is then kicked as Sarah's foot enters the frame. Though "directing the scene" (writing shots and angles directly into the script) is forbidden of screenwriters, such subtle manipula-tions of grammar are an acceptable way to suggest a visualization without overtly stating how the scene must be shot.

Finally, screenwriters should never use phrases such as *"we see* Tom look outside," or *"the camera* moves closer to reveal..." Not only does this make the writer sound amateur, but any acknowledgment of the existence of a camera or viewing audience removes the reader from the story's world by pointing out its artificiality. The script no longer reads like a story, but a blueprint of instructions. It is difficult for the reader to get mentally involved in the script with this technical garbage in the way. Just don't do it.

THE CURSE OF DIALOGUE

"Wise men speak because they have something to say. Fools
because they have to say something." - Plato

You are not writing a novel. You are also not writing a stageplay! Theatrical plays must depend upon dialogue as their primary storytelling tool. This is because a play's action is limited by what can be physically produced on stage. A play can have only so many sets and locations, the curtain can open and close only so many times, and effects are limited to that which can be produced in front of a live audience. Cinema, however, has no such limitations. A cinematic story can jump across the world at the push of a button. Its action is limited only by the storyteller's imagination. Audiences accept the static, talky nature of stageplays because they recognize the stage's limitations. However, a movie made in the same style as a play will bore an audience stiff. Cinema's freedom from the stage has turned it into a medium of visuals and action. Not of talk.

Despite all of this, beginning screenwriters always seem to miss the point. They believe movies are all about dialogue. So, they turn out 130-page scripts bloated with talk, talk, talk. Every scene drags at a snail's pace as characters talk and talk and talk. No action. No visuals. Just talk. Nothing kills excitement like too much dialogue. This is because when people are talking, that is time in which they are not DOING. And when no one is doing anything, the story does not advance. Most film schools forbid the use of dialogue in their students' first films. They do this to teach filmmakers to tell a story with visuals first. If only there was such a ban on first-time screenwriters.

If a picture is worth a thousand words, and actions speak much louder, one can see the relatively low value of dialogue when compared to the alternatives. More can be communicated with a well-chosen image or decisive action than an entire page of speech. Writers are often told to "show and not tell." This means storytellers should first seek to communicate information visually and use dialogue only when this is not possible. The cinema existed for more than thirty years before recorded dialogue was even possible. An over-reliance on talk takes drama a step backwards, back onto the stage.

Visuals and actions are not only a more efficient way to communicate, not only a more dramatic way to communicate, but they are often the only dependable way to express real meaning. Audiences cannot always trust a character's words. People lie. They can be biased, ignorant, or uninformed. A character can talk for hours about who they are or what they believe, but the audience will never become fully convinced until they see the character in action. A story's meaning cannot be communicated through long-winded speeches. True significance can only be found in how events play out through action. Seeing is believing. Characters need to walk the walk, not just talk the talk.

GETTING VALUE FROM DIALOGUE

Whenever a storyteller does use dialogue, he or she must strive for dialogue of *value,* meaning dialogue that benefits the action of the scene. Characters cannot talk just for the sake of talking. Like every other story atom, each line of dialogue must have a legitimate reason to exist. The dialogue must *accomplish something.*

When it comes down to it, dialogue has only three uses. In a well-written scene, everything characters say will either: a. *advance the scene toward its moment of change,* b. *develop character,* or c. *supply the scene with conflict.*

The following is a scene from *The Shawshank Redemption,* written by Frank Darabont, adapted from a story by Stephen King. *Shawshank* is the story of Andy Dufrene, a former banker sentenced to life in prison for the alleged murder of his wife. This scene picks up moments after Andy is released from two weeks of solitary confinement for playing a Mozart record over the prison's loudspeakers. Its function is to communicate Andy's determination to hold onto hope, unlike his fellow inmate Brooks who committed suicide. Though this scene consists almost entirely of dialogue, observe how every line serves the story by performing one or more of dialogue's three essential uses.

```
INT. MESS HALL - DAY

                    HEYWOOD
          Hey. It's the mystero. You couldn't
          play somethin' good? Hank Williams?

                    ANDY
          They broke the door down before I could
          take requests.
```

Even if this were the first scene of the film, the audience would instantly learn something about Heywood and Andy by their opening lines. Heywood is a "Good Ol' Boy" who does not have the refinement it takes to appreciate Mozart. Andy has a resilient character shown by his ability to joke about his punishment only moments after his release.

```
            FLOYD
Was it worth two weeks in the hole?

            ANDY
Easiest time I ever did.
```

This scene will use Andy's reaction to his punishment as a means to express its greater message. Floyd's line sets up this action. Andy's reply launches it.

```
            HEYWOOD
Shit. No such thing as easy time in the
hole. A week seems like a year.
```

Heywood's refusal to believe Andy incites the scene's conflict. Once again, we learn about Heywood by how he speaks. He is the pugnacious sort who shoots straight from the hip.

```
            ANDY
I had Mr. Mozart to keep me company.
Hardly felt the time at all.
```

Challenged by Heywood, Andy picks up the gauntlet. The scene now has a two-sided conflict. This line also establishes the strategy Andy will use to pursue his goal. He wants to convince his friends to his point of view and chooses the metaphor of music to do so.

```
            FLOYD
So they let you tote that record player
down there, huh?
```

If this scene is to achieve its function, someone or something must continually motivate Andy to keep pushing towards his goal. This something is conflict. In this case, it is a simple conflict of understanding. Floyd misunderstands Andy, compelling Andy to continue.

>   ANDY
>   (taps his heart, his head)
>   It was in here...and here. That's the
>   beauty of music. They can't get that
>   from you. Haven't you ever felt that
>   way about music?

Andy's reply creates the first scene beat. In response to opposition, Andy changes strategy; he goes from making half-jokes to launching an argument straight from his heart. Once again, we learn about Andy's character by how he uses his words. He has a spiritual side, evidenced by his poetic words and phrases.

>   RED
>   I played a mean harmonica as a younger
>   man. Lost interest in it. Didn't make
>   much sense in here.

Once again, a bit of conflict gives Andy an excuse to push the scene further. Just like Heywood and Andy, we learn about Red from his opening line. Red is a down to earth, practical sort of guy. While Andy speaks with the lofty notions of an educated man, Red communicates in short, choppy thoughts. He thinks he knows the way things are, and that is that.

>   ANDY
>   Here's where it makes most sense. We
>   need it so we don't forget.

Andy advances the scene by escalating the conflict. He goes from stating his position in the general to taking on Red in the specific. Andy knows Red is the most respected man at the table. If he can win him over, everyone else will follow.

>   RED
>   Forget?

>   ANDY
>   Forget that there are places in this
>   world not made out of stone. That
>   there's something inside of us they
>   can't touch. Something that's yours.

Notice how Andy's line adds drama by providing a hint of mystery. Andy is driving at something, but it is not yet clear what. This causes his friends, and the audience, to lean forward out of a desire to know.

> RED
> What's that?

> ANDY
> Hope.

Andy finally reaches the crux of his argument. Notice that the scene does not achieve its function by making this statement up front and then hammering the audience over the head with it. Instead, there is a slow, dramatic build. As covered in Chapter 9, the scene uses conflict as a logical means to reach its moment of change. Each opposing line of dialogue causes Andy to escalate, like scraps of kindling that turn Andy's original spark into a roaring fire.

> RED
> Let me tell you something, my friend.
> Hope is a dangerous thing. Hope can
> drive a man insane. It's got no use on
> the inside. You better get used to that
> idea.

Red refuses to back down, escalating the conflict to its tipping point. His piece of dialogue draws a line in the sand, causing the scene's outcome to grow uncertain (fostering suspense). At this point, the scene's moment of change could go either way. Depending on Andy's response, the characters will be convinced to either take on Andy's quiet optimism or Red's cynicism.

> ANDY
> (softly)
> Like Brooks did?

Andy's final line creates the scene's second beat, sealing the conflict in his favor. Simple, efficient, and powerful, these three words defeat Red without the need for more argumentation. Though the scene's third act plays out in silence, it is clear by his friend's reactions that Andy has won the conflict and given everyone something to think about. Notice how quickly the scene ends. Once the scene has achieved its function, there is nothing left to be said.

There is no wasted material in this scene. Every word exists to serve the scene's function, whether it be to set up its conflict (Heywood and Floyd's lines), provide material to drive the scene forward (Andy's lines), or supply the resistance necessary to push the scene to a dramatic moment of change (Red's lines).

Dialogue of value takes into consideration not only what characters say, but how they say it. A person's inner character is naturally reflected by how they speak. Amateur screenplays often overlook this fact and create characters who all sound exactly the same. The same generic speech makes all characters appear to be the same generic person. No one stands out as individual or unique. In contrast, *Shawshank* has created three very different people in Andy, Red, and Heywood, a fact the audience can hear every time they open their mouths. Whether it be Andy's poetic soul or Red's blunt realism, each character's inner nature is exposed by how they express themselves to the world. What they say communicates the facts. How they say it communicates character.

TEXT VS. SUBTEXT

Stories put characters into emotional situations. In every scene, they must face conflict and wrestle with stakes. This has an emotional impact upon characters, one the audience must see and understand. However, simply allowing characters to open their mouths and state exactly what they think or feel will not make a good scene or good dialogue. When characters express themselves too directly, their behavior comes off forced and artificial. This is known as LITERAL DIALOGUE.

Literal dialogue creates unnatural behavior. In story, as in real life, people rarely say exactly what they mean. They talk around issues. They keep things hidden. They have wants and needs, but have enough sense to know they will not get them by blurting them out loud. Often, people are not even aware of their needs. They instead react instinctively without knowing why. Yet despite the confusion and subterfuge, the audience must still be able to understand what is going on underneath the surface.

The words people say are known as TEXT. Hidden beneath those words is an undercurrent of thoughts and emotions, known as the SUBTEXT. Often, the best way to understand people's intentions is not by listening to what they say, but how they choose to say it – or in many cases, what they choose *not* to say. For various social and psychological reasons, people rarely express exactly what they think or feel. Instead, we protect our vulnerable inner selves by choosing our words strategically and going about our efforts in an indirect, roundabout manner. There is not necessarily anything dishonest about this. It is how a society functions. What we consider manners or etiquette are really guidelines on how to choose our words and actions so they do not offend others or disrupt pleasant interaction. We have been taught to get what we need not by making demands, but through far more subtle means.

Our training in subtext began at an early age. As children, we had no barrier between our mouth and brain. We would express exactly what we thought, no matter how inappropriate. As we matured, we came to understand it was counterproductive to voice such matters directly. So, we learned to pursue our wants and needs through more palatable behavior which we could use to nudge our interactions in the desired direction.

In screenwriting, subtext is the dialogue behind the dialogue. It is what characters want and why. The text they speak is the strategy they employ to get it. Believe it or not, the best demonstration I have ever encountered on the subject of subtext comes from a 1987 episode of *Saturday Night Live*. In a sketch entitled "Honest Stu," Phil Hartman and Janet Hooks play Dan and Leslie, two budding lovers on the couch after their first date. On the surface, Dan and Leslie's interaction seems quite bland. However, after each line of dialogue, the audience hears a voiceover that communicates what each character is *really* thinking, (in other words, the dialogue's subtext). Its turns out that Dan and Leslie both want to spend the night together, but each are afraid to make the first move. Because of this, they both circle the proposition indirectly.

Then, the sketch takes a turn. Dan's roommate Stu arrives, played by guest host Joe Montana. However, unlike Dan or Leslie, whenever Stu speaks, his thoughts repeat the exact same words that have just left his mouth. When Stu says, "I hope I'm not disturbing you," he really does mean, "I hope I'm not disturbing them." When Stu says to Leslie "I'm glad to meet you," he literally means, "I'm glad to meet her." The joke lies in the fact that Stu's behavior lacks all subtext. There is nothing going on inside his head other than the blatantly obvious. While Dan and Leslie come off as normal, relatable human beings, Stu appears strange, alien, even creepy. He is an empty-headed dolt with nothing under his surface.

Despite the absurdity of Stu's behavior, I time and again find scripts with characters just like him. They express every thought and emotion out loud without a hint of anything existing underneath. Like Stu, these characters appear to be hollow, cardboard cutouts. Underdeveloped characters are often criticized as being "flat." This does not mean the characters lack characterization. Characters feel flat when their words or deeds seem to have nothing greater going on underneath. They behave like open books and are therefore as deep as the pages of the script itself. When there is nothing beneath the surface of a person's words, the audience is led to conclude that there is nothing beneath the person AT ALL. The characters then appear flat and unnatural, lacking the behavior people attach to genuine human beings.

So many developing writers forget to bury their subtexts. They instead leave everything on the surface. Literal interaction undermines drama. It robs the audience of the interactive experience that encourages them to figure out what is really happening and why. Take a look at another scene from *The Shawshank Redemption*. The Warden has called Andy into his office. He has discovered that Andy's banking experience has given him a set of skills that the Warden can exploit for mutual benefit. However, Andy and the audience do not yet know this and assume that a summons to the office can only mean something bad. Notice how subtext brings drama to this scene. No one ever states anything directly, but only hints at what they think and feel. This causes the audience to become involved through their desire to understand.

```
INT - WARDEN NORTON'S OFFICE - DAY

Andy is led in. Norton is at his desk doing
paperwork. Andy's eyes go to a framed needle-
point sampler on the wall behind him that reads:
"HIS JUDGMENT COMETH AND THAT RIGHT SOON."
                    NORTON
     My wife made that in church group.
```

The Warden did not invite Andy into his office to talk about the sampler. However, when he notices Andy eying the rather feminine object, he becomes uncomfortable and feels a need to explain.

```
                    ANDY
     It's very nice, sir.
```

Andy might not think so. He may not even care. However, Andy is nervous, as well as embarrassed that the Warden caught him looking. He tries to be polite and end the matter quickly.

```
                    NORTON
     Do you enjoy working in the laundry?
```

The Warden does not state his intentions directly. Andy's new job is meant to be secret, so the Warden first tries to get a read on Andy by talking around the issue.

```
                    ANDY
     No, sir. Not especially.
```

Andy is cautious. He does not yet know the Warden's intentions, so he guards himself with a half-answer.

```
                    NORTON
     Perhaps we can find something more
     befitting a man of your education.
```

Again, the Warden speaks indirectly. He has heard what he needs and closes the issue. There is no need for a man of the Warden's authority to explain anything to a prisoner. Andy and the audience must wait later to learn his meaning.

There are only five lines in this scene, but five lines are all that is necessary. The words the characters say may have little meaning on the surface, but the underlying subtext speaks volumes. The audience learns not so much by what the characters say, but how they say it.

No speech is one hundred percent literal. No matter how sincere a person may be, behind everything said are invisible urges that motivated the person to speak. People may make small talk because they feel uncomfortable sitting in silence. People may voice their opinions because it makes them feel smart. Someone may make a suggestion because he or she feels a need to take control. Psychological factors affect everything we say. Our speech walks a constant tight rope between what we want and what we consider to be appropriate. The compromises we make between our thoughts and words comprise a significant part of what makes us human. Cinematic dialogue rings true only when storytellers recognize this fact.

WHERE GOOD DIALOGUE GOES BAD

Though dialogue comprises only a small part of a cinematic story, it draws more of the reader's attention than any other element on the page. Because of this, poor dialogue can bring down even the most well-crafted of narratives. Lack of subtext is only one of many ways dialogue can falter. What follows is a selection of the most common mistakes and how to best avoid them.

Overwritten Dialogue

Dialogue becomes overwritten when characters talk too much and say too little. What could be expressed in a few words is instead inflated into entire paragraphs. Too much talk slows a scene and dilutes its content. Remember that pace and momentum depend on the rate which new information is given. Take a look at the scripts of some of your favorite films and you may be surprised at just how little dialogue each scene contains.

Like description, dialogue should be a bullet of information, communicating the most with the fewest amount of words. This does not mean dialogue should be stripped to its bare bones, just that it should be efficient. People often use the word "snappy" to describe good dialogue. This means it is quick, energetic, and packs a punch into few words. If dialogue can be cut down or rephrased without losing its character or meaning, do so. The more streamlined the dialogue, the smoother the scene. The smoother the scene, the more momentum it provides the story as a whole.

In many cases, dialogue is not even necessary to give information. It can be expressed through a nod, a gesture, a shift in posture, or a physical action. Over ninety percent of human communication is nonverbal. Use this fact to keep scenes trim.

Filler Dialogue

"Hello." "Hello." "How are you?" "I am fine. And you?" "I couldn't be better. Would you like to sit down?" "That would be nice." "Now, what can I do for you?" "I'm glad you asked."

Small talk makes small scenes. In the compressed, goal-driven world of the cinematic story, characters do not have time for idle chatter. They need to go after what they want, and do it quickly.

Filler dialogue is any line that seems to exist for no purpose other than to lengthen a scene. Sometimes a writer feels a scene is too thin and will try to expand it with extra conversation. Unfortunately, this only makes the problem worse. The scene goes from short and weak to long and uneventful. Any dialogue that does not either advance the scene, communicate character, or supply conflict amounts to nothing but dead air, spacing out the scene's atoms with useless noninformation. The audience is hungry for the substance of the scene. Don't fill them up on hot air.

Aimless "Witty" Banter

This condition used to run rampant back when every newcomer was trying to imitate the pop culture hits of the '90s, such as *Pulp Fiction* or *Clerks*.

Unfortunately, the result was usually something like a series of bad comedy routines strung together without any intent or greater purpose. Banter cannot exist for its own sake. Unless it advances the scene or communicates new and relevant information, it once again amount to noninformation. Comedy should contribute to story development. It should not be a red light that forces the story to stop just so characters can get their yucks out. Banter, like any other story atom, should have one purpose: to move things forward.

Clonky Dialogue

Clonky dialogue is speech that sounds clumsy or awkward. This is usually because sentences are poorly constructed or contain more words than necessary. Dialogue needs to be streamlined to a point where it flows effortlessly off an actor's tongue. Otherwise, the actors will have to force their words, drawing attention away from the action.

The key to effortless dialogue is to construct lines that not only use the fewest amount of words, but also the fewest number of *syllables.* If it is within character to use tighter phrases, or a shorter synonym in place of a ten-dollar word, this is often preferable. Read your dialogue out loud, or better yet ask someone to read it to you. You should be able to hear where it is smooth and where it grows awkward. The less tongue-wrangling actors must perform, the better dialogue will sound.

Stilted Dialogue

Though the term is often misused, stilted dialogue refers to speech that lacks a natural rhythm or flow, making it sound wooden, stiff, or pompous. Even the best of actors have difficulty giving stilted dialogue without sounding fake.

To avoid this, make an effort to listen to how people speak in everyday situations. Hear the rhythm of their voices and how they stress certain words or phrases. Different people structure their thoughts in different ways, depending on place and circumstance. Age and background also have an influence. It pays to observe of how patterns differ from one social group to the next, especially groups with members of different background than yourself. Again, it helps immensely to ask someone to read your dialogue out loud.

Overly Formal Dialogue

Similar to stilted dialogue, overly formal dialogue occurs when characters speak with the perfect grammar we were taught in grade school. Though we should all write with perfect grammar, rarely does anyone speak with it. Even the most educated of persons will be informal in his or her casual speech. People save time by compressing thoughts into the shortest and most direct form. They use fragments and run-ons. They drop subjects, misconjugate verbs, clip words and phrases, and apply double negatives. People frequently smash words together to create improper contractions, such as "hafta," "gonna," or "woulda," for the sake of speed and efficiency.

Authentic speech is not only flawed speech, but the *right kind* of flawed speech. Speech habits differ a good deal by region. What may sound normal in rural Georgia may sound ridiculous in Boston or the Pacific Northwest – and vice versa. We all mangle the English language in some way, but how we do so depends on our individual backgrounds and personalities.

Expositional Dialogue

Man: "What day is today? Thursday?" Woman: "Yes, one day before my sister's birthday. Don't forget her party." Man: "I don't like that European guy she's dating. There's something strange about him." Woman: "Oh, you're crazy. They've been together for over a year."

This echoes back to Chapter 10. The least natural way to give exposition is to have it come directly from a character's mouth. If exposition must be given through dialogue, it should be done indirectly. Rather than state exposition explicitly, good dialogue hints at the information in a way that allows the audience to grasp the general meaning without having it shoved in their face. Here is the same scene, this time with indirect exposition:

Woman: "Don't forget to get a gift for tomorrow." Man: "I'm not sure I want to go." Woman: "You have to! It's my sister's big 3-0." Man: "Is she still dating what's-his-name?" Woman: "Jean Phillipe? What have you got against Jean Phillipe?" Man: "I don't know. Nothing, I guess."

Repetitive Dialogue

This one is simple. Do not waste time with characters repeating information the audience already knows. Hearing information a second time will add nothing new, no matter how extraordinary that info may be. If a scene requires one character to fill in another on what has already occurred, have this action occur off-screen and then cut to the scene with both characters already in the know. The audience only needs (and wants) to hear things once.

On-the-Nose Dialogue

Closely related to literal dialogue, dialogue becomes on-the-nose when it states information in a way that is unnaturally plain, obvious, or direct. If a character is angry, the most on-the-nose thing to say would be, "I'm so angry!" If a building is about to collapse, it would be on-the-nose to yell "That building is about to collapse!" On-the-nose dialogue uses characters like ventriloquist dummies. Rather than react naturally to the context of events, characters become tools to narrate information the audience can figure out through other means. Though it may be easiest to state things out loud, doing so will appear artificial. Instead, find ways to communicate through visuals and action, or through subtext and inter-character conflict.

Dull, Unemotional Dialogue

Cinematic stories put characters into the most dramatic situations of their lives. Every event threatens to alter their world with terrible consequences. This creates an emotional urgency that should reflect itself in the character's speech. Yet despite this, I time and again encounter scripts with characters who act aloof and unattached from the beginning of a story to its end. If even the characters cannot become emotionally invested in the situation, how will the audience? The audience receives its emotional cues from a story's characters. If characters do not react to events with the proper amount of emotion, it provides nothing to pass along to the audience. Communicate drama through your character's words. Remember conflict. Remember stakes. Characters must seem to care about their situation. The more they care, the more the audience will care as well.

Preachy Dialogue

Preachy dialogue usually comes from a writer with a personal or political agenda. The writer wishes to press an idea upon the audience, so he or she puts that idea directly into the characters' mouths. Audiences do not react well to this. They want to hear a story, not a sermon. The purpose of art is not to tell people what to think, but to encourage people to think for themselves. If a storyteller wishes to convey a particular message, the proper way to do so would be to supply evidence through plot, character, and conflict, and then allow the audience to draw their own conclusions. The moment art goes from encouraging the search for truth to telling people what the "truth" should be, it ceases to be art. It becomes propaganda.

Unnatural dialogue creates unnatural characters. The reverse is also true. Since the words people say are a natural reflection of who they are, character and dialogue are inseparably linked. If one wishes to improve dialogue, the first place to look is to the characters themselves. Deeper dialogue must come from a deeper source. Ask yourself, is every character fully dimensional? Do you clearly understand each character's wants, needs, flaws, and fears? Is the dialogue a natural expression of these wants, needs, flaws, and fears? Or do the characters simply speak to move things along?

In the same way, improving a character's dialogue will improve the audience's *perception* of that character. If you have put considerable effort into developing a character, yet he or she still falls short on the page, dialogue may be the problem. Audiences can only understand characters by their words and deeds. If those words are flat, unemotional, overwritten, or contain any of the problems that can turn dialogue sour, the audience will be unable to see through those words to the deeper character underneath. Character and dialogue rely on each other to create one total package. Underserve one and it will harm the other.

As if it needs to be said again, half of story is in the telling. Storytelling is an act of communication, and this ultimately comes down to the very words put on the page. Though it should be the farthest thing from the storyteller's mind when he or she starts the creative process, the wise and judicious use of language will ultimately become an essential part of communicating the story in a way others will find clear, effective, and emotionally satisfying. Great words make a great script.

CHAPTER 12
AFTER THE FIRST DRAFT

Congratulations! You have completed your first draft. You have endured months of labor and given birth to a 90-120 page bundle of joy. Take a moment to pat yourself on the back. Many never get this far.

However, do not think your work is finished. Far from it. In fact, it has just begun. No child is ready for the world straight from birth, and neither is your screenplay. You must now take your newborn script and nurture it to maturity.

Recall from Chapter 1 how no script is perfect the first time around. The first draft merely gets your ideas down on the page. Now that those ideas are laid out in structured form, you can observe how the story takes shape, identify its flaws, and then remold it into perfection. For many, this is when the real inspiration kicks in.

Nevertheless, many writers feel overwhelmed at the revision stage. They see a 120-page monster riddled with holes and crippled by flaws and have no idea where to start. They then launch a haphazard campaign to fix everything at once, often creating more problems than when they started.

If writers are to get the most from the revision process, they need an organized approach. This starts with the right attitude.

First, be honest with yourself. Do not look at your first draft with rose-colored glasses just to spare your own ego. If it stinks, fine. It stinks. Admission is the first step to recovery. What you have now is nothing but raw material. With proper time and effort, any rough stone can be polished into a jewel.

Second, be critical. Put your creative brain aside and let analysis take over. Use the principles contained in this book to decide how well each element lives up to the requirements of a good story. Try to remain objective. Look at the script for what it really is, not what you wish it to be.

Finally, remain optimistic. Each draft is only one step in a long process. Be confident that your work will pay off in the end. Do not fall in love with your first draft, but don't beat yourself up over it either. Your honest, critical, optimistic attitude should be, "What is bad, I can fix. What is good, I can make better."

Writers often have trouble evaluating their work because they have become "too close to it." When in the thick of it, writing a script can feel like being stuck inside a hedgemaze. Viewed from the outside, it may be obvious which direction to go, but inside the maze, all writers can see are the walls around them. Writers need to distance themselves from their work at the start of each revision, both physically and emotionally. Objectivity is essential. Like a mother and child, writers often become so emotionally attached to their work that they become blind to its flaws. Take a step back and give your script some tough love. Be hard on it. Cruel even. This is the only way to make it better. Do you think Army Drill Sergeants are so hard on their recruits just to be mean? No. They act this way because they know it is the fastest method to get soldiers ready for combat. Think of the revision process as basic training for your screenplay. If you want it to survive, you have to be just as tough.

THE REVISION PROCESS

Stage 1: Evaluation

The revision process differs with every script. Each story has its own particular needs, and every writer has a way of working he or she finds most comfortable. However, it is generally beneficial to prepare for each new draft with the following steps.

First, take a break. If you have just finished, take a week or two away from the script to busy your mind with other things. This will help gain objectivity so you may return to the script with a pair of fresh eyes. Do not take too long, however. Like many things, the writing process has momentum. Stop working for too long and it may be difficult to get that momentum back again.

Once time has passed, read your script from start to finish, in one sitting if possible. This will allow you to experience the story in the same way an audience would, as one continuous whole. For now, resist the urge to make corrections along the way. This is a sure way to catch scene-itis. Instead, try to get a sense of the story's overall shape and form, and how well each element fits into the whole. Pay attention to areas where things seem to be lacking, such as points where momentum slows or where structure feels out of whack. Jot down some general impressions after you have finished.

With that done, read the draft a second time, this time paying close attention to each individual scene. Make notes as you go on what needs improvement or any changes you would like to make. Remember to focus not only on the scenes themselves, but on how well each scene works to support and develop the story as a whole. It is okay to make small corrections at this time. If there are mistakes or pieces of dialogue you cannot stand, feel free to fix them as you go. However, leave significant changes for later. The purpose of this read-through is not to edit, but to compile a set of notes that will guide you in the next stage. Problems are easier solved if identified ahead of time. By gathering this information, you will be able to organize the revision with a clear, systematic approach.

Stage 2: Starting the New Draft

There is no set way to go about making changes to your script. You might start on page one and plow straight through to the end, or you might begin by fixing the major problems, and then jump from one area to the next. Try to be thorough. Address all problems identified in your notes and make an effort to improve everything the best you can at the moment. Be willing to put in the proper amount of time. Rewriting requires the same discipline it took to finish the original draft, maybe even more. Work left behind is just more that will have to be dealt with in the next pass.

Keep in mind that "re-writing" means to literally *write it again.* If some part of the script is unsatisfactory, a writer must not be afraid to throw it out and begin anew. Beginners have the tendency to cling to their original material out of a fear that they will be unable to come up with something better. They make a tweak here and a tweak there, but the flawed material remains intact. An experienced writer is not afraid to "slash & burn." If material is not good enough, he or she will not hesitate to throw it away and start again. Do not worry. All you are throwing away are words. You have an unlimited supply. However, clinging to poor words is like clinging to a sinking ship.

Many writers are afraid to make major changes to plot or character because they see their story as a house of cards. If they change one thing, they must also change everything else or the whole story will collapse. Yes, it is true that a screenplay is holistic. Everything is connected to everything else, so a major change in one area may force a drastic rewrite of the entire script. When some writers realize this, they chicken out and decide they would rather stick with the flaws rather than put in the extra work. This reluctance becomes a permanent obstacle to success. Do not be afraid to go the extra mile. Your goal is to construct the best story possible. If this means you must strip the script down and give it a complete overhaul, then so be it. The dozens of extra hours necessary to make a script great will always out-value the hundreds of hours wasted on a script that never meets its full potential.

Writers also have the tendency to hold onto the "little moments" they know the script is better off without. This might be a clever exchange of dialogue, an imaginative side-scene, or a funny additional character. Writers can fall in love with such bits and pieces, but unfortunately these moments are sometimes extraneous to the plot and slow the story down. There is a saying amongst screenwriters, "Sometimes you have to kill your babies." This is a rather extreme way to put it, so let us instead say, sometimes you have to let things go. Imagine you are the boss of a company. You have an employee named Josh. Everybody loves Josh, but Josh is just not cutting it when it comes to his work. His poor performance is dragging everyone else down. Though you may hate to do it, you have to let Josh go. It is for the good of the entire company.

Stage 3: Successive Drafts

Though a writer should try to be thorough with each revision, it will be impossible to fully address every element within a single draft. As you realize by now, screenwriting is a complicated craft, and every area can bring a multitude of problems. Trying to tackle them all at once will give the writer nothing but a splitting headache.

Because of this, the revision process is best accomplished in a series of levels. After the initial revision, the writer should work to improve his or her script one element at a time. There should be drafts solely dedicated to structure, others dedicated to character, a draft dedicated to theme, and so on. This allows the writer to see through the clutter and develop the finer details of each element in a way that would not have been possible in a generalized revision.

In the early stages, the writer's primary concern must be the fundamentals of storytelling, namely the Story Spine and plot structure. Everything else has little significance until the story "works" on a basic level. Therefore, writers should not move forward until these fundamentals stand on solid ground.

Begin by identifying the protagonist. Is it perfectly clear that this is the protagonist? It may sound odd, but I have encountered many scripts where this is far from obvious. Are you *sure* this is the protagonist? It is not uncommon for beginning writers to mistakenly consider one character the protagonist, when it is in fact another character that actually drives the narrative. When this happens, the writer should either reconsider his or her protagonist or rewrite the narrative so the proper character takes center stage.

Next, identify the Story Spine. What are its five components? Do all five components exist? Are they clear and obvious? Is each strong enough to sustain dramatic tension for the story's entire length?

Now, look at plot structure. What are the Major Dramatic Turning Points? When do they occur? Where is the inciting incident? Does it establish the Story Problem and force the protagonist to take action? What about the climax? Does it resolve the Story Spine in a way that is both conclusive and satisfying? Look at story sequences and turning points. Does the plot have sufficient development? Does each sequence have a spine that supports the main narrative? Does every sequence end with a moment that escalates conflict and turns the story in a new direction?

Is there conflict in every scene? Is each scene relevant to the Story Spine? Are there any holes in your story logic? Is there causality? Does every event alter the narrative in a way that is both plausible and necessary? Does momentum lag at any point? Is there any extraneous material which does not belong?

As you can see, there is much that needs to be addressed. It may take a number of drafts before every structural problem has been fixed. Take all the time you need. You do the script no favors by removing it from the oven half-baked.

Once confident in your story's foundation, shift focus onto character. Character development is often overlooked until plot is locked down, so it is necessary at this time to shine a spotlight on the characters to help them grow. Focus on one character at a time. You may even want to dedicate an entire draft to each major character. Use this opportunity to get inside each character's head and see the story from his or her point of view. Explore the conflicting wants and needs that drive the character's behavior in each and every scene. When finished, scenes will be dramatically improved now that every character pursues clear goals and acts according to well thought-out psychological needs.

Start each character draft by identifying the character's spine. Label his or her problem, goal, path of action, conflict, and stakes. Again, are all five components present? Are they strong enough? Are they clear enough for the audience to understand? Map out each character's internal arc. What is the internal need? What is the flaw? How do story events cause the character to change? What are the specific moments that trigger this change? Keep in mind that though every character should have a spine, not every character requires an internal arc. Some characters, such as the antagonist, refuse to change or are incapable of internal growth. In this case, identify the factors or flaws that prevent change from taking hold.

It may be helpful to write biographies for each character. This exercise allows you to explore your characters in dimensions that may have never occurred to you before. Fully-dimensional characters have inner lives and emotional histories that extend far beyond the events of the plot. Ask yourself: Where was the character born? What was his or her childhood like? What about relationships with family? How does the character see the world? What factors have led him or her to think this way? Explore the character's personal life both inside and outside of the story's events. What does the character do when not engaged in conflict? What are the character's likes? Dislikes? What do they want out of life? Why? What do they need emotionally? Why? Are they aware of this need? Why or why not?

After the character drafts, it is up to the writer to decide what still must be done before the script is complete. Maybe there are some lingering problems that need to be addressed. Maybe a few more drafts are necessary in response to reader feedback. Once all elements have been developed to satisfaction, it is a good idea to perform another draft to focus on cohesion. Revising one step at a time often has the unwelcome side effect of leaving the script a bit disjointed or rough around the edges. This revision gives an opportunity to bring everything back into harmony. Keep an eye out for inconsistencies. While making improvements, you may have neglected to clean up the details attached to each change. There may remain passing references to scenes that have been altered, or lingering elements from previous drafts that have since been removed. Watch out for loose story threads. You may have set something up but neglected to carry it through, or possibly created a new event without returning to an earlier point to establish a proper setup.

Before finishing the process, it is strongly recommended to perform what is known as a line revision. Look over the script line-by-line, paying close attention to every piece of description, action, and dialogue to make sure you have communicated your information as clearly and efficiently as possible. At this point, you are preparing your script for readers, so you want to make sure every word flows as smoothly as possible. Look for typos. Make use of stronger, more visual language. You have no doubt made improvements with every revision, but this is one last chance to smooth out the wrinkles and make the script as presentable as possible. After a week or two, it is advisable to perform a second line revision. The more polished the script, the more professional it will appear. Never overlook the details. A sloppy script will make a writer look amateur, regardless of how great the story may be.

As you can see, the revision process takes time. But, when is the script finished? Most will say this is a trick question. The script is never finished until it is shot, edited, and put on screen. Even then, the writer will wish he or she had one last chance to make improvements. The real question is, when is the script ready to show the world? Again, there is no definite answer. The best indication, however, will come through reader feedback.

SOLICITING FEEDBACK

Outside opinions can be invaluable to a screenwriter. Completing a script without feedback is like styling your hair without a mirror. You would like to believe everything is in the right place, but you will never know for sure unless someone tells you.

Though feedback can be helpful at any stage (although I do not recommend allowing anyone to read your first draft), it becomes most crucial once the writer has reached a point where he or she believes the script to be finished and ready to show the world. Because quite often, it is not. Writers often see through obvious flaws or ignore problems right under their noses. Even worse, the way the writer sees the script in his or her own head may not be anything close to how it actually exists on the page.

You may be surprised that storytellers can be this ignorant of their own work. However, there is a reasonable explanation. As far as the writer is concerned, every screenplay exists within two separate realities: a SUBJECTIVE reality, and an OBJECTIVE reality. The subjective reality is what you, the writer, *think* your script accomplishes. The objective reality is what the script actually *does* accomplish on the black and white of the page. As surprising as it may seem, there is often a striking difference between the two.

To relate: I am sure that most of you are familiar with the reality TV phenomenon "American Idol" (or one of its international incarnations). As fans know, each season begins with auditions from thousands of young singers who believe they are qualified to become contestants. Some are clearly talented. Others are so painfully bad that one swears the audition must be a joke. Yet, it is no joke. Those lacking talent honestly believe they are great singers, and are shocked – SHOCKED – to hear otherwise.

What is wrong with these people? Are they delusional? Insane? Just plain stupid? Maybe. However, the real cause of their delusion is that, much like you and your screenplay, their singing ability exists in two simultaneous realities: the subjective reality of what these people *think* they sound like, and the objective reality of how they actually sound to others. This is why writers need feedback. Writers need someone to judge their work because they are unable to accurately judge it themselves. Feedback pulls writers away from their subjective point of view and shows them the reality of their accomplishments in the cold light of day.

Receiving feedback can be a confusing, disheartening, even aggravating experience, especially when that feedback is negative. No one likes to be criticized, even when they ask for it. Rather than accept the reader's comments, insecure writers will become angry. With egos bruised, they throw a fit, questioning the reader's intelligence, ultimately rejecting any benefit the feedback may give.

The worst thing a writer can do is get mad at the people who have so graciously volunteered time and effort to evaluate someone else's work. Criticism is not meant as a personal attack, but an attempt to help the writer make his or her work the best it can possibly be. When a writer asks for feedback, he or she implicitly admits that the script is not perfect and needs help. The writer asks to be criticized. It makes no sense to get angry at someone for doing what you asked him or her to do! If all you want is an ego boost, look elsewhere. This is not what feedback is for. Feedback's purpose is to tear a script open and root out its flaws so it may be improved. If you want a truly great script, you must not only accept criticism, but welcome it with open arms.

To whom should you give your script? Ideally, you want to find readers with a level of experience equal to or greater than your own. Readers with no story experience can tell if a story works on a gut level, but they are rarely able to identify specific problems or suggest practical improvements. Writers with less experience than yourself may be even less helpful. Beginners often feel the need to prove their own talent, and treat feedback as an opportunity to do so at the author's expense. Amateur feedback can also be rooted in an inferior knowledge of the craft and may mislead the author with suggestions that are not dramatically sound. The most useful feedback comes from those more knowledgeable than yourself. Find these people if you can.

Get feedback from three to six different sources before making significant changes. Feedback from one source may not be reliable. Each reader's opinions are shaped by personal tastes that may not be shared by others. The best strategy is to compare results from multiple readers and look for patterns. If one reader out of five asks for broad sweeping changes, changes not even hinted at by others, you can probably chalk up these comments to personal taste. However, if more than one reader makes a comment, it is probably a valid point. The more who agree, the more serious the issue. Though you may not share the opinion, it must be looked into. There is a saying, "If one person tells you that you have a tail, that person might be crazy. If five people tell you, you had better check your rear end."

Unfortunately, analyzing feedback is not always a simple task. Reconciling the opinions of multiple readers with differing backgrounds and levels of experience can be an art in itself. Then comes the challenge of taking these suggestions and matching them with your own intentions without drastically changing the script you wish to create. Luckily, three rules exist to help writers see through the confusion.

THREE RULES TO GET THE MOST OUT OF FEEDBACK

RULE #1: THE READER IS NEVER WRONG

This is not to say the reader is always right. Far from it. This means everything the reader says is a one hundred percent valid impression of the work *as they saw it.*

Readers can only base their opinions off what has been printed on the page. They cannot see the story as it exists in your head. They cannot read between the lines. They only have the information you have supplied, as you have supplied it. If there is a shocking difference between what you see when you look at your script and what they see when they read it, the fault lies with you, the writer. Between the subjective view of the writer and the objective opinion of the reader lies a GAP. A gap of miscommunication. You have somehow failed to communicate your story in a way that will generate the desired response. The writer's job is to find the cause of the gap and fix it.

Many would like to blame negative feedback on the reader. The reader is too stupid, or jealous, or has the wrong attitude to understand what you have put on the page. Thinking this way is nothing more than sour grapes. Never argue with feedback. Never tell the reader he or she is wrong. Your readers may not all be experts on screencraft, but every one of them is an expert on their own feelings. If reading your script made them feel one way or another, then that feeling is valid and true. The reaction may not be universal, but as far as personal opinions are concerned, it is the objective truth of what has been placed in front of them.

RULE #2: IS IT THE STORY, OR THE TELLING?

If an idea falls flat with a reader, it may not be the idea at fault. Perhaps the fault lies in how that idea was executed on the page. Let's say a reader tells you a certain sequence does not make sense. To you, it makes perfect sense, but for some reason the details have flown over the reader's head. The flaw then lies in communication. You must go back into that sequence and rewrite its material so everything becomes clear.

Recall from Chapter 11 how a writer must take the sights and sounds as they exist in their imaginations and transcribe them into written words. If this process is done poorly, ideas that are originally clear to the writer become garbled and confused on the page, preventing the reader from visualizing events as the writer intends. You might call this *transcription error.* If a reader finds fault with a certain idea, the writer must figure out if the reader is reacting negatively to the idea itself, or how that idea was executed on the page. Often the original idea is solid. There is just a problem with presentation.

The reader will not be able to tell you which is the case. It is up to you to figure this out. Often the best indicator is how well the reader's impressions match your own. Let's say a reader says she dislikes your "bitter, antisocial protagonist." These comments come as a surprise, since you think of your protagonist as shy and sympathetic. There has clearly been an error in communication. To fix this problem, you must go into the script and find what moments may have given the wrong impression. On the other hand, if it was your intention to create a bitter, antisocial protagonist, the reader is reacting negatively towards your original ideas. In this case, you may wish to change your protagonist to make him or her more appealing.

RULE #3: NEVER TAKE FEEDBACK LITERALLY

Writers are rarely lucky enough to receive feedback that spots a script's exact cause of failure. You would like to hear something like, "Your second act drags because the force of antagonism fails to escalate after each turning point." Instead, you get "The middle was slow and boring." Instead of, "You have not created a strong internal need to motivate the protagonist's actions," you get, "Your main character did things kind of randomly."

To get the most out of feedback, the writer should not focus on what the reader has said, but figure out what caused him or her to say it. Most of the time, feedback comes not from readers' intellect, but their gut. They know they felt a certain way, but cannot tell you why.

To do this, a writer must take on the role of a doctor. A patient does not come to a doctor and state "I have a viral infection." Rather, the patient gives a list of symptoms: a cough, a headache, a fever... Now, a poor doctor would treat only the symptoms. He or she would give the patient an aspirin and some cough syrup and send the patient on his or her way. However, the patient would still be sick. The condition may get worse and harm the patient in many other ways. A good doctor, on the other hand, uses symptoms as clues to diagnose an underlying cause. The doctor treats the disease, not just the symptoms. In the same way, a flawed script is a sick script. Feedback gives a list of symptoms. The writer could take suggestions literally, but doing so would treat the symptoms and not the disease. The underlying flaws will still remain and will continue to damage the script. Instead, the writer should think of suggestions as clues that point to the script's real problems.

As an example, let's say a reader thinks your climax falls flat. You could rewrite the climax in an attempt to make it more exciting, but this may not solve the actual problem. Instead, dig deeper into the craft and ask, "What made the reader think that?" A number of flaws could cause a disappointing climax, such as insufficient conflict, weak stakes, or an event that fails to fully resolve the Story Spine. However, only one of these will be the actual culprit. Look into the script to find the answer. The reader got his or her criticisms from the page, so it will be on the page where you will find their cause. Such critical analysis takes thought and experience, but most of the knowledge required has already been covered in this book. By treating the disease, and not just the symptoms, the entire script will improve. It will not only fix the reader's complaint, but remedy any other problems the flaw may cause now or in the future.

As previously mentioned, between the subjective reality of the writer and the objective reality of the reader there lies a gap. The goal of rewriting is to close that gap so the story the writer wishes to give is the same as the one readers ultimately receive. The writer does not do this by giving into the readers' suggestions like a list of demands. This would compromise the writer's original vision and may turn the script into something the writer never wished it to be. Instead, writers must find the causes of this gap and then fix the associated problems so the audience receives the mental and emotional satisfaction they require, while maintaining the integrity of the narrative the storyteller wishes to give.

A writer cannot do this without a strong grasp of the craft. The craft exists to serve the needs of both the audience and the storyteller. It balances the needs of each side to bring the two together. Fix the broken craft, and you and the audience will connect as one.

CHAPTER 13
ON THEME

Every story, regardless of genre or type, communicates a larger meaning that goes far beyond the events of its plot. Whether the storyteller realizes it or not, every choice he or she makes conveys subtle, underlying messages to the audience. Therefore, a responsible storyteller should make an effort to recognize his or her message and how best to give it.

This message is known as the THEME. As you know by now, stories play an important role in society. Part of this role is to impart the society's rules and values through the use of plot and character. Every story reflects the society that created it. For example, American culture traditionally prizes values such as individualism, personal freedom, self-achievement, respect for the family unit, and monogamous love. Thus, it is no surprise that most Hollywood films contain stories that support these themes. (*Rocky, Star Wars, Raiders of the Lost Ark,* and *The Godfather* are all good examples.) Films produced outside of the United States express slightly differing themes, ones that support values their own societies hold dear. By acting as a medium through which important values are expressed, storytelling helps maintain social order and unite its audience under a shared identity.

However, storytellers are not slaves to the society in which they live. Storytelling, like any other art, is a means of personal expression. Each individual story is influenced not only by society's rules and values, but the storyteller's personal opinion of those rules and values. If the storyteller is critical of his or her society, he or she will create stories with themes that challenge social norms. Thus, story is not only a tool of social stability, but also one of social change. A storyteller's dissenting opinions can influence the audience's views, slowly pushing society in a new direction.

As you can see, theme can be a powerful thing. And, whether you realize it or not, your story will have one. It does not matter if you are writing a serious political thriller or a light-hearted adventure. The story's characters and events will say something to the audience. It is your responsibility as a storyteller to recognize this message and communicate it in the most dramatically effective way possible.

You may wonder why I have waited this late to discuss the topic of theme. Why after a chapter on the revision process, rather than while discussing character or plot? The truth is, theme is not a physical component of storytelling as are plot, character, or dialogue. Theme is instead a natural outcome arising from the combined and total use of all other elements. Theme is not an ingredient. It is an end result. Many times, the storyteller does not have a particular message in mind when he or she begins work on a story. Despite this, meaning will inevitably emerge from how he or she uses plot, character, and other storytelling elements. Because of this, it is sometimes impossible for the storyteller to recognize his or her theme until well after the first draft, after plot and character have grown solid and clear.

You may wonder how a storyteller can generate a theme and not know it. The reason is simple. Writers are drawn to tell particular stories in particular ways as a result of their *personal psychology*. Along with shared social values, we all possess a unique set of personal beliefs that influence our likes and dislikes, our opinions and points of view. This personal psychology expresses itself through what we choose to write and how we write it. Take a moment to think about it. What drew you to tell your particular story? What about its content appealed to you? Why did you choose a teenage girl as protagonist and not a middle-aged man? Why do you like science fiction but not romantic comedy (or vice versa)? Why do you conclude your story with an up-ending or down-ending? These choices are all based upon how you see yourself and the world. There is a part of the storyteller in every protagonist he or she creates. Genre preference is based on how the writer prefers to see the world. Choice of ending communicates the storyteller's final opinion of a story's events. Every decision you make in your writing is in some small way an expression of yourself. Taken together, it forms a larger picture of what the storyteller believes or how he or she perceives the world.

Take a closer look at your script and you may be surprised by what it says about you. You may find that you are a silly romantic, or maybe more cynical than you realize. Your story may show you have radical beliefs, or that you are surprisingly old-fashioned. Whatever your story says, embrace it. Your theme is an expression of yourself.

The key point is that theme grows *organically* from the choices a storyteller makes. Theme emerges from plot and character, not the other way around. Some writers get this backwards. They begin a story with a particular message in mind. They then try to orchestrate character and plot to intentionally communicate this theme. However, this approach rarely meets success. Theme cannot be forced upon a story. When this happens, the tone becomes too preachy. Subtext becomes text as the writer attempts to speak directly to the audience. The story world then loses its illusion of reality as each character and event is used as a blunt instrument in service of its lesson. A great story cannot be created from a preconceived theme. A great theme comes naturally from a great story.

This is not to say a storyteller cannot recognize his or her theme early in the writing process. Some discover the seeds of their message while brainstorming or outlining the first draft. This is perfectly fine as long as the writer remembers his or her highest priority is creating an effective and entertaining narrative. Theme, like all other elements, exists to serve the story as a whole. It is part of the total experience, not the point of the experience itself.

At its best, theme is invisible. It is not a physical thing, but a shadow that resides behind the story's events. In many great films, the theme is never expressed out loud. *The Bourne Identity* is a story about the importance of maintaining one's sense of self. This is not expressed through speeches, but through character and action. Jason Bourne is a man who has allowed his sense of self to be corrupted by the CIA. In response, Bourne's mind wipes itself clean so he may find his identity all over again. Thematically, the story can be summarized as a battle between a man who wishes to regain his personal sense of self versus malevolent forces who wish to steal it away. Was this the idea that inspired *Bourne?* Probably not. A spy with amnesia simply seemed like an intriguing premise. Nevertheless, this theme grew from the original premise, one the storytellers had the wisdom to embrace.

As you can see from *Bourne,* great themes are not reserved solely for "serious" films. Even the wildest of action flicks or most raucous of comedies can be elevated with a well-developed theme. For example, if one looks deeper into *Die Hard,* the movie reveals itself to be a statement on how traditional, hard-working values can protect American society against foreign threats. This is all communicated through subtext, of course. To put the film into historical perspective, 1988 was a period of economic anxiety for the American public. For the first time since World War II, the United States was no longer the economic powerhouse of the world, falling behind former foes Germany and Japan. Working-class Americans took this especially hard, since it seemed to suggest that their traditional values were no longer good enough. American audiences needed a reason to believe in themselves again. Part of *Die Hard'*s monumental success came from the fact that it tapped into the anxiety of the times and dramatized it on the screen. John McClane is a hard-working "All-American guy" whose health and happiness are first threatened by a *Japanese* corporation, and then *German* terrorists. *Die Hard'*s blue-collar heroes (McClane, Sgt. Powell, Argyle) then use American-prized values such as courage, ingenuity, and perseverance to overcome the cold, ruthless efficiency of their foreign threats. There is no way to tell to what degree the anxieties of the time were on the minds of *Die Hard*'s storytellers as they created exploding rooftops and escapes down elevator shafts. However, it is almost certain these feelings were in the back of their minds, as they were for most of the American public, causing this theme to naturally emerge from the story's characters and events.

THEME & PLOT

A great theme does not express itself as a one-sided affair. A storyteller does not merely establish a message and then hammer on it with every story event. Doing so would be tiresome and transparent. A well-executed theme expresses itself as a *conflict*. Like the plot, the theme grows and develops by way of a battle between two opposing sides. But unlike the plot, this is an invisible battle that resides behind and works through the story's physical events.

This battle is called the THEMATIC ARGUMENT. On one side of the argument is the value or message the story wishes to express (courage, community, generosity). On the other side is that value or message's exact *opposite* (cowardice, isolation, selfishness). This opposing value is called the ANTI-THEME. Like yin and yang, each thematic value is dramatically counter-balanced by its opposite. A story about hope is opposed by an anti-theme of despair. A story about justice is met by the anti-theme of injustice. The theme and anti-theme then battle each other through the story's physical events. This means for the thematic argument to exist, the story's plot must contain not only material that supports its intended message, but an equal amount of material that seems to suggest its opposite. A story on the importance of family can and should contain moments when characters reject their families. A story about honesty should contain characters who profit from lies. An equally-weighted thematic argument turns the plot into not only a physical battle between its characters, but also a moral battle between love and hate, law and chaos, selfishness and charity, or any other duality. As the plot's conflict develops and escalates, so will the thematic conflict, building in intensity until the main story climax. The climax will then decide not only the winner of the physical conflict, but the thematic conflict as well.

To illustrate: *Chinatown* presents a thematic argument of CORRUPTION vs. INTEGRITY. Jake Gittes' world is filled with corruption of every shape and size. Corrupt business dealings, corrupt marriages, corrupt legal and political systems. Primary amongst this corruption is a plan to build an unsafe dam, initiated by a shady group of conspirators who wish to manipulate the system to gain control of much of Los Angeles County. Counteracting this corruption is a force of integrity, Hollis Mulwray. Mulwray opposes the dam, and seeks to root out the corruption which chokes his department. Because of this, the forces of corruption fool Jake Gittes into taking photographs of Mulwray that they use to corrupt Mulwray's good name.

However, it turns out that Jake Gittes, in his own way, is also a man of high integrity. Though Jake may sometimes behave in an ethically dubious manner, he takes extreme pride in his work, so much that he is willing to come to blows with anyone who questions it. When Jake learns he has been played for a sap, he becomes furious – not out of a sense of right or wrong, but because someone has corrupted his reputation. It is this sense of professional integrity that first motivates Jake to take action.

The thematic battle between corruption and integrity escalates as the plot unfolds. When Hollis Mulwray is found dead, Jake's sense of ethical integrity is summoned as well. Something really stinks, and Jake is going to find out what. Though Jake realizes the danger in sticking his nose where it does not belong, his integrity will not let him stop. He receives several opportunities to abandon his quest and walk away unharmed; when Mrs. Mulwray drops her lawsuit, when Jake is roughed up by thugs, when Noah Cross offers him more money; but doing so would force Jake to corrupt his integrity – something he cannot do. So Jake refuses these opportunities, each time forging a stronger commitment to his side of the thematic argument.

Though corruption and integrity clash with escalating intensity as the story progresses, a winner cannot be decided until the story's main climax. As the third act draws to a close, it seems as if Jake's sense of integrity will win. Only then, everything goes wrong. Jake is detained by Lt. Escobar. Mrs. Mulwray is shot trying to escape. Noah Cross gets away scott-free. Jake can do nothing but walk away in defeat. Corruption has won.

Here we see that a story's message is ultimately decided by how the main conflict is resolved at the story climax. Until the climax, the thematic battle hangs in the balance. The story's message could go either way. Thus, the climactic event decides not only who wins the main story conflict, but the thematic conflict as well. Who wins and why brings the gavel down and declares the theme's final verdict. Because of this, if one changes a story's ending, he or she will also change the story's message even though everything else in the story remains the same. Few know that *Chinatown* had an alternate ending. In the unused version, Mrs. Mulwray kills Noah Cross and saves her daughter. This victory allows Jake to expose Cross's corruption and find justice. Though still dark, this alternate ending would have drastically altered the film's message. The fact that the corrupt Cross met punishment in the end would have reversed the story into a win for integrity. Instead of a tale on the incurable rottenness of modern society, *Chinatown* would have been a story on how morals and ethics will always win out in the end. Thus, any change to a story's climax should not be taken lightly. Change the ending and it may change the audience's entire perception of the film.

THEME & CHARACTER

Theme expresses itself not only through a story's plot, but also its cast of characters. In any good story, all characters will represent in various degrees one side of the thematic battle or the other. The cast is then split down the middle, on the dark side or the light, lined up against each other like pieces in a game of chess.

Primary amongst these pieces is a *white knight*. A white knight is a character who wholly embodies the positive, morally-uplifting side of the theme. In *Chinatown,* this is Hollis Mulwray. In *Star Wars,* this is Obi-Wan Kenobi. In *The Godfather,* it is Kay. The white knight is the story's center of moral good. Leading the other side of the battle is the *blackhat* – a character who embodies the negative, harmful values the story warns against. This is Noah Cross in *Chinatown,* Darth Vader in *Star Wars,* and Virgil Sollozzo in *The Godfather.* The blackhat is the story's heart of darkness, a character who wishes to drag others down to his or her moral depths.

While some characters are a solid black or white, all others exist as various shades of gray. Though each represents some facet of the theme or anti-theme, they do so in varying levels of intensity. *Chinatown's* characters are not all white knights or blackhats. They instead exist somewhere within a spectrum between absolute integrity and absolute corruption. On the side of integrity are Lieutenant Escobar (a police detective who plays everything by the rules), Kahn the butler (a man dedicated to Mrs. Mulwray, but often unfair in that duty), and Mrs. Mulwray herself (she has a sense of integrity, but is willing to lie like crazy to protect it). The corrupt side of the spectrum runs from Ida Sessions (a woman willing to ruin a man's reputation, but comes clean when it leads to murder), to Deputy Chief Russ Yelburton (a man who covers up the conspiracy to promote his career), to Mulvihill (a rival private eye completely lacking in moral fiber).

Themes can be complex issues. A diverse cast of characters gives a storyteller the opportunity to not only explore the values of theme and anti-theme in various levels of intensity, but also the many ways these values can manifest in human behavior. In *Die Hard,* John McClane, Holly, Sgt. Powell, and Argyle all support the heroic side of the theme by demonstrating their care for the common man. However, each character demonstrates this value in different ways: John as a lone champion, Holly as a protecting mother hen, Sgt. Powell as a kindred spirit, Argyle as a buddy willing to go the extra mile. Likewise, Hans Gruber, Ellis, and the Agents Johnson all demonstrate facets of the anti-theme with their reckless disregard for others. However, how Hans shows this quality is much different than Ellis, and how Ellis shows it is different than the Agents. Such a diverse cast of characters allows the theme and anti-theme to be expressed in detail and present a far more well-rounded argument.

Only in the most melodramatic of stories is the protagonist the white knight. Instead, he or she usually begins a neutral gray. As conflict ensues, the protagonist is pulled from one side of the thematic argument to the other, as characters on each side attempt to influence his or her behavior. This moral tug-of-war continues until the protagonist *chooses a side.* Once aligned, the protagonist becomes a warrior for that value, using it as his or her main weapon to overcome the story's conflict. While Jake Gittes makes his choice rather early in *Chinatown,* it is not uncommon for the protagonist to wait until the end of the second act or even later to decide which path to follow.

Michael Corleone is one such protagonist. Michael's Story Goal is to find a way to achieve the permanent and lasting safety of his family. On one side of the thematic argument are forces that urge Michael to solve his problems through patience and temperance, primary amongst them his girlfriend/wife Kay, and to a lesser degree, his father Vito and Tom Hagen. On the other side are those that insist the only way to succeed is by brute force. These include Michael's brother Sonny, Clemenza, Virgil Sollozzo, and the heads of the remaining Five Families. When finally forced to decide, Michael chooses darkness over light, achieving his goal through a flurry of bloodshed.

DECIDING FACTORS

As seen in *The Godfather,* the protagonist does not always choose light over darkness. And as seen in *Chinatown,* just because the protagonist chooses a side, this does not mean that side will always win. The combination of these two factors – which side the protagonist chooses, and whether or not this choice allows the protagonist to reach victory – ultimately decides what message the audience will take away from a film.

This creates four possible story endings, each communicating a different message on values, ethics, and the world. Here are these endings, ordered from those that give the most positive message to the most negative.

1. The protagonist embraces a positive value, and succeeds. (Luke Skywalker in *Star Wars*)

This type of ending celebrates the importance of a positive value by demonstrating how the acceptance of that value will lead to happiness and success. It supports social norms by telling the audience that good will come to those who embrace good.

2. The protagonist embraces a negative value, and fails. (Jerry Lundegaard in *Fargo*)

This ending turns a story into a morality play. It promotes a positive social value by showing the terrible consequences which come from embracing its opposite. It acts as a warning by demonstrating the punishment that comes to those who cannot behave in a socially-acceptable manner.

3. The protagonist embraces a positive value, yet still fails. (Jake Gittes in *Chinatown*)

This is the stuff of tragedy. More complicated than the previous types, this ending communicates the importance of a positive value, while at the same time implying that society is fundamentally flawed in relation to that value. Social criticism is the result.

4. The protagonist embraces a negative value, and succeeds. (Michael Corleone in *The Godfather*)

This ends a film with the most cynical world view. It suggests that society's supposed values have grown illusionary and no longer function as they should. The story becomes a grim command to reevaluate oneself and the values society is supposedly built upon.

THEME AND THE REVISION PROCESS

Theme can be difficult to work with, primarily because of its abstract nature. This is why I recommend leaving its full consideration to later drafts. Focus on creating a great story first – one with a solid Spine, sufficient conflict, and capable structure. Develop characters who influence the story through motivated action. Do this well, and a theme will take root on its own accord.

Once this is achieved, look into the story and identify your theme. In some cases, the theme is easy to spot. In others, it can be far more difficult. In early drafts, the theme is often vague and unclear due to out-of-place story elements or distracting material. In this case, the theme is best found by focusing on the basics. Who are the two sides in conflict? What values do their actions seem to embody? Who wins the conflict and why? What values are necessary to reach success? What is the protagonist's internal need? What is the fatal flaw? How do the need and flaw connect to story events? Is the protagonist able to attain his or her need? Does doing so allow the protagonist to succeed in the end? A story's message originates from its most basic ingredients. Focus on them, and the shadows of theme will begin to take form.

Once you have found a common thread, express it in a clear, simple sentence that will unify all of the story's events. Identify the positive value and its opposing value. Recognize which value the protagonist ultimately chooses and whether or not this value allows the protagonist to achieve victory in the end. Taken together, these factors express your story's theme. Strive for simple clarity. You can elaborate if you wish, but the clear simplicity of your message will be essential in the next stage of your work.

Once the theme is identified, start a new revision. The purpose of this draft will be to unify all story elements under the theme. Everything within the story should somehow relate to the thematic argument. Identify elements that distract from the theme. Distracting elements are those that seem to express a second, unrelated message. If a story on the importance of family is interrupted by a scene condemning capitalist greed, something does not fit. Such material should be altered or removed. There can only be one theme per cinematic story. Novels may have the length and breadth to explore multiple themes, but a 90-120 page screenplay must keep things simple. Multiple messages will only interfere with each other like two radio stations broadcasting on the same frequency. Rather than enrich the story, they will cause confusion.

The best themes permeate every element of a story. Look for thematically neutral events and find ways to incorporate them into the overall message. Look at your cast of characters. Does every one of them, through action or behavior, demonstrate the theme or anti-theme? Look at plot structure. Does every turning point serve as a victory or loss for the thematic battle as well as the main conflict? Look at the minor details. Can they be used to express a greater meaning? *Chinatown* is a film that never misses an opportunity to support its theme. Even the smallest of details play upon the concepts of corruption or integrity. Jake's face is corrupted by Cross's goons. Mrs. Mulwray admits to corrupting her marriage with repeated affairs. Jake notices a black spot that corrupts Mrs. Mulwray's green eyes. Noah Cross even corrupts the integrity of Jake's name, constantly calling him "Mr. Gits." Every disconnected element is a missed opportunity to enrich a story with deeper meaning and draw it together into a cohesive whole.

Though plot and character are the main communicators of theme, visuals and dialogue can also strengthen its presence. Well thought out visuals or pieces of action can do much to unobtrusively suggest meaning without distracting from a story's events. Symbolism can be employed. Take a look at how Captain Miller's hand shakes whenever he checks his compass in *Saving Private Ryan*. This is symbolic. A compass finds direction. A person's ability to tell right from wrong is known as a "moral compass." Miller's shaking hand symbolizes his difficulty to tell right from wrong in the moral ambiguity of war. However, any use of symbolism should not be too overt, or else it will appear cheap or hackneyed. Any symbols should be an organic part of the natural action of the scene. It is natural that a military commander should check his compass from time to time, but if Jake Gittes were to perform the same action in *Chinatown,* the symbolism would be too obvious.

Theme can also be communicated through dialogue. However, this can be tricky. If too overt, the audience will gag as meaning is forced down their throats. Like symbols or metaphors, statements on theme must be weaved into the natural action of a scene. They should not stand out, but only gain meaning in retrospect. Should a line punch the theme on the nose, the storyteller's heavy hand becomes visible, causing the message to feel forced and artificial. Keep in mind that thematic visuals and dialogue should only be used to augment the message already communicated through plot and character. It should not be used to force a message upon a story in which it does not already exist. The best themes should only become apparent only once the story has reached its end. It is only after the climax that the audience should be able to look back on the story and get a sense of what it was all about.

CHAPTER 14
BECOMING A BETTER WRITER

Facts and theory provide only the basics a storyteller needs to master his or her craft. The rest is up to the writer. Screenwriting is more than an ambition. It is a lifestyle. The dedicated screenwriter will not only study the craft, but take advantage of all the little ways he or she can enrich his or her skills in daily life. The world has far more to offer a cinematic storyteller than can be contained in books. What follows are nine simple ways writers can expand upon their study of the craft to take their storytelling abilities to a higher level.

1. Write.

Writers write. Period. Anyone who does not cannot call themselves a writer. This may seem obvious, but it is surprising how many aspiring writers never take the necessary time and effort to practice the craft. One can read every book on the subject, one can attend film school or pay for expensive seminars, but until he or she sits down and puts this knowledge into practice, it is like trying to learn how to swim without ever getting into the water. I often hear people say, "I *want* to be a writer." Want to? Well, what is stopping you? Write something!

Sure, we all have excuses not to write. We're too busy. We can't spare the time. It's HARD. However, professional skill is not something that will fall into your lap. It requires practice. Do you think professional athletes reach such heights on talent alone? Of course not. They hone their skills through practice, day in and day out. If you really want to write, you must take the time to do the same. Set aside a few hours to write every day. No distractions. No excuses. At first, you will feel resistance. There will be days when you do not want to write. There will be days when nothing seems to come. You must push through this resistance. Set a schedule and stick to it. Writing will eventually become a habit. You will *want* to write every day. The thought of a day without it becomes unimaginable. It is only then that you can truly call yourself a writer.

2. Read.

Reading improves writing. I do not just mean books on the craft. Read everything. Fiction, nonfiction, textbooks, plays, newspapers, magazines. Absorbing the words of others will build your vocabulary and improve your ability to communicate. Novels, short stories, and stage plays can expand your grasp of narrative and character beyond the clichéd formulas found on movie screens. Great storytelling has existed for centuries. Why limit yourself to one tiny area of its expression?

Nonfiction is also extremely helpful. Great writers are well-versed in many fields. They know history, science, politics. They take interest in languages, cultures, and world events. The more you know about, the more material you have to draw upon in your work. Expand your sphere of knowledge into as many areas as possible. Beginners are often told to "write what they know." This is not an order to limit yourself to your currently narrow range of experiences. It is rather a command to *learn more*. Every field of study offers a rich, vibrant world, overflowing with resources waiting to be tapped. The more you know about these subjects, the more authenticity you will be able to bring to the world of your story.

3. Watch movies like a writer.

Do not just watch a movie. View it through the eyes of a storyteller. Analyze how the story is put together. Identify the Story Spine and Major Dramatic Turning Points. How are the scenes constructed? How does the storyteller create mystery, surprise, or suspense? Watch the same film twice, the first to experience the story, and then a second time to analyze its craft. Recall what the film made you think and feel during the first viewing. Then, take a closer look to find out how this was accomplished.

If the movie is a bad one, figure out why it is bad. Where did the story-teller go wrong? What are its flaws? If you were hired to fix the script, what would you do differently? An observant writer can learn just as much from the bad movies as he or she can from the good.

4. Read the screenplays of films you admire.

Watching a movie is one thing, but seeing it on the page without the distractions of actors, camera, or sound provides a different experience altogether. The best way to learn is by example. If certain films inspire you, find their scripts and study them. Thousands of popular shooting scripts are available online. Many have also been published as books. By providing the movie before it was a movie, shooting scripts give writers the oppor-tunity to see how the best in the business physically communicate their stories on the page. Reading the script allows you to take in the story at your own pace, break down its structure, and observe the construction of its scenes. You will come to understand how great writers use their words to evoke thought and emotions.

Reading great scripts is also the best way to learn how to write effective action and description. A writer's use of language is lost when his or her work is transferred to the screen. One could watch films all day and not learn anything in this area. The shooting script, however, demonstrates the strong, vivid language necessary for action to leap off the page and into the reader's imagination.

5. Work as a script reader.

The rules of screencraft will always seem theoretical and abstract when confined to the pages of a book. To gain a full understanding, a writer must see the successes and failures of the craft in action. The quickest and easiest way to do this is by analyzing the scripts of other writers. Hundreds of them. From every type and genre. This may seem like a tall order, but luckily, the film industry already has a system in place that allows developing writers to do just this – and gain valuable job experience along the way.

Studios, production companies, and entertainment agencies are flooded every day with dozens of unproduced screenplays, ranging in quality from the very good to the unreadably bad. Unable (and often unwilling) to read all these scripts themselves, companies hire readers to comb through these submissions to separate the good from the bad from the ugly. Though one of the lowest positions on the industry totem pole, this job can give writers a hands-on education no film school can touch. Not only are readers exposed to every type of script from writers of every background, they are also expected to analyze each script with a written summary of what is good or bad, why it is good or bad, and what might be necessary for improvement.

Critiquing screenplays gives writers an unparalleled opportunity to sharpen their critical skills while learning the craft from the inside-out. They learn the correct way to construct a screenplay by seeing all the ways a script can go wrong. They learn how to appeal to readers by experiencing first-hand what turns a reader off. With constant exposure to screencraft in action, a script reader's grasp of the subject quickly turns from vague and theoreticl to practical and concrete.

Paid reader jobs require experience, and most unpaid internships require enrollment in a college or university. However, there are many small companies or script competitions in constant need of volunteers. If you cannot get one of these jobs due to your current location or availability, there is nothing to keep you from replicating the experience on your own.

There are many online communities where developing screenwriters post their work for feedback. This is a win-win for both parties. The writer gets advice while the reader gets to practice his or her critical skills. If you would rather cut your teeth on something a little more polished, you could even find professional scripts online (ideally from films that have not yet been produced or that you have not yet seen) and write your own mock analysis. Just make sure to get the most of the exercise by putting your thoughts in writing. No education is complete without homework.

6. Watch documentaries.

A screenwriter is expected to portray reality with drama, authenticity, and originality. Watching films can help this. However, if a writer's experience with drama is limited only to formulative Hollywood films, his or her work will often become stale and derivative since the writer has little to draw upon but the clichéd and artificial. Because of this, it can be quite helpful to add documentaries to the mix. Documentaries also present drama. But unlike fictional films, they present the drama of real life. They contain real people struggling with real problems, many as rich and complex as that found in any fictional film. Like reading, documentaries expose writers to subjects and areas of experience rarely explored in traditional feature films. By observing the genuine behavior of persons dealing with real-world conflicts, screenwriters can enrich their own ability to create authentic characters and dramatic, true to life situations.

7. Read biographies and autobiographies.

The media typically presents famous (or infamous) persons in only one dimension. A rock star is just a musician or addict. A politician is just the policies he or she supports. An actor is little more than the roles he or she has played. Biographies and autobiographies allow readers to see larger-than-life persons for who they really are in multiple dimensions. They explore the subject's past and delve into the influences that shaped the person into who they came to be. Drama often takes center stage, with a focus upon the obstacles these people had to face and the intimate thoughts, fears, and emotions they experienced in the process. A great storyteller must understand his or her characters with the same intimacy as these books portray their subjects. If a storyteller wishes to create larger-than-life characters who captivate the audience as celebrities do the public, it does him or her much good to explore similar persons as they existed in real life, with the fears, flaws, and psychological hang-ups intact. Without such depth, these characters will remain as one-dimensional as the media portrays its public figures.

8. Make an effort to understand human psychology.

Creating great characters requires a great deal of personal empathy. The storyteller must be able to take the viewpoint of any character at any time, regardless of that character's age, gender, race, cultural background, or sexual orientation. The storyteller must think how the character thinks. Feel how the character feels. See the world from the character's eyes.

This is difficult without a basic understanding of human psychology. A storyteller cannot create believable human behavior on the page without first understanding it in real life. Stories are about people. They explore humanity. To find success, storytellers must be students of human nature. By understanding how wants, needs, fears, traumas, and past experiences shape a person and influence behavior, storytellers can inject authenticity into characters and their actions. Knowing the ins and outs of the human mind helps a storyteller understand what any character will think or feel in any possible situation, and how that particular person might react to any given event. Audiences will then better connect with characters because those characters seem genuine. They act just as we would expect others to act in real life.

9. Write more.

Writing is not easy. It is not glamorous. It demands such time and energy that only the dedicated will survive. This is why above all things a writer must LOVE to write. A real writer does not write only for money (though money is nice), nor does he or she write for fame (few ever attain it). A writer writes because he or she genuinely wants to write. Within the writer is a deep, burning desire to express his or her thoughts and ideas to the world. Life without writing seems incomplete. There is only one possible word for this impulse. That word is PASSION.

It is passion alone that will get you through your growing pains. Those without passion never have the guts to start. Those who cannot maintain their passion will give up along the way. But those with true passion have the faith in themselves to keep writing, keep improving, and never stop. You will only find success if you love what you do and have the dedication to keep doing it. Like the medieval monk cloistered in his cell, the writer chooses a humble existence of scribbling in solitude, not for money or fame, but because his or her passion demands it. Putting dreams on paper makes the writer happy. And, God willing, that passion will pay off in the end.

So with that, to all my fellow scriptmonks, I bid farewell.

Scribble on.

INDEX

Made in the USA
Coppell, TX
26 May 2022